Landscaping Wish List

A landscape plan begins with your wish list. Use this list for ideas, but don't stop here — use your imagination to customize your landscape to your family's needs.

- Enough lawn to play catch.
- A brick patio or wooden deck.
- An outdoor barbecue.
- A privacy hedge.
- A fenced-in yard.
- A swimming pool or spa.
- A storage shed or potting shed.
- A compost pile.
- A fish pond or reflecting pool.
- A place where butterflies and birds come to visit.
- A private retreat with a hammock.
- A flower-cutting garden.
- A rose garden.
- A fresh herb plot or scented garden.
- A vegetable garden or fruit orchard.
- A rooftop garden.
- A bulb garden with flowers that announce the start of a new season.
- A patio garden with different pots full of colorful plants.
- Wildflowers.
- A drought-tolerant garden.

Planning Steps

Use the following process to plan your landscape. Chapters 1 through 3 provide more detail.

1. Measure your current landscape and draw a rough plan on paper.
2. Review your wish list.
3. Determine your budget.
4. Add potential structures (patio, deck, shed, bench, fence, pool, or pond) and pathways to your plan.
5. Determine the sun, partial shade, and shade availability for each area that you plan to grow plants. Determine your hardiness zone (see Chapter 12).
6. Add plants and trees to your plan.
7. Check costs and availability of materials and plants.
8. Call your local governing body and ask about permits.
9. Enlist a landscape contractor, if necessary.
10. Begin building and planting!

FOR DUMMIES™

BESTSELLING
BOOK SERIES
FROM IDG

Landscaping For Dummies®

Cheat Sheet

Buying the Best Plants

The following tips help you make smart purchases on your landscape plants. Flip to Chapters 8 through 12 for gobs more tips on buying and planting trees, shrubs, vines, flowers, bulbs, and grasses.

- ✔ Plan your landscape on paper before you set out to purchase plants — you'll know exactly how much to buy.

- ✔ Establish a budget before you arrive at the nursery.

- ✔ Choose plants suited to the amount of sun, partial shade, or shade in your garden.

- ✔ Avoid plants that don't grow well in your zone (see Chapter 12).

- ✔ Buy plants that, when mature, are the right height, shape, and color for the scale of your landscape.

- ✔ Choose plants that are compact, healthy, and (if applicable) just starting to flower. Avoid weak, spindly, or insect-infested plants.

- ✔ Avoid buying plants that are rootbound or have outgrown their pots.

- ✔ Note any special conditions before purchasing plants — soil requirements, watering needs, invasiveness, smells, and messiness (especially with berries).

Hardiness Zone Table

Most trees, shrubs, vines, and flowers are labeled with a *zone* that indicates in what areas of the world the perennial plants grow best. See Chapter 12 for more on hardiness zones.

Zone	Minimum Temperature	
	Fahrenheit	Celsius
Zone 1	Below −50°F	Below −46°C
Zone 2	−50°F to −40°F	−46°C to −40°C
Zone 3	−40°F to −30°F	−40°C to −34°C
Zone 4	−30°F to −20°F	−34°C to −29°C
Zone 5	−20°F to −10°F	−29°C to −23°C
Zone 6	−10°F to 0°F	−23°C to −18°C
Zone 7	0°F to 10°F	−18°C to −12°C
Zone 8	10°F to 20°F	−12°C to −7°C
Zone 9	20°F to 30°F	−7°C to −1°C
Zone 10	30°F to 40°F	−1°C to 4°C
Zone 11	40°F and up	4°C and up

IDG
BOOKS
WORLDWIDE

Copyright © 1999 IDG Books Worldwide, Inc.
All rights reserved.

Cheat Sheet $2.95 value. Item 5128-0.

For more information about IDG Books,
call 1-800-762-2974.

...For Dummies: Bestselling Book Series for Beginners

Praise For *Gardening For Dummies,* 2nd Edition

"Despite the humorous title, *Gardening For Dummies,* 2nd Edition is a valuable book full of down-to-earth gardening advice. I've been gardening most of my life and I still found something new in this well-organized book."

— Laurence Sombke, Public Radio's *Natural Gardener*

"Packed with down-to-earth gardening advice that both novice and experienced gardeners will find useful."

— Doug Jimerson, VP Editor-in-Chief of garden.com

"*Gardening For Dummies,* 2nd Edition offers the perfect map for a new generation of gardener . . . with this book and a little time practicing in the garden, you won't be a 'gardening dummy' for long!"

— William Raap, President, Gardener's Supply Company

Praise For *Vegetable Gardening For Dummies*

"This book contains all of the basic requirements for the average American to plan and maintain a healthy and hardy vegetable garden. The chapters are comprehensive, witty, and easy-to-read. Planting and culture descriptions of individual vegetables are excellent with colorful descriptions and scrumptious recipes."

— Michael D. Orzolek, Professor of Vegetable Crops, Pennsylvania State University

Praise For *Flowering Bulbs For Dummies*

"What a joy it is to have this book available to all gardeners. Bulb gardening has now been reduced to a simple pleasure."
— Dan Davids, President, Davids & Royston Bulb Co., Leading Flowering-Bulb Wholesaler

"Flowering bulbs are one of nature's close-to-perfect perennial plants. This book, with its easy, well-written style, covers just about every aspect of bulb gardening that the home gardener may encounter and should assure gardening successes with bulbs for all who read it!"
— Brent & Becky Heath, authors of *Daffodils for American Gardens*

Praise For *Houseplants For Dummies*

"Indoor gardening, quite an intimidating prospect for the brown-thumbed novice, comes alive under the user-friendly guidance in *Houseplants For Dummies*. Larry Hodgson has succeeded in making interior plantscaping accessible for both the novice and the seasoned professional."
— Matthew Gardner, President, California Interior Plantscape Association

"Finally — a book that takes the mystery out of how to keep houseplants alive! Even a veteran black-thumber will turn a shade of green after reading this concise, clearly-presented houseplant primer. Following the right-on information presented in this book on how to take care of your houseplants when you're gone more than pays for the price of the book in saved plants."
— Steve Frowine, President, The Great Plant Company

Praise For *Lawn Care For Dummies*

"I recommend this book to anyone starting a new lawn or improving an existing one."

— Kevin N. Norris, Director, National Turfgrass Evaluation Program

"This is the one book you should have, keep handy, and use often!"

— Doug Fender, Executive Director, Turf Resource Center, Rolling Meadows, Illinois

Praise For *Decks & Patios For Dummies*

"Thorough and thoughtful, with plenty of solid, on-the-ground advice. Bob Beckstrom will have you thinking like a landscape architect, a carpenter, a mason, and an artist. If you're considering finally living to the limits of your lot line, this book is required reading — it's the guidebook to turning your yard into your favorite getaway destination."

— Bill Crosby, Editorial Director, ImproveNet

"This is an exceptionally complete guide. It treats decks and patios not as isolated projects but as features that should fit with the entire property, and it helps homeowners avoid later disappointments by covering details often overlooked in the eagerness to enjoy outdoor living. You know the book is thorough when it goes so far as to recommend that, before digging post holes by hand, you do some physical workouts!"

— Huck DeVenzio, Advertising Manager, Wolmanized wood

 ™

References for the Rest of Us! ™

BESTSELLING BOOK SERIES FROM IDG

Do you find that traditional reference books are overloaded with technical details and advice you'll never use? Do you postpone important life decisions because you just don't want to deal with them? Then our *...For Dummies®* business and general reference book series is for you.

...For Dummies business and general reference books are written for those frustrated and hard-working souls who know they aren't dumb, but find that the myriad of personal and business issues and the accompanying horror stories make them feel helpless. *...For Dummies* books use a lighthearted approach, a down-to-earth style, and even cartoons and humorous icons to diffuse fears and build confidence. Lighthearted but not lightweight, these books are perfect survival guides to solve your everyday personal and business problems.

> **"More than a publishing phenomenon, 'Dummies' is a sign of the times."**
> — *The New York Times*

> **"A world of detailed and authoritative information is packed into them..."**
> — *U.S. News and World Report*

> **"...you won't go wrong buying them."**
> — *Walter Mossberg, Wall Street Journal, on IDG Books' ...For Dummies books*

Already, millions of satisfied readers agree. They have made *...For Dummies* the #1 introductory level computer book series and a best-selling business book series. They have written asking for more. So, if you're looking for the best and easiest way to learn about business and other general reference topics, look to *...For Dummies* to give you a helping hand.

8/98i

LANDSCAPING

FOR

DUMMIES®

LANDSCAPING FOR DUMMIES®

by Philip Giroux, Bob Beckstrom,
Lance Walheim, and The Editors of
the National Gardening Association

Contributions by Michael MacCaskey, Bill Marken,
and Sally Roth

IDG Books Worldwide, Inc.
An International Data Group Company

Foster City, CA ♦ Chicago, IL ♦ Indianapolis, IN ♦ New York, NY

Landscaping For Dummies®

Published by
IDG Books Worldwide, Inc.
An International Data Group Company
919 E. Hillsdale Blvd.
Suite 400
Foster City, CA 94404
www.idgbooks.com (IDG Books Worldwide Web site)
www.dummies.com (Dummies Press Web site)

Library of Congress Catalog Card No.: 98-89727

ISBN: 0-7645-5128-0

Printed in the United States of America

10 9 8 7 6 5 4 3 2 1

1B/QW/QR/ZZ/IN

Distributed in the United States by IDG Books Worldwide, Inc.

Distributed by Macmillan Canada for Canada; by Transworld Publishers Limited in the United Kingdom; by IDG Norge Books for Norway; by IDG Sweden Books for Sweden; by Woodslane Pty. Ltd. for Australia; by Woodslane (NZ) Ltd. for New Zealand; by Addison Wesley Longman Singapore Pte Ltd. for Singapore, Malaysia, Thailand, and Indonesia; by Norma Comunicaciones S.A. for Colombia; by Intersoft for South Africa; by International Thomson Publishing for Germany, Austria and Switzerland; by Distribuidora Cuspide for Argentina; by Livraria Cultura for Brazil; by Ediciencia S.A. for Ecuador; by Ediciones ZETA S.C.R. Ltda. for Peru; by WS Computer Publishing Corporation, Inc., for the Philippines; by Contemporanea de Ediciones for Venezuela; by Express Computer Distributors for the Caribbean and West Indies; by Micronesia Media Distributor, Inc. for Micronesia; by Grupo Editorial Norma S.A. for Guatemala; by Chips Computadoras S.A. de C.V. for Mexico; by Editorial Norma de Panama S.A. for Panama; by Wouters Import for Belgium; by American Bookshops for Finland. Authorized Sales Agent: Anthony Rudkin Associates for the Middle East and North Africa.

For general information on IDG Books Worldwide's books in the U.S., please call our Consumer Customer Service department at 800-762-2974. For reseller information, including discounts and premium sales, please call our Reseller Customer Service department at 800-434-3422.

For information on where to purchase IDG Books Worldwide's books outside the U.S., please contact our International Sales department at 317-596-5530 or fax 317-596-5692.

For information on foreign language translations, please contact our Foreign & Subsidiary Rights department at 650-655-3021 or fax 650-655-3281.

For sales inquiries and special prices for bulk quantities, please contact our Sales department at 650-655-3200 or write to the address above.

For information on using IDG Books Worldwide's books in the classroom or for ordering examination copies, please contact our Educational Sales department at 800-434-2086 or fax 317-596-5499.

For press review copies, author interviews, or other publicity information, please contact our Public Relations department at 650-655-3000 or fax 650-655-3299.

For authorization to photocopy items for corporate, personal, or educational use, please contact Copyright Clearance Center, 222 Rosewood Drive, Danvers, MA 01923, or fax 978-750-4470.

About the Authors

Philip Giroux is a second-generation Californian who developed his desire for planting and his love of gardens watching his father, an avid gardener, and graduated from the University of Arizona with a degree in landscape architecture and ornamental horticulture. He established his landscape designing and building firm in 1978, specializing in custom residential installations, including the estates of Rupert Murdock and Henry Mudd. Philip is responsible for numerous large-scale commercial projects, such as the Los Angles County Museum of Arts Sculpture and Japanese Pavilion Garden. His garden column in the *Manhattan Beach Reporter* is both a practical guide for weekend gardeners and a garden travelogue from such faraway places as Japan, France, England, Canada, and Israel. Philip has served as L.A. Chapter President for the California Landscape Contractors Association and is a member of the Royal Horticulture Society.

Bob Beckstrom is a licensed general contractor, living in northern California. He enjoys building things, spending time outdoors, and sharing what he's learned with other people. His first building experience was as a VISTA volunteer in 1968, as the coordinator of a self-help housing project in rural Alaska. He taught elementary school for ten years; has taught adult courses in house building and remodeling at The Owner Builder Center in Berkeley, California; and has written and edited extensively on home-improvement topics, including *Decks & Patios For Dummies*.

Lance Walheim has been gardening most of his life. He got his start when his father forced him to turn the soil and plant tomatoes in the family vegetable garden as punishment for a deed he can't recall. Funny thing was, he found that he enjoyed working in the soil and has been doing it ever since. In 1975, he graduated from the University of California, Berkeley, with a degree in botany. Shortly after, he started writing and researching books on gardening and since has written or contributed to more than 40 gardening books on subject ranging from citrus to roses (including *Roses For Dummies*). He has also written extensively about lawns and lawn care — check out his book, *Lawn Care For Dummies*. He also has served as a writer for *Sunset* and *National Gardening* magazines and is part owner of California Citrus Specialties, marketers of specialty citrus fruit. But his true loves are family and gardening, the "composts" that enrich his heart and soul.

The **National Gardening Association** is the largest member-based, not-for-profit organization of home gardeners in the United States. Founded in 1972 (as "Gardens for All") to spearhead the community garden movement, today's National Gardening Association is best known for its bimonthly publication, *National Gardening* magazine ($18 per year). Reporting on all aspects of home gardening, each issue is read to some half-million gardeners worldwide. For more information about the National Gardening Association, write to 180 Flynn Ave., Burlington, Vermont, U.S.A.; call 1-800-LETSGRO (1-800-538-7476); or check out the NGA's Web site at www.garden.org.

About the Contributors

Michael MacCaskey is a Los Angeles native who relocated five years ago to Burlington, Vermont to become editor-in-chief of *National Gardening* magazine (published by the National Gardening Association). He is also the author of *Gardening For Dummies,* 2nd Edition, and has served as NGA's editor-in-chief for the other *...For Dummies* gardening books. While he claims that the 95-day growing season is still a shock to his system, he adores Vermont's natural beauty and spectacular summers, and is hard at work landscaping his new home.

Bill Marken, a native of the San Francisco Bay Area, is the editor of *Rebecca's Garden Magazine,* based on the popular syndicated television series. He is the former editor-in-chief of *Sunset, The Magazine of Western Living.* He is the author of two books in the *...For Dummies* gardening series: *Container Gardening For Dummies* and *Annuals For Dummies* (both published by IDG Books Worldwide, Inc.).

Sally Roth was raised in Bethlehem, Pennsylvania and lived in Oregon before settling into her current home in New Harmony, Indiana. She's a lifelong naturalist, gardener, and writer. Her writing credits include books and magazine articles for several publishers. When she isn't digging in her garden or out walking in the woods looking at birds, Sally listens to blues and folk music, reads, and plays a mean Scrabble.

About the Photographers

Crandall & Crandall Photography supplied all of the photos for this book, except those listed below.

Michael S. Thompson: Figure 2-2 and color photos 3, 22, 24, and 28

Michael Landis: Figures 11-1 and 11-10

Margaret Hensel/Positive Images: Figures 5-1d, 7-6a, and color photo 17

Pam Spaudling/Positive Images: Color photo 16

Karen Bussolini/Positive Images: Color photo 18

Harry Haralambou/Positive Images: Color photo 19

About the Landscape Architects and Designers

Sara Jane von Trapp designed all of the landscape plans in Chapters 13, 14, and 15.

Ronald J. Allison & Associates designed the landscape in color photo 23.

Lani Berrington & Associates designed the landscapes in color photos 30 and 32.

Blue Sky Designs designed the landscapes in color photos 6 and 36.

Hugh Dargan & Associates designed the landscapes in Figures 2-1, 8-2, 10-11, and color photo 35.

Barbara Fealey designed the landscape in color photo 3.

Ruben Flores designed the landscape in Figure 9-1.

Michael Glassman & Associates designed the landscapes in Figures 7-7, 16-2, 16-3, and color photo 13.

Erik Gronborg designed the landscape in Figure 2-4.

John Herbst, Jr. & Associates designed the landscapes in color photos 21, 26, and 31.

Elizabeth Lair designed the landscape in Figure 2-2.

Mario Mathias designed the landscapes in Figure 2-3 and color photo 2.

Marcella Moore designed the landscape in color photo 28.

Paradise Designs, Inc. designed the landscape in Figure 2-6.

Rathfon Designs designed the landscape in color photo 33.

Sarah Robertson designed the landscape in color photo 24.

Rogers Gardens designed the landscapes in Figures 2-5, 10-8, and color photo 37.

Polly and Gary Weber designed the landscape in color photo 22.

ABOUT IDG BOOKS WORLDWIDE

Welcome to the world of IDG Books Worldwide.

IDG Books Worldwide, Inc., is a subsidiary of International Data Group, the world's largest publisher of computer-related information and the leading global provider of information services on information technology. IDG was founded more than 30 years ago by Patrick J. McGovern and now employs more than 9,000 people worldwide. IDG publishes more than 290 computer publications in over 75 countries. More than 90 million people read one or more IDG publications each month.

Launched in 1990, IDG Books Worldwide is today the #1 publisher of best-selling computer books in the United States. We are proud to have received eight awards from the Computer Press Association in recognition of editorial excellence and three from Computer Currents' First Annual Readers' Choice Awards. Our best-selling *...For Dummies*® series has more than 50 million copies in print with translations in 31 languages. IDG Books Worldwide, through a joint venture with IDG's Hi-Tech Beijing, became the first U.S. publisher to publish a computer book in the People's Republic of China. In record time, IDG Books Worldwide has become the first choice for millions of readers around the world who want to learn how to better manage their businesses.

Our mission is simple: Every one of our books is designed to bring extra value and skill-building instructions to the reader. Our books are written by experts who understand and care about our readers. The knowledge base of our editorial staff comes from years of experience in publishing, education, and journalism — experience we use to produce books to carry us into the new millennium. In short, we care about books, so we attract the best people. We devote special attention to details such as audience, interior design, use of icons, and illustrations. And because we use an efficient process of authoring, editing, and desktop publishing our books electronically, we can spend more time ensuring superior content and less time on the technicalities of making books.

You can count on our commitment to deliver high-quality books at competitive prices on topics you want to read about. At IDG Books Worldwide, we continue in the IDG tradition of delivering quality for more than 30 years. You'll find no better book on a subject than one from IDG Books Worldwide.

John Kilcullen
Chairman and CEO
IDG Books Worldwide, Inc.

Steven Berkowitz
President and Publisher
IDG Books Worldwide, Inc.

Eighth Annual Computer Press Awards 1992

Ninth Annual Computer Press Awards 1993

Tenth Annual Computer Press Awards 1994

Eleventh Annual Computer Press Awards 1995

IDG is the world's leading IT media, research and exposition company. Founded, in 1964, IDG had 1997 revenues of $2.05 billion and has more than 9,000 employees worldwide. IDG offers the widest range of media options that reach IT buyers in 75 countries representing 95% of worldwide IT spending. IDG's diverse product and services portfolio spans six key areas including print publishing, online publishing, expositions and conferences, market research, education and training, and global marketing services. More than 90 million people read one or more of IDG's 290 magazines and newspapers, including IDG's leading global brands — Computerworld, PC World, Network World, Macworld and the Channel World family of publications. IDG Books Worldwide is one of the fastest-growing computer book publishers in the world, with more than 700 titles in 36 languages. The "...For Dummies®" series alone has more than 50 million copies in print. IDG offers online users the largest network of technology-specific Web sites around the world through IDG.net (http://www.idg.net), which comprises more than 225 targeted Web sites in 55 countries worldwide. International Data Corporation (IDC) is the world's largest provider of information technology data, analysis and consulting, with research centers in over 41 countries and more than 400 research analysts worldwide. IDG World Expo is a leading producer of more than 168 globally branded conferences and expositions in 35 countries including E3 (Electronic Entertainment Expo), Macworld Expo, ComNet, Windows World Expo, ICE (Internet Commerce Expo), Agenda, DEMO, and Spotlight. IDG's training subsidiary, ExecuTrain, is the world's largest computer training company, with more than 230 locations worldwide and 785 training courses. IDG Marketing Services helps industry-leading IT companies build international brand recognition by developing global integrated marketing programs via IDG's print, online and exposition products worldwide. Further information about the company can be found at www.idg.com.

10/8/98

Dedications

Philip dedicates this book to the memory of his mom and dad, whose understanding and appreciation for the world around them cultivated his curiosity and instilled in him his desire to design and build a better environment. **Bob** and **Lance** dedicate this book to the idea that making this world a better place to live begins in your own backyard.

Authors' Acknowledgments

Philip Giroux: I am indebted to my team of coauthors and contributors for their professionalism and their unbending patience, especially to Mike MacCaskey, for guiding me through my first book. To Grace Skidmore, Disney horticulturist, marketing consultant and good friend, who advised me and provided invaluable information; Stephen Ormanyi, landscape architect, mentor, and friend; Arnold Dutton, who taught me that less is more in many landscape solutions; Dan Guzman, masonry contractor and friend; Ann Videriksen, for her attention to detail; Joe Linesch for his influence in solving difficult design situations through the use of plants; and Lynn Potter for her encouragement and support during this project. I also wish to thank the many employees of my company, whose caring and attention to detail established our reputation as a premier landscape design and construction company. Finally, thanks to my two children, Todd and Samantha, for enriching my life and being so special to me.

Bob Beckstrom: I am indebted to a great number of building contractors, building inspectors, landscape designers, homeowners, and do-it-yourselfers — too many to list here — for virtually all of the information about hardscaping in this book. I am especially grateful to my father, Randy Beckstrom, my brother Lyle, and my brother-in-law Jerry for instilling in me a can-do attitude at an early age, and for the encouragement of my wife, Linda, as I wrote the hardscaping chapters of this book. I also wish to acknowledge the pleasure of working with project editor Tere Drenth and members of The National Gardening Association, who contributed to this book.

Lance Walheim: I would like to thank all the great plantsmen and plantswomen (there are way too many to mention) whose knowledge was invaluable in writing the "green sections" of this book. Also thanks to the University Cooperative Extensions throughout the United States. Their expertise and generosity of time always help make any book so much better. This book would not have been possible without the patience and level-headed guidance of Tere Drenth at IDG Books and all my friends at *National Gardening*. Thanks to them. I would also like to thank my wife Laura, and daughters Ashely and Teale, who put up with dad and his crazy deadlines.

Publisher's Acknowledgments

We're proud of this book; please register your comments through our IDG Books Worldwide Online Registration Form located at http://my2cents.dummies.com.

Some of the people who helped bring this book to market include the following:

Acquisitions, Editorial, and Media Development

Project Editor: Tere Drenth

Acquisitions Editor: Holly McGuire

General Reviewer: Roger Fiske, Fiske Landscaping, Inc.

Technical Consultant: Janet S. Dunn

Editorial Manager: Mary C. Corder

Editorial Coordinator: Maureen Kelly

Special Help

Sarah Kennedy, Jonathan Malysiak, Suzanne Thomas, Robert Wallace

Production

Project Coordinator: Valery Bourke

Layout and Graphics: Lou Boudreau, Linda M. Boyer, Angela F. Hunckler, Brent Savage, Kate Snell, Brian Torwelle

Illustrators: Ron Hildebrand, Joanna Koperski and JAK Graphics Ltd., John Padgett, Mark R. Zahnd

Proofreaders: Kelli Botta, Michelle Croninger, Betty Kish, Ethel M Winslow, Janet M. Withers

Indexer: Sherry Massey

General and Administrative

IDG Books Worldwide, Inc.: John Kilcullen, CEO; Steven Berkowitz, President and Publisher

IDG Books Technology Publishing: Brenda McLaughlin, Senior Vice President and Group Publisher

Dummies Technology Press and Dummies Editorial: Diane Graves Steele, Vice President and Associate Publisher; Mary Bednarek, Director of Acquisitions and Product Development; Kristin A. Cocks, Editorial Director

Dummies Trade Press: Kathleen A. Welton, Vice President and Publisher; Kevin Thornton, Acquisitions Manager

IDG Books Production for Dummies Press: Michael R. Britton, Vice President of Production and Creative Services; Cindy L. Phipps, Manager of Project Coordination, Production Proofreading, and Indexing; Kathie S. Schutte, Supervisor of Page Layout; Shelley Lea, Supervisor of Graphics and Design; Debbie J. Gates, Production Systems Specialist; Robert Springer, Supervisor of Proofreading; Debbie Stailey, Special Projects Coordinator; Tony Augsburger, Supervisor of Reprints and Bluelines

Dummies Packaging and Book Design: Patty Page, Manager, Promotions Marketing

◆

The publisher would like to give special thanks to Patrick J. McGovern, without whom this book would not have been possible.

◆

Contents at a Glance

Cartoons at a Glance

By Rich Tennant

page 7

page 45

page 143

page 255

page 297

Fax: 978-546-7747 • **E-mail:** the5wave@tiac.net

Table of Contents

Introduction

· ·

We figure that you can find two kinds of people in the world — those who have waited and waited until they have a home or some property that they can landscape, and those who never gave landscaping a second thought and suddenly find themselves having to do just that. Whichever camp you belong to, welcome — this book is for you.

Good landscaping can do many things for you and your home. A well-planned landscape beautifies your house, wedding it with the surroundings and making it a part of a neighborhood or native terrain. And doing so increases the home's value. Landscaping also makes your house and yard more useful and better able to complement your family's lifestyle, whether you hardly ever step foot in your backyard or want to spend every possible moment outdoors.

Appropriate landscaping can also be functional. Trees can shade your home to reduce energy use. Thorny shrubs can create an impenetrable barrier against possible intruders. Lawns reduce dust from bare ground and are the perfect play area for children. You can entertain or eat outdoors on a patio or deck. And if you leave room for a vegetable garden, you can have fresh salads to enjoy on that patio or deck.

A good landscape also solves problems, providing privacy from nearby neighbors, preventing erosion on steep ground, or channeling water out of soggy, low spots.

About This Book

In this book, you get a mixture of ideas, step-by-step instructions, and answers to practical questions like:

- ✔ "Do I have enough space for this?"
- ✔ "Will this look all right with the style of my house?"
- ✔ "How much time will I need to spend taking care of this?"
- ✔ "Can I really afford this?"

If all you really want is a shady, secluded spot to hang a hammock, this book can help you. If your plans are more grandiose and include a large brick patio, sweeping flower beds, and a potting shed, we can get you there, too.

You see, the steps to designing any landscape, whether simple or sophisticated, are the same. And there are no shortcuts here. This book takes you from the beginning to the end of the landscaping process — from dreaming up ideas, putting them on paper, and estimating costs to choosing plants and building permanent structures like patios, decks, and walls. We also know you may not be able to do all the work yourself, so we also tell you where to get help and how to make sure the job is getting done properly.

The only thing we can't do is come over next weekend and help.

Conventions Used in This Book

When you take on your landscape project, you're dipping into several different disciplines, each with its own peculiar language. The design phase uses words like unity, formal, and landscape architect, which we define or explain as we use them. The planting phase uses common gardening terms like watering, fertilizing, and pruning which most people understand, at least in a basic way.

The specific names of plants, however, are a little trickier. To be sure you know which plants we're talking about, gardeners have a system of plant naming based on Latin and Greek. Following conventional garden naming, we list the common name of plants in normal type (redbud, for example). From there it gets a bit more complex.

- Every plant is a member of a larger horticultural family. For instance, the *family* name for redbuds is *Fabaceae*. Common garden peas and beans are members of the same family, as are locust and mesquite trees.

- These plant family names are divided into groups of closer relatives, indicated by a group or *genus name*. This genus is always written in italics and with the first letter uppercased. Thus the genus name for redbud is *Cercis*.

- The next name is the *species* name. Like the genus, it is written in italics, but the first letter is lowercase. Usually, a plant species name tells something about the plant's shape, color, leaf form, fragrance or some other peculiarity. The genus for the eastern redbud is *canadensis,* which means "of Canada," where the tree is common. (Note that a genus followed by the word "species" means we're referring to numerous species within that group, such as *Cercis* species.)

✔ The final common part of a plant's name is the *variety* name. These are enclosed in single quotation marks. An example is *Cercis canadensis* 'Forest Pansy'. A variety usually has some desirable feature that distinguishes it from the species. In the case of 'Forest Pansy', it has purple leaves instead of the more common green leaves.

The construction part of landscaping also has some conventions that you should be aware of.

✔ When you see something like "2x4," it refers to a piece of lumber with a specific thickness and width — in this case, 2 inches thick by 4 inches wide. Actually, these aren't true dimensions, because what you get at the lumber yard isn't quite 2 inches by 4 inches. We get into that in Chapter 4.

✔ When we say "1-by lumber" or "2-by lumber," we mean lumber that is one inch by something or two inches by something. So a 2-by board can be a 2x4, 2x6, 2x8, or… you get the picture.

✔ Nails have an arcane sizing system based on *pennyweight,* an antiquated British system, which has an even more outdated symbol *(d)* that stands for an even more outdated object — the Roman coin, denarius. What you need to know is that a 4d, 16d, and so on refer to "four-penny" and "sixteen-penny" nails. The good news is that smaller numbers represent smaller nails, larger numbers larger nails, so the system has some logic.

How This Book Is Organized

We designed *Landscaping For Dummies* so that you can pick it up and start anywhere to get at the information you need. Still, because we have no idea where you may need to begin, the following sections tell you how the book is organized — from front to back.

Part I: Designing Your Landscape

This part is where you get acquainted with what you already have in your landscape, and decide what you want to do with it. We take a close look at your property, both the good and the bad, and see how we can solve problems while creating something that fits the "outdoor living" needs of your family. We go over the basic principles of landscape design and get you familiar with tricks that professional designers use to create beautiful, private, and useful gardens. We also show you how to put your ideas on paper, how to estimate costs, and how to plan the whole installation.

Part II: Building Hardscape into Your Yard

A well-designed landscape contains surfaces like paths, patios, and decks; enclosures like fences, arbors, and walls; and things that make a garden unique and useful, like outdoor kitchens, gazebos, custom-built containers, and children's play structures. This is the stuff we call *hardscape* and this part shows you how to design and build it all. But even before you can do that, you may have some other work to do, like installing irrigation. We show you how to do all that in this part as well.

Part III: The Planting o' the Green

Here we're talking out the green stuff. This part covers different kinds of plants — trees, shrubs and vines, annuals, perennials, bulbs, container plants, plants with texture, grasses, ground covers, shady plants, and hardy plants. Each chapter includes hard-core information on how to choose and plant different species, and describes the best kinds for your area.

Part IV: Putting It All Together

Just to show you that everything we tell you in this book really works, we include a whole part of specific landscape designs (including drawings and plant selections) created by a real landscape architect for real people like you. These designs give you ideas for your whole lot — front, side, and back; for special situations like designing a hillside garden, landscaping around low-water areas and pools, or creating a balcony garden; and for theme gardens that attract wildlife, help kids garden, grow vegetables and herbs, or create a water garden.

Part V: The Part of Tens

The Part of Tens includes, well, the leftovers — things you may want to know and things we certainly want to tell you, but we just couldn't find room for them anywhere else. We include ten ways to make your landscape unique, ten landscaping techniques that conserve energy, and ten easy ways to increase your home's resale value.

Appendix

Just as an added bonus, we include a handy list of landscape resources, everything from suppliers of irrigation equipment, specialty plants, and garden ornaments to organizations that can help you get the job done right. It also includes lots of great Web sites that are full of useful information and products for landscaping.

Color photo section

What's a landscaping book without some pictures that show examples? Not much, huh? That's what we figured, so we've included a color section in the middle of this book.

The key feature in these photos that we'd like you to notice is that these aren't exclusively photos of fabulous gardens created by professionals. They are, for the most part, real landscapes created by homeowners with limited budgets. They're examples of what you can create around your own home.

But keep in mind that these are only examples. As with any creative endeavor, you can come up with your own, equally-good ways to make a path, bench, flower bed, deck, or shed.

Icons Used in This Book

Throughout this book, you can find *icons* — small pictures next to the text that point out extra-important information. Here's what they all mean:

This icon highlights all of the jargon that you need to know, either to communicate with your contractor or to buy materials and plants for yourself.

For gems of accumulated wisdom — often the kind learned by painful experience — follow this icon.

Consider this icon like a stop sign — when you see it, stop and pay extra attention, because we only use it to help you avoid serious mistakes or bodily harm.

Suppose you're trying to do the right thing for the environment. Problem is, you may not always know what's right and what isn't. When you see this icon, we're pretty certain that we're steering you in the proper direction.

Where to Go from Here

Hopefully, you're starting to feel excited about your new landscape and the creative juices are starting to flow. So, now what? For some of the tricks you can use to turn dirt, plants, and paving into a something-special design, flip to Part I. For ideas on building patios, decks, paths and other hardscape parts of the landscape, check out Part II.

Part III is full of ideas for selecting plants and putting them in the ground. To see how plans, plants, and hardscape come together, go to Part IV — there you see entire landscape plans that help you solve special problems. For quick, easy tips, check out Part V (the Part of Tens). And for instant inspiration, flip to the color section, located near the center of this book.

Part I
Designing Your
Landscape

In this part . . .

1 If you're a dreamer, this part of the book is for you, because these three chapters are about letting yourself go and not being inhibited. Why? Because it's all on paper. Saying "So, we'll put the pool over here and the second deck off the guest bedroom" is a perfectly acceptable way to start. Get your landscape dreams on paper and who knows, they just may come true.

In order to figure out what you want to do, you have to know what you want. You also need to know what you already have and what you need — that's Chapter 1. In Chapter 2, we introduce you to some of the words and concepts that designers use so that you can analyze your plans the same way that a professional does. It's not until Chapter 3 that we ask you to become very real with plans on paper and start thinking about what it may all cost. So take a deep breath, relax, and dream on. If all goes according to our plan, you'll be so deep into designing your landscape that you'll never notice all the work that you've done!

Chapter 1

Plotting Your Landscape Design

*1*n this chapter, we show you how to create a *site plan* — a drawing of your existing property — and then help you sketch in your landscaping wish list.

But this isn't just any old wish list. Your landscape should be perfect for you and for the people living in your house. The *hardscape* (the parts of your landscape that are physically hard, like a deck or fence) should create an outdoor room for you and your family. The plants in your landscape should provide beauty, privacy, sunblock, or little maintenance — whatever you're looking for in your yard.

So, go ahead and start dreaming — the rest of this book helps you turn those dreams into reality.

Site Analysis — Assessing What You Have

Your first landscape project is to come to grips with your property the way it is now.

✔ What are its strengths and weaknesses?

✔ What do you like or dislike about your yard?

✔ What kind of problems does your landscape have that you need to find solutions for?

This process of assessing your yard is called *site analysis* — an important process when designing a landscape. To begin your own site analysis, here's what you do:

1. **Get a piece of paper (at least 8$\frac{1}{2}$ by 11) and a pencil and make a rough drawing of your property.**

   Be sure to include your house with windows and doors, existing plants, and general north/south directions. Although you should try to draw to scale, your rough drawing doesn't have to be very precise. To do some serious drawing — with dimensions — check out Chapter 3.

2. **Put the drawing on clipboard and walk around your yard at different times of day, making notations of the following:**

   • **Sun and shade:** Mark areas that are sunny or shady, and at what times of the day. When you're ready to purchase plants for your landscape (flip to Chapters 9 and 10), this notation helps you match plants with appropriate light conditions. Noting sunny and shady areas may also give you ideas about creating more comfortable outdoor living space. In midsummer, the south and western sides of the house will be sunniest and warmest. If you live in a cool summer area, that's something you may want to take advantage of. If you live in an area with hot summers, these may be places for shade trees (see Chapter 8) or arbors (see Chapter 7).

   • **Views:** Note good and bad views — ones that you may want to preserve and ones you may want to block. Good views — surrounding hills, the coast, maybe just the nearby skyline — are easy to recognize. Bad views, on the other hand, take a little more eyeballing. Can the neighbors see in your yard or can you see in theirs? Do you have things on your own property, like a utility or storage area, that you'd rather not see? What will you see if you put in a raised deck? Are utility poles visible? Does the view change when deciduous trees lose their leaves?

   • **Prevailing winds:** Note if you regularly feel winds that you may be able to block with fencing or plants.

   • **Slope and drainage:** Put in some arrows that give you a rough idea of the contour of your yard. Sloping ground or uneven terrain can be an interesting part of a landscape, especially if you accentuate it with walls or plants combined with stone to simulate a dry stream bed. High points may also provide some views that you want to take advantage of. On the other hand, sloping ground can also mean erosion or drainage problems that can threaten your house or yard. Be sure that water drains away from all of the walls of your house. Mark down any areas that seem overly wet or where moss or algae is growing. If you can stand getting wet, go outside in a rainstorm and watch where excess water flows. But don't take your clipboard with you!

- **Existing plants:** Draw in large trees, shrubs, vines, and perennials that you may want to preserve.

- **Interesting natural features:** If you're lucky enough to have a small stream or handsome rocks protruding from the ground, they can become special landscape features.

- **Noise, smells, and lights:** Let your senses go and write down anything that you notice — lights at night, noise from next door, and even unpleasant odors. You may be able to do something about them.

3. **Make notations of what you see from *inside* the house:**

- **Views:** Note the good views and the bad. When you look out windows, what do you see? A nice view of the yard or the neighbors back porch? Who can see in the windows from the street or next door?

- **Sunlight:** Does sun blaze through your windows, heating the house in the afternoon? Or do you get a pleasant light that's cast on the kitchen table as you drink coffee in the morning?

- **Lights:** Do car lights or signs shine through your window at night?

4. **You're done!**

Figure 1-1 is a sample of what your site analysis may look like when you're finished. Now you know what you have to work with and can begin dreaming about what improvements will be there soon.

Dreaming Up Your Ideal Landscape

A landscape can be whatever you want it to be. If you want to turn the whole place into a miniature golf course, go right ahead — it's your yard! But experienced landscape designers often say "form follows function," which means that a landscape should meet the needs of the people who use it. In other words, you can design the most elaborate landscape with thousands of dollars of beautiful plants and expensive paving, but if you can't find a comfortable place to set up the barbecue and you *love* to barbecue, what good is your yard to you?

The following sections help you dream up a landscape that's perfect for you.

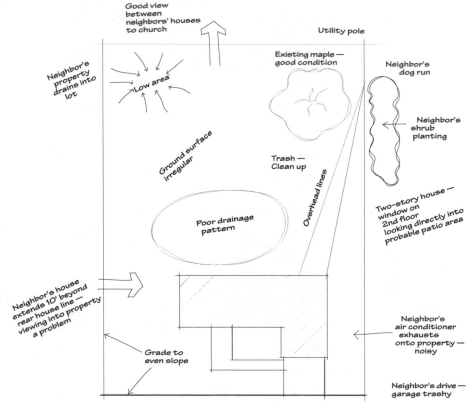

Figure 1-1:
A completed site analysis notes significant features of the property.

How long do you plan to stay in your house?

How long you plan to live in your house influences your landscape planning. If you're only planning to live in your house a couple of years, concentrate on fast-growing trees and shrubs to give you a more powerful effect, sooner. Expensive projects like a deck or pool may add to the value of your home, but you may not recoup those costs before you're ready to move.

In general, the shorter your stay, the less complex your landscape plans should be. If you plan to stay in your house for a long time, tackle more difficult projects, such as adding a deck, fence, pool, or patio (see Part II).

How much of your yard can you use?

Most houses are plunked somewhere in the middle of the lot. Though the surrounding areas may vary in size, you almost always have a front yard, a back yard, and two side yards — that's called a *four-sided landscape*.

Think of your entire yard as potential living spaces. At first, you may have a tough time overcoming the tradition that back yards are where you actually live, front yards are for show, and side yards are mostly ignored. Instead, why not make your entire landscape your living area?

✔ Shield the front yard with walls of greenery (see Chapters 8 and 9) or a privacy fence (flip to Chapter 5), and on weekend afternoons when the rest of the neighborhood is carousing in their back yards, you'll have the front all to yourself. (See Chapter 13 for a great front yard landscape plan.)

If you think that's too bold of a step (and it may well be for your neighborhood), at least you can move some of your ornamental garden beds to the front instead of having a boring, look-good lawn. You may be surprised at how quickly a beautification copycat campaign can start up after the neighbors see you puttering among the flowers and butterflies.

Be aware that you may need to keep your front yard neat to avoid neighborhood resentment — in fact, your local municipality may even have a word with you about this. If you're inspired to plant a prairie or a naturalistic woodland out front, talk to your neighbors first (and call your local government) so that they know what you're doing. Keep well-groomed paths so that the landscape looks guided instead of frighteningly wild. (The reaction that you're trying to avoid is "Oh no! What if those weeds come into my yard?")

✔ Back yards are usually best for children's play areas, because you don't want them to chase balls into the street. If you're a veggie grower with kids, put your garden near the play area so you can keep one eye on them while you weed the zukes. (Check out Chapter 13 for a back yard plan and Chapter 15 for a great vegetable garden plan.)

Vegetable patches don't have to be relegated to the back yard — put them wherever the light and soil and convenience are best. A well-tended patch, planted in an interesting design of diagonals or squares with vegetables that are interspersed with flowers and herbs, has a lot of curb appeal. (Keep in mind that vegetable gardens definitely have an off-season that is less attractive.)

✔ Side yards are often narrow, sometimes shady, and they're usually overlooked as nothing more than a way to get from the front yard to the back. Give yourself reason to linger in your side yard by jumping on a hammock or moving a tea table and chair to the area. If your side yard is sunny, it can be the perfect place for a strawberry patch or a row of raspberries. Your side yard can be a surprise to be discovered — a whimsical garden ornament of some kind or another (here's the place for your pink flamingo), a small garden pool, a dollhouse — and your side yard will become a destination on its own instead of a waystation. (For more ideas, flip to the side yard plan in Chapter 13.)

Using your entire yard allows you to take advantage of different times of the day when one part or another of your landscape is at its best. If your back yard is baked on summer afternoons, you can retreat to the cool respite out front. If the under-eight crowd swarms over the swing set, you can move around to the side yard where you can discreetly keep an eye on the goings-on without being accused of spying. If the neighbor is laboring over his acre of lawn grass out back, you can either stay at your garden retreat to sip lemonade and snicker surreptitiously, or you can move around to the front yard so that he doesn't become too envious.

What will you use your yard for?

To customize your landscape to your life, start by developing a landscaping wish list. The following list is just a start, though — keep working on your own list until you've dreamed up everything you want to do in your yard.

✔ Play catch (or fetch) on the lawn

✔ Cut fresh flowers

✔ Entertain dozens of guests

✔ Grow vegetables and fruit for canning

✔ Swing in a hammock with a good book

✔ Play sports such as basketball, tennis, and badminton

✔ Enjoy the garden after the sun goes down

✔ Swim in a pool or soak in a spa

✔ Watch fish in a small pond

✔ Watch kids play in a sand box, play structure, or fort

✔ Compost lawn clippings, raked leaves, and kitchen scraps

✔ Grow prize-winning roses

✔ Grow fresh herbs or scented flowers

> ✔ View colorful flowers or container plants
>
> ✔ Walk through a meadow of wild flowers
>
> ✔ Hold barbecue parties

Finding ideas

Gathering new ideas for your landscape design is in many ways a treasure hunt. Try the following:

✔ Plan weekend outings to nurseries to give you ideas on what plants flourish in your area. Plants are often displayed at nurseries according to their needs for sun or shade. For example, ferns are displayed in a shade house, while daylilies are displayed in full sun. After a visit or two, you soon figure out which plants you like and where to plant them.

Many nurseries offer lectures during weekends. These talks are usually free and are valuable for gathering information on plants.

✔ Visit local botanical gardens and arboretums to see a great variety of plants (much of it unusual, but proven in your climate).

✔ Join a garden club or plant society. These groups frequently have informative speakers at their meetings and periodically offer garden tours. The garden tours offer you the opportunity to observe the use of various landscape elements, both with the hardscape and with plants. Your local nursery should be able to hook you up with garden clubs or societies dedicated to specific plants, like the Rose Society or Rhododendron Society.

✔ Visit your neighbors and ask them to give you a garden tour of their yards. Seeing the level of landscape in your neighborhood gives you a benchmark on the level and quality of landscaping that the neighborhood warrants.

✔ Subscribe to garden magazines to increase your warehouse of knowledge on plants and their uses. Of course, after you subscribe to a magazine, you soon receive every mail-order plant catalog in the country. That's great for you. Cut out the articles that interest you and make folders organized by plant type. Here are labels on some of the folders we keep: bulbs, perennials, annuals, evergreen trees and shrubs, deciduous trees and shrubs, vines, tools, lawns and ground cover, bugs (both good and bad), plant diseases, decks and patios, garden paths, and garden furniture.

Magazines and catalogs can also alert you to problems in the care and maintenance of plants in the landscape.

✔ Flip to Part II of this book for information on building hardscape and Part III for ideas on plants. You can also find valuable information in *Gardening For Dummies, Roses For Dummies, Perennials For Dummies, Lawn Care For Dummies,* and *Decks & Patios For Dummies*, all written by the Editors of the National Gardening Association and published by IDG Books Worldwide, Inc.

✔ Check out the Internet for a wealth of information in Web sites and in chat rooms. Flip to the Appendix for sources.

Who will use your yard?

Before finalizing any wish list ideas into concrete plans, consider who will use the yard:

- ✔ If you have young children, safety is a big consideration. A swing set in a fenced back yard makes sense. You may also want to include a storage bench for their toys.

- ✔ Do you spend a lot of time barbecuing in the summer? You could really use a built-in barbecue as close to the kitchen door as possible. How about an outdoor sink? (Wait, if that means that the grill master has to wash his or her own dishes, forget the outdoor sink.)

- ✔ What about Fido? You may want to fence in an area or put in a dog run.

Tailor your wish list to your friends and family, so that your landscape is designed to be useful by the people who use it.

Where do you need to walk?

You may already have thought about what friends and family intend to do in the yard — picnicking, socializing, growing tomatoes, making compost, playing in the sandbox, and so on — but you may also want to think about how you and your family move through your yard.

Your list of outdoor wants and needs — eating, playing, sitting — is a lot simpler to divvy up when spaces are already separate, thanks to the geography of the yard and house. Chances are, you already know where the best flat lawn is for that pitch-and-catch area you need. You also know the most discreet place to hide the compost heap and trash cans. You know which neighbor will hate having to see the dog run out his bedroom window and which one will sneak Fido a steak bone when he's out. You know where the sun beats down on late summer afternoons — perfect for the herb garden — and where the neighbor's oak tree casts a cool pool of shade for those patio cookouts that you can't wait to indulge in.

As you begin to get an idea of where the best places are for all the things on your wish list, stroll around and figure out the routes that will get you and others from one area to the next. As you begin fiddling with potential pathways, you may discover that they can make your garden seem bigger. Obscured by shrubs, ornamental grasses, or other tall plants, paths can double back, twist and turn, and run along for much longer than you may think in a limited space. (Chapter 5 is chock-full of information on building pathways.)

Consider the following when planning your paths:

✔ Your kids, your dog, and the pizza guy probably aren't interested in meandering trails, no matter how intriguing and artistic they are. They want to get to the sandbox, the Frisbee, or the front door in a beeline. Don't forget other humdrum daily activities — getting from your house to the mailbox or making a way for the meter reader.

You probably want an easy-access, straight-arrow path, too, for getting to your car in the morning or lugging in groceries after work.

✔ Guests at your patio party enjoy wandering paths through neighboring flower beds and greenery (you can even add nighttime lighting — covered in Chapter 7 — for more romance).

✔ Plan a wide, flat, solid path to trundle a wheelbarrow full of compost, manure, grass clippings, and other goodies from one place to another.

✔ Try to make your pathways link up with each other, so that your landscape isn't full of dead ends. Although friends and family — and the dog — will soon develop favorite routes, it's fun to have more than one choice about which way to go.

✔ The width of paths affects the speed at which people walk them. Wide paths are not only practical for two people to stroll along, they encourage lingering. Narrow paths tend to make people unconsciously uncomfortable, feeling that they have to hurry along.

✔ Paths don't have to be made of paving materials — they're just clear routes to get you from here to there. A swath of lawn that winds through garden beds is as much a path as that beautiful brick herringbone path that you lay through an herb garden.

✔ If you're planning to include fenced areas in your landscape (covered in Chapter 5), make sure that they don't block access to other parts of the yard. Include gates where they make sense or leave sections open for easier access.

If you're having trouble visualizing your paths, use oatmeal or flour to sprinkle a biodegradable path through your yard — you can see in a minute whether your path design works.

How much privacy do you want?

Even if your neighbors aren't the busybody type, you may still find relief in building in privacy as you create your landscape plan.

✔ Tall hedges (covered in Chapter 9), fences (see Chapter 5), and arbors (flip to Chapter 7) work wonders at making your yard your own space.

✔ Privacy structures and walls help to keep your noise in and other noise out, so that you don't have to keep shushing your kids or resenting the neighbor's kid with his souped-up car.

✔ Privacy structures define the boundaries of your landscape. Imagine decorating your living room if it had no walls. A little tricky to make it feel cozy, isn't it? Outdoor living rooms work the same way. Walls make the furnishings — in this case, the plants and ornaments — look better by providing a backdrop. Put that dream fountain you invested in against a wall of lush greenery and it becomes much more appealing than if the sidewalk or the street forms the backdrop.

Chapters 9 and 10 have lots of good plant choices for creating privacy. If you're working with a limited budget, you can use fast-growing annuals like sunflowers and castor bean plant to make a quick, temporary barrier. Rampant vines, though more expensive, are also ideal for creating privacy while saving money. Fast-growing annual vines swarm over whatever support you give them, totally hiding it from view, so feel free to pinch pennies by making privacy screens of plastic garden netting for your scarlet runner beans or moonflowers.

When will you use your landscape?

When dreaming up your ideal landscape, think of the times of day and the times of year in which you plan to uses your yard. For example:

✔ If you plan to be outdoors in the late afternoon, where will you be most comfortable at that time of day? Maybe the shady spot under the big oak tree out back. But if the sun shines hot where a patio is or may be, maybe you need an overhead structure for shade, or need to plant shade trees.

✔ If you like to use the garden (or view the garden) at night, good outdoor lighting is a must.

✔ If you like to be outside during the rainy season, consider creating a covered patio.

✔ If bugs like to use the yard at the same time that you do, a screened-in porch or patio will keep them at bay.

✔ If you like to get outdoors early in the spring, keep or plant trees and structures that don't block the sun.

✔ If you enjoy every minute of summer outdoors, choose trees, shrubs, and flowers that bloom throughout the season.

How much maintenance are you ready for?

Planning your landscape, installing the structures and plants, and admiring your efforts of the finished project are the most gratifying parts of the landscape process. Then comes the reality of maintaining your efforts. Landscape maintenance is an ongoing event — it's the insurance policy that can guarantee success or failure of the landscape. However, you can design low maintenance into a landscape. For example:

- ✔ If you're often away, traveling for business or pleasure, you may want a yard with hardscape and very few plants. (See Part II for more on hardscape.)

- ✔ Avoid overplanting or using fast-growing plants that get too large for their space. They'll need more pruning later on.

- ✔ Having cut flowers in annual beds adds baskets of color to your yard but you'll need to replant these beds a minimum of two times per year. Use lower-maintenance perennials or flowering shrubs instead.

An *annual* is a plant that completes its life in a single season. They are planted once a year. Examples include snapdragons, pansies, marigolds, zinnias, and petunias. A *perennial* grows back year after year. Chapter 10 explains this in more detail.

- ✔ If you're planting a new lawn, plan on mowing it weekly during its growing season. Otherwise, consider ground cover. Check out Chapter 11 for ground cover ideas.

- ✔ If you plan to build wooden landscape elements like decks and fences, plan on painting or applying preservatives every two to three years. Masonry (brick and concrete) needs less maintenance.

- ✔ If you install your planting without an irrigation system, you end up having to water everything by hand unless you live in a climate where rain keeps the garden wet enough. An *automated irrigation system* (see Chaper 4) can water even when you're out of town.

Chapter 2

Thinking Like a Designer

How'd you decide what to wear when you hauled yourself out of bed this morning? Chances are, without even consciously thinking about it, you eliminated those unique plaid pants and awning-striped shirt that your brother-in-law gave you for your last birthday, and you went for an outfit that's a little more stylish. Then you added a scarf or a tie or a couple of pieces of jewelry for a little flash.

Hey, you're a designer! The principles that you use to get dressed every day are exactly the ideas behind good landscaping — a put-together look without major clashing elements, accented by attention-getters here and there. In the language of landscaping, you've just achieved unity; used the appropriate proportions and a correct sense of scale; and balanced color, texture, and form. (And here you thought you were just getting dressed.)

Landscaping lingo may sound like mumbo-jumbo at first, but if you can dress yourself in the morning, you can understand the rules that help change your yard into something more satisfying. Oh, and if you prefer a little more pizzazz than a plain landscape offers — don't worry, we've written this book for all kinds of personal idiosyncrasies to shine here. If you want a flock of pink flamingos parading before shrubbery clipped to look like poodles and giraffes, go for it. (Just don't move in next door to us.)

This chapter includes everything that you need to know to really annoy the next professional landscaper — sometimes called a *landscape architect* or *landscape designer* — that you come across at the next patio party in your redone backyard.

Unity, Blessed Unity

Unity is what keeps all those separate parts of your landscape tied together, so that the eyes and feet of visitors flow from one part of the yard to another. To achieve unity in your landscape, do the following:

- **Clearly define pathways.** Pathways are a first step to unifying your landscape.

- **Link greenery.** A couple of shade trees and a forsythia bush stuck here and there in your lawn do *not* create a unified landscape design. Plant a bed of vinca or other ground cover or even a thick layer of wood chips at the feet of all three to visually link them together, continue the same ground cover along the fence and around the corner to the patio, stick a couple more forsythias at the corner, and presto! Unity.

- **Have a style.** Be clear about what you want the garden to say about you.

  - If your tastes run to formal precision, for instance, you probably want clipped hedges, classic statues, brick or stone pathways, and symmetrical plantings that provide calming mirror images.

  - A cottage garden jumble of exuberant flowers with rustic fences, bent-twig benches, and a concrete frog along the path tells visitors that you're more of a free-spirit type.

A combination of the two styles looks disjointed and has a disquieting effect on your landscape. But having unity in your landscape doesn't mean that you can't have your formal rose garden and your wildflower meadow — just don't put them side-by-side. Separated by a hedge, on opposite sides of the house, or linked by a transition zone that gradually makes the shift from control to wilderness, your gardens can be as fickle as your little heart desires.

Figure 2-1 shows a unified backyard.

Repeat After Me

Repetition of hardscape materials — including brick, wood, stone, concrete, wood chips, and fencing — is a simple way to make your garden look like it's all one piece, even if the areas are distinctly different.

- Manmade materials — basically, anything other than plants — carry great weight in the landscape, because they draw viewers' eyes like a magnet. Select your hardscape materials to match your garden style and repeat them throughout the landscape.

For example, you can use a single section of diagonal, framed lattice to support a climbing rose along the wall of your house; an L-shaped couple of sections to shield the compost pile from view; or three or four linked sections to serve as a privacy screen along the patio, as shown in Figure 2-2. Depending how large your yard is, you may want to repeat the lattice theme in variation by installing solid, vertical-board privacy fence topped by a narrow strip of lattice.

✔ Sticking in the same plants here and there (think, "Here a shrub, there a shrub") is an easy trick. Simply repeat backbone plants that perform well most of the year, like evergreens (discussed in Chapter 8), ground covers (covered in Chapter 11), and shrubs (see Chapter 9), to tie your garden areas to each other.

✔ Repeating shapes helps pull things together, too: curved outlines of beds, undulating paths, bosomy urns, and mounds of plants. Or, if your yang side is doing the designing, try no-nonsense point A to point B paths, yardstick-straight bed edges, spiky plant forms, clipped hedges, or vertical board fences.

Figure 2-2:
Simple
devices,
such as
these
screens,
help create
repetition.

✔ That great repetition catchall also covers color: by repeating colors throughout the landscape, you make it look like it's all one piece — the unity thing again. Stick in clumps of yellow flowers here and there in various beds, pots, or plantings across your back yard, and you'll find your eye travels from one patch of yellow to the next in a seamless, satisfying way. But if the most eye-catching plant in one bed is red, the next one yellow, the next one white, your poor eyes get confused. You can combine colors of plants with colors of house or hardscape, too, for unity's sake. For example, paint a lattice cobalt blue and match it with big folk-art blue-and-yellow flower pots, and you can use that two-tone color scheme to run through the garden.

Play with Color

Hot colors — white, bright pink, yellow, orange, and orange-red — jump out at you, making distances seem shorter. Cool colors — blues, purples, deep reds, and pastels — recede, making spaces seem longer. If you want to make a small yard seem bigger, plant hot colors at the entryway and cool colors across the garden at the far end, where they'll look like a misty watercolor painting.

To make wide-open spaces seem smaller, plant bright, hot colors across the way, where they'll seem to jump forward. Just be sure to choose colors in the same palette. You can use vivid orange and golden yellow dahlias at a gate, for instance, then soften the hue into apricot and pale sulphur yellow as the plantings recede.

The color photo section, near the center of this book, has lots of ideas about color.

Get Some Rhythm

Repeating elements — whether it's color, leaf shape, plant forms, curved or straight lines, hedges, or ground cover — create a rhythm in your land-scape, a pacing that you can control by your plant choices just like turning the dial to a different radio station. If you want slow, smooth-flowing music, choose quiet colors and wide stretches of greenery. To jazz it up, look to bright hues and vertical forms, such as sword-leaved irises, vertical clumps of ornamental grasses, and decorative posts and columns.

Want to see this in action? Take a look at Figure 2-3.

Figure 2-3:
Repeating
elements
create
rhythm.

The rhythm of your landscape can be as energetic as "Rocky Top" or as elegant as "The Blue Danube." Any eye-catchers in the garden, if accompanied by neighboring plants of lower voltage, work to create a lively rhythm. Clipped shrubs, grasses, vertical plants, big-leafed plants, anything bigger, brighter, taller, or otherwise strikingly different than its neighbors — they're all showoffs that grab attention. Use them to make your garden dance with a lively beat. Restful rhythm makers include stretches of greenery, such as fern beds, shrub plantings, ground covers, and cool-colored flowers in shades of blue, purple, or pastels.

How Many Pink Flamingos Are Enough?

Manmade objects carry much more weight in the garden than plants — our eyes are instantly drawn to them. That's why a single urn or birdbath draws the eye like a magnet, even in the midst of the most beautiful garden (see Figure 2-4 for an example). The rule with garden ornaments is the same one that mothers teach their daughters about jewelry — when it comes to adornment, less is more.

You can still have your gazing globe, your collection of birdhouses, your gargoyles, and your angel fountain, but keep them separate visually with intervening shrubbery or bends in the path so they don't all burst on the scene at once. Your eye should know exactly where to look. Place your *objets d'art,* then walk out of the garden. Do something else for a while, then go back to the garden as if you're seeing it for the first time. If your gaze hops around from one outrageous, er, wonderful piece of lawn art to another, you have too much stuff.

Pay Attention to Hardscape

The patio, deck, walkways, fences, trellises, and other hardscape elements of your landscape are just as important as the plants. Whether you're shopping for store-bought or creating your own, make your hardscape elements as attractive as your planting beds.

Remember that you'll be looking at them unadorned in the off season, when leaves have fallen and plants are dormant. Soften them in all seasons by planting woody shrubs, vines, ornamental grasses, and trees nearby. A patio without softening plants may look fine in summer surrounded by lawn grass, but in winter, it can look pretty bleak without a few natural plant forms to anchor it to the earth.

Figure 2-4:
Use manmade objects in your landscape.

TIP

Shopping for hardscape and for the materials to make it can be a rude introduction to sticker shock. Bricks, arbors, benches, fences, and all those other "extras" can be a much bigger investment than the plants. Considering how valuable they are in transforming an average garden into a great one, though, hardscape is well worth the investment. Search out the most beautiful arbor in the world, and you'll love your garden forever. Skimp on the deck, and you'll rue your miserly impulse for years.

Focus on the Details

You may have some favorite plants that you want to include in your new landscape. *Before* you plant is the time to acquire an appreciation of the subtler details of those plant.

- Look at the leaves with an eye toward design attributes — after all, unless you're growing only annuals, your plants will be mostly leaves much of the time.

- Begin to notice the texture of foliage: broad and strappy, flat and wide, ferny and delicate, fuzzy, velvety, or shiny.

- Consider the form of the flower — is it simple and flat like a daisy, emphatically spiky like gayfeather, or soft and wide like yarrow? Also, consider that most perennials bloom for just a few short weeks. What will they add to your garden the rest of the time?

- That young plant at the garden center will grow into a garden member of distinct height and habit. Cast a critical eye toward the mature shape of the plant, which may end up being upright, mounded, arching, single-stemmed, branching, swordlike. Find out if it stays in a clump or travels to form a colony.

When you make your choices, contrast and combine plants so they make the most of one another. Put frilly ferns next to plain-leaved hostas, so they can both show off without competing with each other. Partner upright growers like iris with mounders and sprawlers so that they can stand like punctuation points. Echo colors, leaf shapes, forms to create beds of delicious texture. Play with your plants! And don't worry if you don't get it picture-perfect on the first try. The best part of gardening is that if you decide you don't like a combination, hey, there's the shovel.

The Goldilocks Theory

Not too big, not too small — just right. That's the strategy behind selecting plants that are the right scale for your yard and the right proportions to each other. Fill a small yard with great big plants, and you create a feeling of being overwhelmed. Instead, use small-leafed plants of small stature to stay in scale and make the most of your limited space. If you must have that large plant or tree, make it a focal point by partnering it with low-key plants that don't compete in size and stature, as shown in Figure 2-5.

Choosing the right trees for your yard is where the Goldilocks rule must be obeyed. Judging by the number of mismatched, butchered, hacked-off trees that you see along the streets, and the number of houses swamped in blue spruces or hemlocks planted too close to the dwelling, many folks apparently think the cute little tree they're planting stays that size forever. Wrong.

Never overlook one of the most important lines on the nursery tag — the ultimate size of the tree. Remember what happened to the Three Bears and choose trees that fit your yard. Big yard, big tree. Small yard, small tree.

Figure 2-5:
Select
components
that are the
proper
scale for
your yard.

Layer upon Layer

Big, old shade trees are a great asset, but they can be frustrating to work into a landscape plan because their size makes them stick out. A little trick called *stepping down* anchors your big tree to the rest of the garden. Here's what you do: plant smaller trees beside your giant — redbuds beneath a maple, perhaps — and shrubs beside the shorter trees, so that your gaze makes a transition to the tops of the trees in graduated steps instead of one giant leap. You can also use horizontal visual weight to balance height. Notice the large tree in Figure 2-6 that's flanked by smaller trees on each side, which are surrounded by flowers and shrubs that are smaller yet.

Figure 2-6:
Layering
connects
the trees,
the patio,
and the
planting
beds.

Think of your yard as a big ice cream sundae: layers of good things piled on top of each other to create a breathtaking effect. Okay, so it's not all crammed in a parfait glass, but layering your landscape with plants of different heights definitely improves the look of your landscape. Ground covers and grass form the lowest layer, followed by flowering perennials and annuals, then by shrubs, then small trees, then medium trees, then venerable tall trees. Structures can also substitute for any of the plants: a pedestal birdbath for a midheight shrub, for instance, or a vine-covered wall or fence for a small tree.

Think of layers as you plan the general look of your landscape. Your pencil plan shows only a flat oval for a flower bed, but in your mind, that flat shape should be three-dimensional, with roses or other flowering shrubs rising above the perennials, and small trees or trellises adding even more height to the bed. Layering not only adds height to your landscape, which instantly makes it more interesting, but it lets you wedge in a lot more plants than a design that calls for side-by-side planting.

Chapter 3

Getting Serious about Your Design

· ·

· ·

*O*ne reality about landscaping is that you need a plan — on paper. This is easy if you're artistic, a little tougher if you're not. (Also difficult for the non-*artistes* is visualizing what the plan will actually look like. That's why we tell you to take chairs and a ladder into the yard to create the semblance of your planned landscape.) This chapter shows you the ropes.

Other realities that this chapter helps you face include neighbors, public agencies and their codes, how much your landscape project is going to cost, and who is going to do all of the work. This chapter guides you through it all.

Putting Your Ideas on Paper

Think of your landscape plan as a tool to help you get a handle on the price tag of your project, establish your priorities, and make sure that all the separate parts of your landscape — the barbecue pit, a meditation pool, the kid's area — are present and accounted for. Transferring dreams to paper requires more than a little imagination, but with some practice on perspective, you can tell if your plan is an aesthetically-pleasing one.

In other words, how's the finished yard gonna look?

In order to draw your plan, you may want to pick up a few of the drawing supplies shown in Figure 3-1, but you can get away with just some large-size paper, a pencil, and an eraser. More complicated drawing tools help you keep your lines straight and maintain consistent sizes for the elements of your landscape. Alternatively, you may want to invest in a computer landscape design package (see the Appendix).

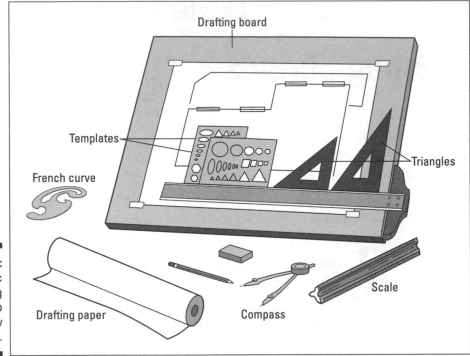

Drafting board

Templates

French curve

Triangles

Figure 3-1:
Basic
drafting
tools help
you draw
your plan.

Drafting paper

Compass

Scale

You may also want to consider using graph paper, which has a printed grid of squares that makes transferring real-life elements to a flat piece of paper much easier. You can, for example, transfer your measurements to the graph paper using a 1-foot to $^1/_4$-inch ratio — a 1-foot-long line in real life covers $^1/_4$ inch on graph paper, a 4-foot-line is 1 inch long on graph paper, a 20-foot-long line in real life is 5 inches long on graph paper, and so on. If you need to, you can tape sheets of graph paper together so that your plan fits.

Draw the base plan

Before you can start adding your wonderful new landscape features, you have to map what's already there, so that you don't end up with your new Victorian knot garden sprouting out of your roof. Here's how to do it:

1. **Measure the lengths of all edges of your property and draw the outline of your yard on paper.**

   Taking measurements may sound like a pain in the neck — and we won't try to fool you, it is — but you're far ahead of the game when you get estimates for what this new design is actually going to cost. Without measurements, you'll have no idea how much concrete, wood chips, topsoil, bricks, ground cover, plants, or other material that you need.

Measurements are also vital when adding new elements to your yard. Sure, you can eyeball your yard and make your drawing fit, but when you try to execute the plan, you may find out how fallible your eyeballs really are. Measurements eliminate guesswork and give you the confidence of knowing that your plan will work.

Invest in a 100-foot tape measure to avoid the frustration of marking off 12-foot lengths and adding them up to get a reading on your 400-foot side boundary. Enlist a helper when you're ready to measure, to make the job go quicker.

If you have the original map of your property, skip the measuring and trace that. No need to reinvent the wheel.

2. **Measure and draw in the outline of your house.**

   Be sure to place the house exactly where it sits on your lot.

3. **Measure and add the garage, yard barn, outhouse, chicken coop, or whatever other outbuildings currently exist.**

   Some of the measurements are easy to take, such as the length of building walls. Start with these. Then draw in other elements and show their locations in relation to known measurements.

4. **Measure and draw in whatever paving is already in place and that you want to keep — the driveway, front walk, basketball court, and so on.**

   Don't assume that right angles and parallel lines that are formed by walls, fences, driveways, and property lines are always perfect. Verify the distance between objects with as many measurements as you can.

5. **Measure and draw existing fences, big trees, hedges, perennials, vegetable garden, and any other current features you want to keep right where they are.**

   Indicate the precise location of a tree trunk or plant by measuring the distance from it to two known points, such as two corners of the house.

Now trot down to your local copy shop and run off a half-dozen or so copies.

Dreaming on paper

Sharpen your pencil, stock up on erasers, and put a copy of your old, unimproved landscape sketch in front of you. In this section, you transfer your dreams into a plan. No Rembrandt needed here — just use circular or oval balloons or *goose eggs* and write inside the circles what they are ("shed," "play area," "vegetable garden" — you get the idea). Make the balloons about the same proportional size that they are in real life. Create a big balloon for the badminton lawn, say, versus a small balloon for the herb garden — or vice versa depending on your priorities. Here's what to add to your drawing of the existing landscape features:

- **Plan activities.** Add goose eggs for all the special activities that you eventually want to enjoy in your yard — if you ever get this blasted plan finished!

- **Sketch paths.** Draw any paths that you'd like to add, drawing lines to indicate their shapes and widths.

- **Add hardscape.** Sketch in fences, a spa, a patio, a deck, front porch improvements, and any other hardscape elements you've chosen.

- **Draw plants.** Add goose eggs for flower beds, shrubs, vines, new trees, vegetable gardens, and so on.

After you have all of the parts of your new design in place, you should have something that looks like Figure 3-2.

Taking your design for a test drive

When you're satisfied with your paper sketch, you need to test your design. Now you get to play with a bunch of weird objects to make your landscape look alive. Pull your garden hoses out of their perpetual nest-of-snakes tangle, collect a handful of tomato stakes or wire cages, get the rope from the garage, drag out the plastic lawn chairs and buckets, prepare a wheelbarrow load of leaves or a bale of straw, and get ready to play make-believe. Work on one section of the plan at a time. Here's how to do it:

- Outline curving paths with hose or rope, or sprinkle a path of oatmeal or flour so that you can see the direction it takes.

  To make a straight line, invest in a *chalkline,* a device that looks like a tape measure, but is filled with chalk. The chalk powders a string that you pull out. Tie the chalked string between two uprights, clip the end, and — this is the fun part — lift the taut string in the center with your thumb and forefinger and let it ping hard toward the ground. It snaps against the grass or soil, leaving a perfect straightedge. Use the chalkline to mark potential beds and paths when you're drawing your design, then use it again later when you start digging.

- Put lawn chairs where you plan to add shrubs or young trees.

- Pound in tomato stakes to show the future homes of roses or large perennials in your flower beds.

- Rake the leaves or straw into the outlines of your new beds. If you have a bounty of fall leaves, grass clippings, or straw, you can spread them out to fill in the outlines so you can easily get a feel for your new beds.

- A step ladder makes a good fool-your-eye representation of an arbor.

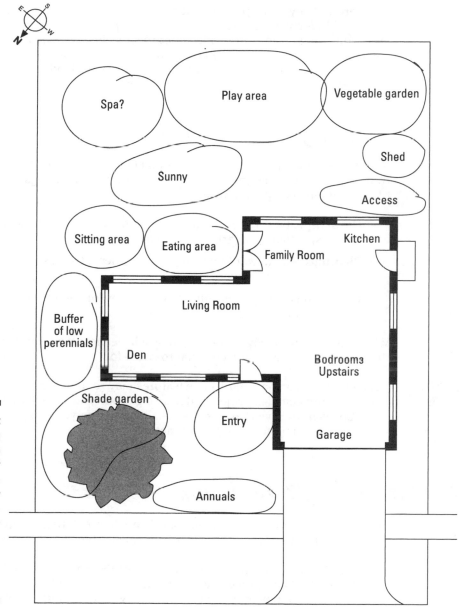

Figure 3-2:
Using tracing paper over your base plan, draw shapes to identify what you have and what you want.

By this time your property will no doubt be ringed with throngs of curious neighbors who will be sure that this time you've totally lost it. Fill them in, if you feel inclined, or let them wonder as you walk around your new "land-scape." Squint your eyes, throw your imagination into full gear, and check the position of the elements you've placed from every vantage point you can think of. Remember, that's not a plastic chair: It's a graceful hemlock. Five-gallon bucket? No — a beautiful holly, resplendent with red berries.

Move around any of the parts of your portable garden until you like the way it looks. When you have this part of your yard arranged to your satisfaction, mark your rough plan with revised lines to show bed edges, plant placement, and any other niceties that you want to note. Then move on to the next section of yard and do it again. Repeat until your landscape plan is — gasp! — finished.

Creating the final plan

After you're comfortable with each section of your proposed landscape, transfer your ideas to paper in real form — not just goose eggs. Your final plan should include the following:

- ✔ **Hardscape:** Be sure to include deck, patio, benches, fences and gates, paths, spa, tool shed, arbor, and so on.

- ✔ **Plantings:** Add flower beds, vegetable gardens, trees, shrubs, vines, lawns, and ground cover.

- ✔ **Dimensions:** Add dimensions for the house, for each element, and for the entire yard.

While the example in Figure 3-3 may look a little more professional than your drawing, it gives you an idea of what to shoot for.

Keep in mind that some hardscape features may require *construction drawings*. For more complex projects (decks, big arbors, and the like), you probably want to have these professionally drawn so you can get construction bids, obtain permits, and order materials.

Stocking Your Tool Box

Every job has its tools, and landscaping is no different. Depending on what projects you plan to tackle, consider investing in the following:

- ✔ **For planting perennials, annuals, and bulbs:** Shovel or spade, stiff-tined rake, hand trowel, hand pruner, and a hose and spray attachment. Optional equipment includes garden gloves, knee pads, plant labels, soaker hose or other irrigation system, bucket, and a bulb planter.

- ✔ **For planting trees, shrubs, and vines:** Square-nosed shovel or garden spade, hoe, stiff-tined rake, and a garden cart or wheelbarrow.

- ✔ **For hardscape:** Posthole digger, pick, digging bar, hammer, handsaw, square, nail set, chisel, plane, circular saw, power drill, power sander, power screwdriver, caulking gun, sawhorse, and stepladder.

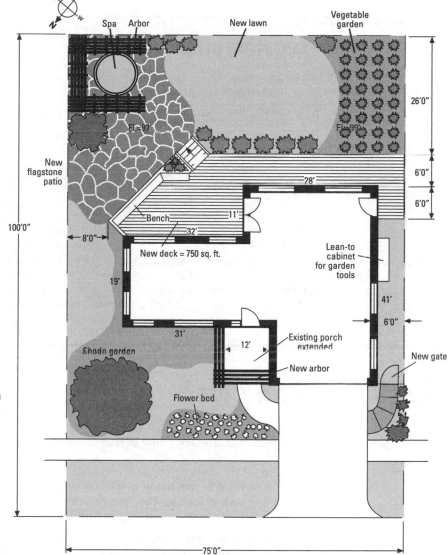

Figure 3-3: The final site plan incorporates needs and features into a functional landscape.

✓ **For planting lawn seed or sod:** Sharp knife, roller, broadcast spreader, and soil preparation equipment, including a rotary tiller and heavy rake. (See Chapter 11 for more on planting seed and sod.)

✓ **For maintenance:** Lawn mower, trimmer, hedge clippers, hand pruner, loppers, pruning saw, hoe, lawn rake, and stiff-tined rake.

Locating property lines

You don't find your property lines drawn on the ground. If you're lucky, though, you can find *monuments,* or markers, at the property corners. These markers may be conspicuous posts driven into the ground, but more likely, they're small pipes or brass medallions, often covered by several inches of accumulated soil. Property corners at the street are usually marked by small crosses inscribed in the concrete curb or gutter.

Keep in mind that your actual property line may be set back several feet from these markers; check your deed to see whether the street occupies an easement along the front of your property (an *easement* essentially means that your city, county, or neighbor can use the space if it ever needs it). Refer to your deed's legal description of your property. It may be a "metes and bounds" description based on known landmarks or a reference to a lot number on a subdivision map that's recorded with the appropriate agency, such as the county recorder's or tax assessor's office.

If you can't find your markers easily, ask your immediate neighbors or long-time residents living nearby. As a good-neighbor policy, you may want to conduct the search with your immediate neighbors anyway, especially to clarify the ownership of fences. If you can't verify the property lines, hire a surveyor, perhaps sharing the cost with neighbors. If your neighbors don't want to cooperate, you can still hire a surveyor yourself and seek his advice about any disputes.

What's It Gonna Cost?

Divide your landscaping project into logical sections according to that list of priorities you established at the beginning of this chapter, and start your tally.

1. List the plants you want to use in each section of the project, and either collect your own prices by shopping nurseries and garden centers or ask a nursery to give you a quote on the whole shebang.

2. Use your plan to measure the areas where you want to install brick, pavers, concrete, or other hardscape materials, and take your measurements to a supplier to get estimates on materials.

3. Make a checklist of the costs of each section of the project, including hardscape items — such as paving, benches, and fencing — and the plants.

4. Consider what, if any, new tools you need to buy.

Visit a building supply store, taking your lists of figures along with you. There, you can find an expert who can calculate exactly what each part of your project will cost. Be sure to find out the delivery charge, and get an estimate on installation, too. Although you may decide starting out that you want to do it all yourself, you may feel better knowing what the installed price is, in case you run out of steam. Fill out a checklist like the one in Table 3-1 for each section of your landscape and then tally up a grand total.

Table 3-1:		Pricing Checklist	
Element	*Price*	*Delivery charge*	*Installation charge*
Plants			
Topsoil			
Mulch			
Concrete			
Lumber			
Bricks			
Gravel			
Sand			
Stone			
Pavers			
Fence			
Lattice			
Trellises/arbors			
Outdoor furniture			
Lighting			
Irrigation system			
Tools			

The advantage to having separate price tags attached to the various sections of your plan is that you then have an idea of how big a bite each new step will take out of your budget. Keep in mind, though, that the estimates you start with may change — go up, that is — by the time you actually begin the next phase.

Cut your landscape project into bite-sized pieces

Renovating your entire yard in one fell swoop can overwhelm even the most dedicated gardener, unless you have an unlimited budget or a staff the size of Martha Stewart's.

✔ **Establish your priorities.** Plan to work on the areas that you will use the most. Only you know whether you get more pleasure out of a patio or an herb garden.

✔ **Have a long-term plan.** Redo your yard on the two-to-five-year plan. Use your budget estimates to decide which parts of your plan you can have this year, and which have to be deferred.

✔ **Do a little at a time.** Landscaping can be a bite too big to chew in a weekend of hard labor. If you're doing the work yourself, focus on one small area at a time. Complete it before you move on to the next. Otherwise your entire yard will be torn up for longer than you're probably comfortable with.

Before You Break Ground

Before you begin your landscaping project, call your local governing body — town council, zoning board, or any other likely agency that you find in the commercial pages of your phone book — and ask what permits are necessary for the work you're planning. Tell them what kind of job you're undertaking; chances are, you have some red tape to get through.

You may also want to let your neighbors know what you're planning — before the backhoe arrives. Also, before beginning your landscape project, consider which tasks may be too time-consuming — or require too much expertise — for you to tackle alone.

Dealing with City Hall

Local restrictions vary greatly from one place to the next, as the neighbors of the Sultan of Brunei found out when he painted his Beverly Hills palace hot pink and added statues of naked dancing girls along the street. Your plans, of course, won't come close to those of His Highness, but you'll still have to clear them with the authorities before you proceed. In many communities, for instance, the height of a fence is a matter of law. Better to find out ahead of time that 5 feet tall is the limit before you invest in 6-foot privacy walls. Ponds and pools, even small ones, may require a fence to keep neighborhood toddlers or the meter reader from falling in. You may need to have an inspector check your work. At the very least, you'll likely need permits for erecting any kind of permanent structure.

The term *setback* is a popular one with zoning departments. The setback is the distance from an adjoining property line that a structure can be erected. Before you dig, make sure you're putting it in the right place. Building a deck is hard work. Taking it down and moving it two feet inward is plain aggravation. Keep things easy on yourself by finding out the rules before you begin.

Penny-pinching ideas

You can shave hundreds of dollars off of your landscaping price tag with a few cost-cutting tricks:

✔ **Buy from the source.** Eliminate the middleman and you're likely to get a bargain. Look for brickyards, paving makers, stone and slate quarries, gravel yards, and other nearby sources of raw materials. Let your fingers do the walking to locate such suppliers — they're probably listed in your phone book. Do some comparison shopping and know how much you need — before you ask for a price.

✔ **Find a friend with a pickup truck.** Don't strain the springs of your own or a friend's truck with stone or other ultra-heavy materials, but do haul your own lumber and anything else that you can safely carry. You save big on delivery charges.

✔ **Combine brick with concrete.** Instead of installing costly all-brick walks, combine brick with concrete. Use the brick as decorative strips in the walk.

✔ **Eliminate mortar between pavers or bricks.** Set the materials into a frame made of rot-resistant lumber or strips of concrete. Set bricks or pavers into a sand base between the edges of the frame and brush sand into the cracks. The frame prevents the paving from shifting.

✔ **Salvage cool stuff.** Visit architectural salvage dealers for real buys on fencing, arbors, ironwork, and neat decorative touches. It's a matter of chance what you can find, but we defy you to come away empty-handed. If your phone book doesn't list "Architectural Salvage," check under "Junk Dealers."

✔ **Make a faux stone wall out of free concrete.** Pieces of broken concrete sidewalk can look a lot like fieldstone when you stack them for a dry wall. Next time you see a sidewalk being ripped out, ask if you can have the broken pieces. Most contractors will gladly dump the stuff in your yard so that they don't have to haul it to the landfill, where they pay a fee for dumping.

✔ **Ask for wood chips from tree services and utility companies or road crews clearing roadside right-of-ways.** You can often get a truckload for zero cash. Use the chips for path surfaces and for long-lasting mulch.

Call before you dig

You've probably seen it on a million little signs plastered to telephone poles or set along the byways: "Call before you dig." Utility companies have a lot going on under the ground, including gas and water mains, electric lines, fiber optic phone cables, and other related goodies. Follow the advice of those cautionary signs and dial the numbers on them to get the okay from those companies. If you think the cost of bricks is high, wait'll you get the bill for slicing through a phone cable! Play it safe, even if all you're doing is planting a tree.

Keeping the neighbors happy

Keep peace in the neighborhood with a very simple action — talk to your neighbors. Let them know what kind of work you're planning, so that they don't panic about how it will affect their property. Talking it over with them works wonders at alleviating apprehension.

Neighbors are as territorial about their own places as pit bulls. Pay attention to how your changes may affect them. Before you plant a row of 12-foot evergreens or put up a privacy fence, consider whether you'll be blocking their view or creating a shade problem for them. Will your improvements be a positive thing for them, too, or will they be left staring at the ugly backside of your new fence or swatting mosquitoes attracted by your garden pool? Put yourself in their shoes.

Doing it yourself or calling in the big guns

You probably can't do it all. Before you tackle a new project, such as laying a patio, assess your physical strength and your skills, and how trainable you are. Read the helpful pamphlets at building supply stores, or read more in how-to books, then take a merciless look at your un-Schwartzeneggeresque biceps and your already jam-packed free time, and decide whether you and the task are compatible.

Even if you're a beginner, with a little dedication and energy, you can have success with the following projects:

- Making a path of wood chips or gravel (see Chapter 5)
- Laying a brick, flagstone, or concrete paver walkway (see Chapter 5)
- Planting small trees, shrubs, perennials, and other plants (see Chapters 9, 10, and 11)
- Installing sod or spreading grass seed (see Chapter 11)
- Planting a ground cover (see Chapter 11)
- Building a raised bed (see Chapter 7)
- Installing low-level outdoor lighting (see Chapter 7)
- Building a lightweight shade structure, arbor, or trellis (see Chapter 7)
- Making a bench or planter (see Chapter 7)
- Installing a preformed garden pond (see Chapter 7)

Bigger jobs, requiring more time and heavier labor, include those that follow. Feel free to tackle them yourself if you're inclined, but you may want to get professional help.

- Installing a fence and gate (see Chapter 5)
- Building steps (see Chapter 5)
- Installing an irrigation system (see Chapter 4)
- Building stone or stacked-concrete walls (see Chapter 5)
- Planting large trees (see Chapter 5)
- Doing electrical, plumbing, or gas-line work
- Building large outdoor structures, such as a shed (see Chapter 7)
- Pouring concrete (see Chapter 6)
- Installing a patio (see Chapter 6)
- Building a deck (see Chapter 6)
- Installing a pool

TIP

Who you gonna call?

Should you decide to holler for help, holler in the right direction. When you're ready to call in a pro, talk to trusted friends and neighbors first. Ask for recommendations for companies that have done satisfying work — don't hire Jimmy-down-the-street's cousin just because he's the only name on your list. Ask for references, and check them. A drive-by around a former client's property may be all you need to see if the work is up to snuff.

Work quality isn't the only consideration, though. Ask whether the work was done on schedule, at a fair price, and whether cleanup afterward was satisfactory. Would the client hire the firm again? When you've narrowed down your list, call the Better Business Bureau and see if any complaints have been filed against the pros you're considering.

If you feel at all shaky about your skills as a designer, call in a landscape architect or designer to give you advice or even draw up a plan for you. You can also show the pro your plan and ask for suggestions or confirmation of your own good common sense — all for a fee, of course.

Part II
Building Hardscape into Your Yard

The 5th Wave   By Rich Tennant

"I think Paul was inspired by our trip last year touring the Great Gothic Decks of Europe."

In this part . . .

A landscape usually contain lots of growing things — trees, shrubs, flowers, and so on — but chances are, you're thinking of *building* a few things for your landscape, too. Even if your home has a great expanse of lawn or an abundant garden, you may want a modest fence or a walkway. At the other extreme, you may xdecide to dominate your landscape with a deck or patio, an arbor, a gazebo, a shed, several walkways and steps, a retaining walls or two, and a pond — any kind of outdoor structure that you can think of!

These man-made features, in landscaping lingo, are called *hardscape,* and are usually installed before the plant materials. Whether you're planning a few feet of fence or a backyard building boom, this part is loaded with information on preparing your site for your hardscape, and for planning and building most hardscape features.

Chapter 4
Taming Your Site

• •

In This Chapter

▶ Preparing your site for construction work

▶ Grading your property

▶ Dealing with sloping ground

▶ Getting water to drain properly

▶ Installing irrigation systems

• •

The first step of landscape construction is to prepare your site for plants and structures. Whether your home is surrounded by bare land or by a mature, established yard, before installing your new landscaping, you have to *lay out* (locate and mark) the site improvements, grade the ground for any structures, stabilize slopes, solve drainage problems, and install any underground utilities, such as electrical wiring or water lines for irrigation. This chapter shows you how, starting with some general guidelines for any type of outdoor construction project.

Construction Basics

Outdoor structures are fun to build and many are within the capabilities of a novice builder. Other projects are more complex, requiring an experienced hand. This section provides some basic information for both types of projects — but keep in mind that a simple project won't require most of it.

In either case, a building project shouldn't involve a carefree, anything-goes approach. Whatever you build or install outdoors endures constant exposure to the weather and withstands continuous contact with the ground, which teems with organisms that accelerate rotting. The ground is also subject to the following:

 ✔ *Frost heaves* (buckling of the ground, due to frost, in areas with severe winters)

 ✔ *Natural settling* (natural compaction of soil over time)

✔ *Creepage* (the sliding of soil down a slope over time)

✔ Poor drainage

✔ *Unstable soils* (certain types of soil that don't compact well)

Many structures, such as decks and shade structures (which are sometimes called *arbors* or *pergolas*), must meet strict building code requirements. Irrigation systems are subject to plumbing codes, and lighting and wiring projects are subject to electrical codes. To meet these challenges, observe the following list of construction basics for outdoor projects.

✔ **Investigate regulations.** Contact your local building department to find out which regulations apply to your project and to obtain a permit, if required. Most communities have zoning ordinances that specify how far you can place certain structures from the property lines (called *setbacks*); what percentage of the property you can cover with improvements (called *lot coverage*); and the maximum height of fences, sheds, and overhead shade structures that you can place near property lines. Building codes govern how you must design and build a structure, such as a deck or overhead cover. Tree removal and landscaping along sidewalk median strips may also be regulated. Certain improvements, however, such as decks lower than 30 inches from the ground, fences lower than a specified height, patios, or walks are often exempt from such regulations.

Your home may also be subject to the covenants, conditions, and restrictions *(CC&R)* of a neighborhood association, which often include design guidelines and a design review process.

✔ **Draw plans.** Work out construction details on paper, not on the job, by making scale drawings (graph paper makes this task much easier). For simple projects, such as a walk or retaining wall, a *plan view* (an overhead view) with a few details can suffice. For projects that require a building permit, such as a deck, you may need to add elevations (side views), sections (cutaways that show features that aren't visible in plan or elevation views), and details (enlargements of critical connections or unusual features). Flip to Chapter 3 for details about drawing your site plan. (You may need to hire a professional to draw more complicated views.)

✔ **Design adequate foundations.** Support structures on concrete footings, gravel beds, or similar foundations. Designs vary with local climate, soil, and slope conditions, but the basic principles are to place the weight of the structure on solid ground (below the *frost line* — the depth to which the ground freezes during winter — or unstable surface soil) or on a stable, well-drained bed, and to elevate all rot-prone wood at least 8 inches above grade (ground level).

✔ **Choose lumber carefully.** All wood is not created equal. Only certain grades (called *heart grades*) of certain species (cedar, redwood, cypress, and some tropical woods) are naturally resistant to decay. Many nondurable woods, such as pine and Douglas fir, aren't decay resistant, but are available as "pressure-treated," with preservatives and stains. They are treated for either above-ground use and for ground contact — be sure to use the correct type.

In addition to durability, consider strength. Southern pine, Douglas fir, and cypress are stronger than redwood, cedar, and other pines.

Also pay attention to size. The thickness and width of boards are expressed in nominal dimensions, such as 2x4 or 1x6, but the actual dimensions are $1/2$- to $3/4$-inch less (a 2x4, for example, is $1^1/2$ by $3^1/2$ inches). For length, boards come in 2-foot increments from 6 to 20 feet.

✔ **Use corrosion-resistant fasteners and hardware.** Use nails, screws, and hardware that are *galvanized* or otherwise treated for outdoor use. For galvanized nails, specify HDG (which means *hot-dip galvanized*). Use fasteners that grip, such as spiral-shank nails or galvanized deck screws, for better holding power. One secret to building long-lasting outdoor structures from wood is to nail, screw, strap, glue, and connect the heck out of 'em!

✔ **Choose finishes that last.** Preservatives (which protect wood from destructive organisms), sealers (which repel moisture), semitransparent stains (light-bodied stains that reveal grain pattern), solid stains (which mask the wood), and paints help wood structures last for years. Some products contain two or more finishes, such as stains that contain a sealer, preservative, and ultraviolet-ray blocker. The most effective finishes are those that penetrate the wood, such as water repellents, water-repellent preservatives, and semitransparent stains, and that are designated specifically for outdoor wood structures, not just for general use.

✔ **Manage materials carefully.** Estimating, ordering, obtaining, delivering, and storing materials is a major part of construction. Many materials are readily available from home centers, but you may have to locate a masonry yard, concrete supplier, fencing specialist, or similar outlet for others. Discuss delivery fees with suppliers. Plan your job so that you move materials only once, by storing them six to ten feet from the construction site. Stack lumber on a flat, dry, shaded surface, such as a patio or garage floor, to keep it from warping. (Keep lumber off of dirt or grass.) Create shelf space to store nails, bolts, screws, and similar hardware. Store bags of cement or mortar mix out of the weather. Use a wheelbarrow or arrange for a helper to move sand, gravel, and masonry materials from the street to your yard.

✔ **Consider debris.** Plan ahead of time where to haul your debris, because regular trash services won't pick it up. To make disposal easier, keep trash, clean fill, toxins, and reusable scraps all separated from each other. Arrange for a disposal service to haul away the debris, if you can't do so yourself.

✔ **Tool up.** Be sure you have the necessary tools on the job before you start construction. Besides basic carpentry tools, such as a tape measure, hammer, square, screwdriver, handsaw, power saw, power drill, and chalkline (discussed in Chapter 2), you may need a wheelbarrow, stepladder, and sawhorses. You may also want to rent or borrow a *builder's level* (a telescope-like instrument, mounted on a tripod, that's used for setting elevations), power auger (to dig post holes), scoop loader (for hauling bulk materials), masonry-cutting saw (for brick, tile, or stone), plate compactor (for compacting gravel and sand), or ditch excavator (for irrigation, drain, and electrical pipes).

✔ **Consider a contractor.** If you hire a contractor, have copies of your plans available for bidding and obtain bids from a minimum of three contractors. Choose one that you trust and can communicate with easily. Verify that the contractor you choose is licensed and insured, and check references. Whenever you discuss changes, get a written change order that specifies costs. Don't make final payment until you obtain lien releases from subcontractors, verifying that the landscape contractor has paid them and waiving their right to lien your property. Above all, keep channels of communication open. Discuss concerns as soon as they arise.

✔ **Always think "safety."** Wear gloves, safety glasses, a dust mask, or hard hat as needed. Lift with your legs, not your back, and avoid lifting and twisting at the same time. Keep the work site clear of scraps, idle tools, and other tripping hazards. Make sure that extension cords and power tools are plugged into outlets with GFCI (ground-fault circuit interrupter) protection. Operate power tools with caution, observing the manufacturer's safety recommendations. Unplug tools if you need to change blades or bits. Use common sense.

Plotting Your Plot

On paper, you can easily draw structures that are exactly in the right place and have perfectly straight sides, square corners, and measured curves (see Chapter 3 for more information on drawing your landscape plan). But how do you *build* a perfectly straight 100-foot-long fence? Or keep the angles of a sprawling deck square and true? Or place symmetrical flower beds in the right spot? For that matter, how do you draw plans that reflect your site accurately in the first place?

All of these tasks require measuring, plotting, and layout techniques that are quite easy to do with a few basic tools. You don't need sophisticated surveying equipment, although a builder's level or laser level (which contractors usually use) speeds up the process.

Measuring slope

Which way does your property slope and how steeply? To measure slope, do the following:

1. **Establish a benchmark, or *datum point,* as a reference for vertical measurements. Many designers use the ground floor of the house, to which you can assign an arbitrary elevation, such as 100 feet-0 inches (100'-0").**

2. **Take vertical measurements to the benchmark (such as the ground) from each doorway and mark the appropriate elevations on your plot plan.**

3. **Take *field measurements* (measurements taken in the field, rather than off of a site drawing) of points on your property every five to ten feet and plot them on your plan. Drive stakes or place markers at these points from your field measurements.**

   Include your patio, deck, driveway, and similar surfaces.

4. **To measure the vertical distance between points, place one end of a 10-foot straightedge (for example, a straight board, held on its edge) on the higher point and, holding the board level, measure down from the bottom of the board to the ground at the lower point (see Figure 4-1).**

   A quicker way to take vertical measurements is to rent a *builder's level* (an instrument that looks like a telescope on a tripod) or a *hydrolevel* (a clear tubing that's filled with water; some include a reservoir).

5. **After you plot all of the elevations on your plan, draw lines connecting any points within one or two inches of the same elevation.**

6. **Using these points and lines as a guide, draw flowing contour lines to indicate 1-foot changes in elevation (2-, 3-, or 5-foot changes for steeper lots).**

Laying out straight lines

A *layout* is a system of stakes and stringlines that establishes the precise location of footings and borders for a building project. You normally do layout after grading the site (see the "Making the Grade" section, later in this chapter), but you may need to set a few stakes, using basic layout techniques, to guide the grading.

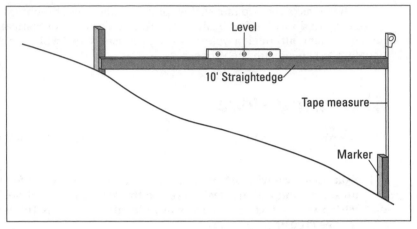

Figure 4-1:
You can measure slope with a 10-foot straightedge, a level, a tape measure, and a marker.

The simplest example of a layout is a string stretched between two stakes to establish a straight line. To build a fence, for example, string a line near the ground and set each fence post carefully against the string — without causing the string to move.

If an obstacle, such as a tree trunk, makes it impossible to string a line between two stakes, move both stakes an equal distance from their original position. Then, stretch a stringline between them. To establish points, such as post locations, where the original stringline would have run, measure an equal distance from the string to the distance that you moved the stakes.

Make sure that you establish precisely what the stringline represents, for example, the inside edge of posts, the outside edge of the finished structure, the center of footings — whatever. It doesn't matter what you choose; just be consistent. Typically, stringlines represent the outside edges of framing members or paving.

Laying out a shape

Laying out a shape, rather than a straight line, involves lots of trial-and-error because you have multiple stringlines to adjust. To help you move the strings back and forth, construct a *batterboard* (horizontal board held in place by two stakes) for each end of each stringline. You can adjust the stringline by untying it and moving it along the board.

Building batterboards

Build batterboards four to six feet behind the approximate end or corner locations of the new structure — far enough back not to interfere with construction. To build the batterboards, follow these steps, shown in Figure 4-2:

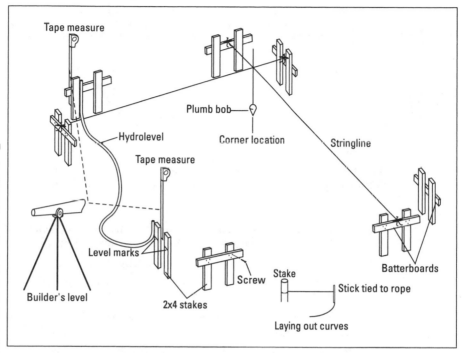

Figure 4-2:
The stages
of building
batterboards
for a
rectangular
structure,
from driving
stakes to
leveling the
cross
pieces.

1. **Drive a pair of sharpened 2x4s into the ground for each batterboard, approximately 3 feet apart.**

   Batterboards at corners can share a common stake.

2. **Using a water level, builder's level, or long straightedge and level, mark all of the stakes at the same level.**

   Mark the stake on the highest ground first, to ensure that all marks are above the grade. Choose a level high enough to clear whatever footings, paving, or other features you plan to construct first.

   A few structures, such as buildings, require that the stringlines be at a precise elevation to establish a predetermined foundation height; for most landscape structures you don't need to worry about this. Just establish an arbitrary height.

3. **Nail a 2x4 crosspiece to each pair of stakes, on the side facing away from the construction site. Align the top of the crosspiece with the level mark that you made on each stake.**

4. **Tack a 6d box nail into the top of each crosspiece where you estimate that the stringline will attach.**

   To locate 6d nails, head to your hardware store and ask for them — the salespeople there will know what they are.

   You move the nail locations as you make final adjustments.

In nailing crosspieces to the stakes, have a helper hold a sledge hammer behind the stake that you're nailing into, so that it doesn't loosen from the ground.

For batterboards located next to an existing fence, wall, or tree, you don't need to pound stakes in the ground. Nail, screw, or wire a crosspiece to the object at the appropriate level. If you're building a deck, the *ledger board* (part of the deck that's attached to the house) serves as a crosspiece.

Stringing lines

With batterboards in place, stretch strings between them to create an outline of your deck, patio, or other structure, using the following steps (refer to Figure 4-2):

1. **Tie nylon string, sometimes called mason's twine, to the 6d nails on the crosspieces located opposite each other. Stretch it tight.**

   The stringlines should form the basic shape of the structure — a simple rectangle, for example. (For decks, the ledger board attached to the house forms one of the sides of the shape.)

2. **Measure the distance between corners to see if each side is the correct length.**

3. **Likewise, measure both diagonals (the distance between opposite corners) to see if the corners are square.**

4. **If the diagonals aren't equal or the sides aren't the correct length, adjust the position of the nails and stringlines until they are correct.**

5. **After you complete the layout, tap the nails firmly into the crosspieces and mark them as "outside edge of framing" or whatever they represent.**

Another method for checking corners is the "3-4-5 triangle." To use this method, mark a point on one string that's 3 feet from the corner; measure from the corner along the other string or the house wall and mark it at 4 feet. The distance between the two marks (the hypotenuse) is exactly 5 feet if the corner is square. For more accurate checking, use multiples of 3, 4, and 5 feet, such as 9, 12, and 15, or 12, 16, and 20 feet.

In some situations, such as attaching a deck or patio to the house, your layout may look cockeyed because the house walls, driveway, or other existing features aren't square. If so, fudge the layout slightly to bring the side of the layout in line with the existing feature.

A few layout tricks

Not all landscape structures are simple rectangles on relatively level ground. The following special situations require different layout techniques:

✔ **Your layout is large or complex.** For large decks, set up batterboards and additional stringlines between the perimeter's stringlines, wherever interior beams or rows of footings line up. For complex shapes, such as a series of small patios or an L-shaped deck, set up batterboards and stringlines for each component, treating it as a separate rectangle.

✔ **Your layout is on a steep site.** Batterboards for most structures are about 3 feet high, but for steep slopes the batterboards on the downhill side may need to be several feet higher to be level with the uphill boards. Rather than build tall batterboards that require step ladders to reach (which is done for home construction), simply build short batterboards and stretch the stringline downhill at an angle. Although the stringlines won't guide you in establishing uniformly level

structures, you can take measurements from the top batterboard or other reference point as you build forms or install posts for such structures.

✔ **Your layout has curves.** For curved corners, run stringlines as if the sides intersected in a square corner. Then, using a rope tied to a stick like a compass, draw an arc on the ground where the curved corner belongs, starting and ending the arc beneath the stringlines. For large curves, drive a stake into the ground where the center of the circle or arc is located. Using the stake as a pivot point, tie one end of a rope to the stake, measure along the rope the length of the radius, tie a stick to the rope at that point, and swing the stick along the ground like a compass to mark a line in the soil. Mark the curve with flour, spray paint, or chalk. For free-form shapes, simply lay a garden hose on the ground in the desired shape, sprinkle flour or chalk along the hose, and remove it.

Transferring the layout to the ground

If the stringlines are for guiding excavation — for fence posts or a patio base, for example — you need to mark the ground for digging. Where such marks must be perfectly accurate, hold a *plumb bob* (a weight on a string — refer to Figure 4-3) close to the ground, with its string brushing against the stringline, and mark the ground directly under the bob with spray paint, flour, chalk, or colored cloth held down with a nail. Make several marks, as needed.

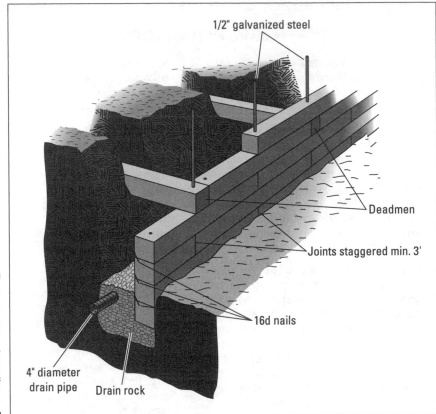

1/2" galvanized steel

Deadmen

Joints staggered min. 3'

16d nails

4" diameter drain pipe

Drain rock

Figure 4-3:
Most do-it-yourselfers can build a low retaining wall out of timbers.

Making the Grade

Grading a site means leveling the soil to the desired contour — usually a flat surface, slightly sloped to allow for drainage. Grading for lawns and planting beds may also include adding soil amendments. Either way, we're talking about pick and shovel work. For small areas, hand tools suffice. For a large patio or complete landscaping project, rent a small tractor with a scoop loader and grading attachments.

The basic rule for grading, especially for patios, walks, and foundation sites, is the Goldilocks rule — not too much, not too little, just right. Built structures must rest on undisturbed soil, so don't overdig. (Planting beds, on the other hand, require breaking up the soil as deep as possible.) Where additional soil is required, compact it carefully to minimize settling.

Don't rely on "eyeballing;" always check your work with a level. For small sites, use a long straightedge and level. For larger sites, use the following procedure to establish the finished grade:

1. **Pound 18-inch stakes 6 to 12 inches into the ground every 10 feet or so.**

2. **Identify the stake at the highest point of what will be the finished ground level for the entire site. Make a reference mark on the stake at the finished grade level.**

   You may have to dig down a bit to make the mark, or make the mark several inches above the existing grade.

3. **Mark the other stakes at the same level as the reference mark. Use a hydrolevel, builder's level, or long straightedge and level.**

4. **At each stake, write how far below the reference mark the finished grade must be — "2¹/₂," for example.**

   For completely level sites, you would write 0" on all the stakes. For most sites, slope the grade at a minimum rate of ¹/₄ inch per foot, for drainage. Around the house, foundation experts recommend that the ground slope, away from the house at a rate of ¹/₂ to 1 inch per foot for the first 10 feet (except for patios and other paved areas, which slope at ¹/₈ to ¹/₄ inch per foot).

5. **Dig and fill the soil, using the measurements written on the stakes as a guide.**

6. **If the site requires extensive grading, use longer stakes and pound them deep enough to penetrate below the finished grade level.**

When excavating, scrape off the topsoil first and place it where you can re-use it in your garden.

For more information on removing a lawn, see Chapter 11.

Taming Slopes

To level a slope, you must cut into the hillside, add fill to the downhill side, or do both. Both options require building a retaining wall to hold back the hillside or the new fill. Walls over 3 feet high require engineering and permits and should be designed and built by professionals, but you can build a low retaining wall yourself out of timbers, stacked stone, or stacked block using the techniques in the following sections.

To relieve the pressure of water building up behind a wall, provide either *weep holes* (small openings) along the base of the wall or a drainpipe behind the wall. Then, install a layer of *drain rock* (large, coarse gravel) against the back of the wall, using filter fabric (available at masonry suppliers) to surround the gravel and drain pipe, so that the soil won't clog them.

Timber wall

To build a retaining wall out of *landscape timbers* (pressure-treated 6x6s specified for ground contact) or used railroad ties, follow these steps that are detailed in Figure 4-3:

1. **Dig into the hill far enough to provide working space — 15 to 18 inches behind the wall.**

2. **Dig trenches into the hill, perpendicular to the wall, for *deadmen* (horizontal braces), every 4 feet.**

   Dig them level and deep enough to place the deadmen in the third or fourth layer of timbers.

3. **Dig a shallow trench for the wall, about 1¹/₂ to 2 times the depth of one timber and twice as wide.**

   Align the front of the trench with the front of the wall. String a line to guide your digging (see the "Laying out a straight line" section, earlier in this chapter. Check the bottom of the trench to make sure it's level.

4. **Place 2 to 4 inches of drain rock or gravel in the bottom of the trench.**

5. **Drill 1-inch diameter holes, spaced 3 feet apart, through each timber as you place it, for the first three layers.**

6. **Set the first layer of timbers on the gravel and level them by tamping them into place.**

   Think of *tamping* as somewhere between tapping and pounding.

7. **Place the next two layers of timbers over the first, aligning the holes.**

   Stagger the end joints at least 3 feet.

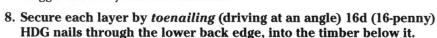

8. **Secure each layer by *toenailing* (driving at an angle) 16d (16-penny) HDG nails through the lower back edge, into the timber below it.**

9. **Drive 6- to 8-foot lengths of ¹/₂-inch galvanized steel (rebar) through the holes (in the timbers) into the ground.**

   Drive them deep enough so that the tops align just below the top of the finished wall.

10. **Install the deadmen along the third or fourth course, or layer. Set the ends flush with the outside of the wall. Attach each deadman to the timber below it with three ¹/₂ by 12-inch lag screws. *Countersink* (set below the surface) the screw heads to make them flush with the top of the deadmen.**

11. **Install the remaining layers of timbers. Drill holes for the pipes and thread the timbers over the pipes.**

12. **Place filter fabric behind the wall, across the gravel, and up the soil bank, but don't cut it yet.**

13. **Place 4-inch perforated flexible drainpipe on the gravel behind the wall, sloping it toward the outlet end.**

14. **Fill the cavity with drain rock to within 8 to 12 inches of the top. Fold the fabric over the top of the rock and cover it with a layer of topsoil.**

Stone wall

Building a 2- or 3-foot high wall of dry-stacked (no mortar) stone requires considerable lifting and adjusting of stones, but is enjoyable work if you aren't in a hurry. It pays off with a handsome wall. Follow these steps, detailed in Figure 4-4:

1. **Dig 15 to 18 inches into the hill, behind the wall, for working space.**

2. **Dig a trench 16 inches deep and wide enough for the broadest stones and a 4-inch drainpipe.**

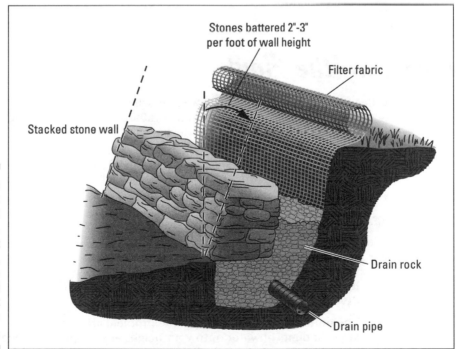

Figure 4-4: Building a stacked stone wall, without mortar, requires careful placement of the stones.

3. **Place 4 inches of road base in the trench and compact it. Lay the drainpipe along the back corner, sloping it toward the outlet end.**

4. **Add 12 inches of rock to the trench.**

5. **Using the largest stones, set the first course in place on the gravel.**

   Tilt the stones back slightly, toward the bank.

6. **Drape filter fabric against the soil bank, behind the wall, and backfill the stones with rock as you lay each course.**

7. **Build up the wall with stones. As you lay each course, lean the wall into the hill at a rate of 2 to 3 inches per foot of wall height. A 3-foot wall, for example, must lean 6 to 9 inches into the hill.**

8. **Within 12 inches of the top of the wall, fold the filter fabric over the drain rock and backfill the rest of the wall with topsoil.**

Concrete block wall

Manufacturers have created decorative concrete blocks that are specifically designed for dry-stacked retaining walls. Modular in dimension, they are easier to work with than stone. Most blocks are designed to be battered and many have predrilled holes for inserting stabilizing pins to lock them together. Follow the manufacturer's instructions for installing them, or use a technique similar to timber and stone walls (see the two previous sections).

Directing the Flow

Unless your entire site has no low spots where rain water and melted snow accumulate, you probably have some drainage problems to solve — especially if water accumulates under decks, around patios and walks, under sheds, or around the house. You can divert water away from low spots by creating *swales* (shallow gullies with gently sloping sides) or ditches along the surface of the ground, or by installing a subsurface drainage system.

Surface drainage

For surface drainage, follow the following steps:

1. **Identify an *outfall* on your own property, to which water can be diverted.**

   The outfall must be lower than the problem areas and must not spill large amounts of water onto your neighbor's property. If necessary, plan a catch basin to collect surface water and divert it underground to a suitable outfall (see the "Subsurface drainage" section for instructions).

2. **Plot a route for a ditch or swale between the problem area and the outfall.**

   Avoid a beeline; choose a meandering course to slow down the flow of water and create an interesting landscaping feature. (See Figure 4-5).

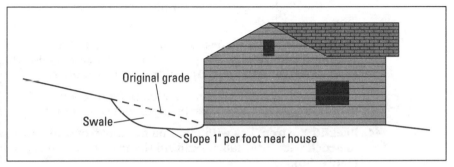

Original grade

Swale

Slope 1" per foot near house

3. **Dig the ditch or grade the swale.**

   Check the bottom with a level and 8-foot straightedge to make sure it slopes 1 inch per 8 feet of horizontal run for bare soil and 2 inches per 8 feet for a lawn or planted beds.

4. **For steeper pitches, or where heavy rainstorms occur, line the bottom of the waterway with a 2-inch thick layer of concrete or strips of PVC (polyvinyl chloride) membrane that are designed for lining ponds.**

5. **For a decorative effect, place stones along the water course to resemble a dry streambed during dry months.**

Subsurface drainage

To install subsurface drainage, follow these steps:

1. **Find a low point in your yard where you can run an underground drain pipe out to "daylight" — the pipe should be 3 or 4 inches in diameter and slope away from the problem site at a rate of $1/8$ inch per foot.**

   The outlet of this pipe must disperse the water into your yard, not your neighbors'. If your property lacks such a low point, you can run the pipe to the street gutter in front of your home or to a municipal storm sewer.

   If that isn't possible, terminate the drain pipe in an underground "dry well," an excavation approximately 8 feet deep and 3 to 4 feet wide that you fill with stones and rubble and cover with top soil. The dry well enables water to percolate into the soil more quickly than from the surface.

Dry wells don't work in deep clay soils with a low percolation rate. There, the only solution is a concrete-lined pit with a sump pump.

2. **After you identify where the drain pipe is to terminate, excavate a trench from that point to the problem site and another trench along the site perimeter, 14 to 16 inches deep.**

   Slope the ditches toward the termination point at a rate of $1/8$ inch per foot.

3. **Place 2 inches of 1-inch smooth *drain rock* (1-inch rocks with no sand) in the bottom of the perimeter trench and lay 4-inch diameter plastic (PVC or ABS) perforated drain pipe on the rock.**

   Continue this pipe to the termination point or connect it to 4-inch diameter (unperforated) plastic pipe, which goes to the outfall.

4. **Backfill the trenches with eight inches more of drain rock, surround the rock with filter fabric, and fill the trenches with top soil (see Figure 4-6).**

Figure 4-6:
Use underground drainpipe and drain rock to provide subsurface drainage.

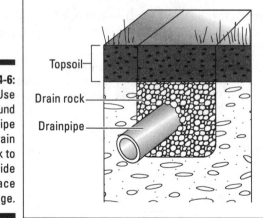

Topsoil

Drain rock

Drainpipe

Water on Tap

Who wants to drag hoses all over the yard? While preparing for your landscape, install plenty of underground pipes for lawn sprinklers, micro-irrigation systems, and entertainment areas. Plastic pipe and fittings make outdoor plumbing fairly simple and inexpensive. Begin with the water supply lines, before you put in your plants, and the excavation is easy. After excavating, branch circuits for sprinkler and irrigation systems.

Installing water supply lines

Plastic pipe and fittings make outdoor plumbing fairly simple and inexpensive. Most systems use PVC (polyvinyl chloride) pipe, which comes in various thicknesses. Use schedule 40 or a heavier gauge for lines under constant pressure. To install water lines, follow these steps:

1. **Find a convenient *fitting* (any one of several contraptions used to join pipe, such as connectors, elbows, and tees) in the existing main line, just before it goes into the house, to connect a new pipe to.**

   Look for a short branch pipe, such as a pipe that supplies a faucet, so you don't have to cut into the main water supply line. In areas with severe winters, this point of connection must be protected from frost, either by locating it within the basement or burying it deep.

   For public health reasons, plumbing codes require a backflow device to be installed between this point of connection and the first outlet for the garden system.

2. **Dig a trench for the new pipe from this connection point to the new faucet or irrigation valve location.**

   For short runs, dig by hand, using a narrow shovel called a trenching shovel. For long runs, rent a ditch excavator.

3. **Lay out the new pipe next to the trench.**

   Pipe comes in 20-foot sections of various diameters. For a single faucet, use $^3/_4$-inch diameter pipe. For multiple faucets or valves, use 1- or $1^1/_4$-inch diameter pipe, depending on the available water pressure.

4. **Plan the fittings that you need.**

   Use couplings for joining pipe end-to-end; 90- and 45-degree elbows for changing direction; tees for branching additional lines off of the main line; adapters for converting from plastic pipe (slip joints) to threaded fittings (MIP or FIP joints — male or female iron pipe); and nipples (rigid pipe threaded at both ends) for short extensions. Although you eventually terminate the water lines at faucets and/or sprinkler valves, you don't need to install those yet — simply attach threaded or slip caps to the ends of the pipe. Where winter freezes are common, install a draindown valve at the lowest point of the system to empty the pipes for winter.

5. **Install a gate valve (manual shutoff valve) where the new piping connects to the old.**

   Shut off the main water valve, remove the existing faucet and riser, and install a tee. Reattach the faucet riser to one outlet of the tee and install the gate valve on the other outlet. Turn on the water and test the valve. (If the valve is underground, place a *valve box* — a prefabricated enclosure for underground valves — over it for access.)

6. **Install the pipe and fittings, starting at the gate valve and working toward the remote locations.**

7. **Turn on the gate valve to test the connections.**

Note: If a test and inspection are required, don't connect the piping to the gate valve. Instead, isolate the system from the valve, attach a pressure gauge at one of the fittings, and pump air into the pipes to the required test pressure — typically around 100 to125 pounds per square inch. The pressure should hold for at least four hours.

8. **After testing the system, fill the trenches with soil.**

If the soil is rocky, cover the pipes with sand to prevent punctures from rocks; then fill the trench with soil.

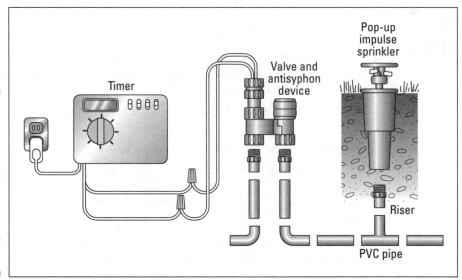

Figure 4-7:
Modern plumbing and irrigation materials lend themselves to do-it-yourself installation.

Installing sprinklers

Planning a sprinkler system requires you to juggle several variables, including the static water pressure of your home's water system, the size of your water supply pipes, the size of your water meter, the spray patterns of sprinkler heads, and the flow rate of sprinkler heads. You can determine these variables yourself, but for best results, have your plan checked by someone who specializes in irrigation systems — either the dealer from whom you buy the system components or a consultant.

Follow these steps to plan and install your system:

1. **Check the water capacity of your home's water system, in gpm (gallons per minute).**

   One way to do this is to measure *static water pressure* (no water is turned on) with a pressure gauge, check the water meter size, check the service pipe size, and consult a water capacity chart for gallons per minute.

   An easier way, if your house water supply doesn't have a pressure reducer, is to fill a bucket with water from an outdoor faucet (while no other water is turned on). Measure the time it takes to fill the bucket (in seconds), divide that time into the number of gallons the bucket holds, and multiply the result by 60 (number of seconds in a minute).

2. **Draw, to scale, the areas that need watering.**

3. **Select the sprinkler head style that best suits your needs.**

   For most yards, choose 3- or 4-inch plastic pop-up heads that spray up to 15 feet. For large areas (over 20 feet wide), consider rotary pop-up heads that spray 30 to 40 feet.

4. **Consulting the manufacturer's specifications, plot the head locations on your drawing.**

   Draw the spray pattern (full circle, partial circle, square, or elongated) for each head, at the radius specified by the manufacturer for your gpm (see Figure 4-8). Overlap sprays so that the water from each head barely reaches adjacent heads. Note that many heads have adjustable *throws* (distance that the spray reaches).

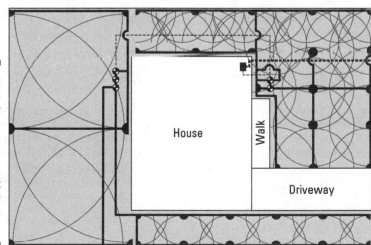

Figure 4-8: This sprinkler system has five separate circuits. Note that the spray patterns overlap.

House

Walk

Driveway

5. **Divide the plan into circuits or zones (groups of heads controlled by a single valve).**

   Plan separate circuits for sunny areas, shade areas, lawns, shrubs, slopes, and flat areas. Cluster heads into convenient piping arrangements, limiting the number of heads to the total available water pressure.

6. **Plan a control valve for each circuit.**

   Group control valves together, as much as possible, for easier installation and access. Locate them as close as possible to the main water line. Use automatic (electrically controlled) valves for convenience and water conservation.

7. **Plot locations for the supply pipes to the valves, and for the circuit pipes from valves to sprinkler heads.**

8. **Plan backflow prevention.**

   Water in the sprinkler system must not be allowed to flow back into the main water supply system when the sprinklers are shut off. Consult with your local building department about required backflow prevention devices. *Antisiphon valves* (control valves that incorporate a backflow prevention device) and *vacuum breakers* (a device installed in the water supply line, at least 12 inches above the highest sprinkler head) are two methods of prevention.

9. **Plan an automatic controller to automate your system.**

   Locate the controller for easy access and near an electrical outlet. Run low-voltage irrigation wiring from the controller to the valves, according to the manufacturer's specifications. Run the wire for each valve in the same trench as the water supply pipe.

10. **Install the pipes, sprinkler heads, and valves. (See the section "Installing water supply lines.")**

Installing micro-irrigation

Unlike sprinklers, which cover large expanses of lawn, micro-irrigation systems deliver water to emitters, microsprinklers, or drip hoses that you place at the bases of individual plants or clusters of plants. The only parts of the system that you need to install during site preparation are the main water supply lines, but most of the system is aboveground and can be installed after you install the plants.

The basic components of a micro-irrigation system include the following items:

✓ A filter (to keep the tubing free of minute debris that can clog the drip holes)

- A pressure regulator (to keep the water pressure in the system constant for optimum performance)

- A backflow preventer (a simple device, usually a vacuum breaker, that prevents water in the system from backing up into the public water supply)

- Valves — manual or electronic (to control water flow to different "circuits")

- An automatic controller (includes valve controllers and a timer)

- Tubing

- Emitters, microsprinklers, or drip hoses

Most manufacturers provide excellent step-by-step instructions for installing their systems. Before you begin planning yours, visit a home center or irrigation supplier and pick up product specifications and instructions.

You can buy components individually or in kits. Kits are less expensive than the same parts bought individually, but may include components that you don't need. The major components, such as the pressure regulator and filter, may also be too small if you intend to expand your system beyond the kit size.

Your main planning task is to decide what type of drip emitter or microsprinkler to use at each plant. These devices are calibrated for different flow rates, such as half a gallon per hour, so that each plant receives an individualized amount of water. Manufacturers provide recommendations for the size and number of emitters to use for certain plants. Most container plants require one emitter rated at a half-, one-, or two-gallons per hour (GPH), depending on size. Some plants, such as ferns or bromiliads, may also require misters (devices that create mist) to keep the leaves moist.

To help in your planning, draw all of the bedding plants and containers that need micro-irrigation and write down the size of emitter for each one. Next, draw a tubing circuit to connect the emitters. It doesn't need to be a continuous circuit — you can run a main supply line and connect branches to it, which enables you to use smaller-diameter tubing that's easier to conceal. Your site may require several circuits. Check the manufacturer's specifications for the maximum "gallonage" per circuit (the total GPH ratings of all emitters), which is typically 600 to 960. Also check for the maximum length of runs for the two common sizes of tubing, $1/4$- and $1/2$-inch. Typically, a single circuit should have no more than 50 feet of $1/4$-inch tubing, with no branch tube exceeding 25 feet. For most installations use $1/2$-inch tubing for the supply line (no more than 200 feet altogether) and $1/4$-inch branches. Plan your layout so that all the circuits originate at the water faucet or valve that you intend to use.

Follow these steps to install your drip irrigation system:

1. **Start by unrolling the tubing and setting it in the sun for half an hour.**

2. **Attach the components to the water valve in the order that the manufacturer recommends.**

   Typically, the order is backflow preventer, timer (for single-circuit setups), filter, pressure regulator, and line connector.

3. **For multiple-circuit systems controlled by automatic valves, connect each valve (which may include a vacuum breaker) directly to the water supply line.**

4. **Attach a filter, pressure regulator, and line connector to each valve.**

   Run concealed wiring from each valve to the main controller, which you can mount anywhere.

5. **Next, attach the main supply tubing ($^1/_4$- or $^1/_2$-inch) to the valve assembly and run it over, under, around, and through the patio or deck area, as necessary.**

   Secure the tubing with clamps.

6. **Attach the $^1/_4$-inch branch lines to the supply line, using tee-connectors for a $^1/_4$-inch supply line or plunge connectors for a $^1/_2$-inch supply line.**

   To connect plunge connectors to $^1/_2$-inch tubing, use a hole punch to make a hole and push the $^1/_4$-inch fitting into the hole until the barb at the end of the fitting is completely inside the $^1/_2$-inch tubing. Use a straight fitting for single branch lines and a tee-fitting to attach two branch lines at the same connection.

   Run the tubing for each branch line and secure it with clamps. Avoid kinking the tubing.

7. **Attach emitters to the branch lines at each plant or cluster of plants.**

   Use in-line emitters if the branch continues to an adjacent plant and end-line emitters where branch lines terminate. Support each emitter approximately 1 inch above the soil, using stakes provided by the manufacturer.

8. **After you connect all of the emitters and tubing, turn on the system for a few minutes to flush it out, then close off the end of the supply line by using a cap or clamp.**

9. **Turn on the system to test it for leaks.**

   Cap leaks with hole plugs and reconnect leaking connections.

10. **Finally, if the system is on an automatic controller, set the timing adjustments to determine the watering cycle.**

Chapter 5

Fences, Walls, Gates, and Paths

· ·

In This Chapter

▶ Putting up a fence

▶ Designing and building a garden wall

▶ Making and installing a gate

▶ Creating pathways

▶ Building steps

· ·

*Y*our property needs boundaries around it and pathways within it. Even sprawling ranches under the western sky have fences around them and a dusty road or two through the sagebrush. In your landscape, fences and walls define areas and provide a background for other features. Gates, paths, and steps enhance movement.

While these elements may not seem to have much in common, they all form the basic infrastructure of your yard. Install them as early in the landscape construction process as possible.

Fabricating Fences

Most fences are variations on a basic design: posts buried in the ground; horizontal rails installed between them; and some kind of fencing attached to the rails — pickets, boards attached vertically, boards attached horizontally, lattice, wire mesh, solid panels, siding materials, bamboo, or wood worked into decorative designs (see Figure 5-1 for examples). Add to those variables the height of the fence and the endless possibilities of color, and you can see why no two fences are exactly alike. To keep these boundless options in check and to narrow your choices, use the following guidelines:

Figure 5-1:
Fence styles, from left to right, top to bottom: picket, rail, alternating board, lattice, solid board, and plastic fencing.

✔ **Height:** 6 feet is standard for side and back yards, but may not be high enough if you have a raised deck or if neighboring houses are close to your property line. You may have to build an 8-foot fence (check your local zoning laws first, though) or solid screen of tall bushes. For front-yard fences, 3 to 4 feet is sufficient for defining your property line. If you have a corner lot with fences along both streets, make sure that neither fence blocks views of traffic. Check your local zoning ordinances for other restrictions, and be sure to discuss the fence with your neighbor.

✔ **Imposing fences:** A long, tall fence may create the feeling of prison walls. To break up the stockade effect, intersperse decorative elements, such as lattice panels or alternative fencing materials, along the fence at regular intervals, or use shrubs (see Chapter 9) or perennial flowers (covered in Chapter 10). Break up the top of a long, monotonous fence with *finials* (round doodads) at the tops of the posts or top the fence sections with scallop shapes to create a wavy fence line.

✔ **Color:** A white or light-colored fence calls attention to itself and brings the fence forward, visually. A dark-colored fence recedes into the background. Painting a fence the same color as the house unifies the two elements. Choosing neutral colors or earthtones for the fence ties your fence to your garden.

✔ **Neighborhood:** In some areas, certain fence styles or materials dominate. In other areas, fence styles reflect eclectic tastes. Respect neighborhood and regional traditions in choosing your style.

Choosing fence materials

Wood, the traditional fence material, varies widely in durability, appearance, availability, and cost.

✔ You can improve the appearance of most wood by staining or painting it, so consider durability and strength first. Some woods, such as the heartwood of cedar and redwood, resist decay naturally. These woods also tend not to warp as much as other species. Although cedar and redwood lack strength for major load-bearing members, such as deck joists, they work well for fences. Choose boards with a high percentage of heartwood (the darker, richer-colored wood) and dense growth rings (at least eight per inch).

No matter what type of fencing you buy, always choose a high grade of the most durable wood for the posts.

✔ Nondurable woods (southern pine and Douglas fir, for example) that have been pressure-treated with preservatives also make excellent fence materials.

Pay attention to the *retention level* (how much preservative the lumber holds). For posts, choose a retention level of .40, which is suitable for contact with the ground. For other fence members, choose lumber that's treated to a retention level of .25. Unless you buy pressure-treated wood that includes a water-repellent stain, you must seal and finish the wood after building your fence.

✔ Use lumber cut to standard dimensions (4x4s, 1x8s, and so on) for your fence, or buy wood that's milled into specialty shapes such as pickets, split rails, decorative posts, or scrolled board patterns.

You can also buy prefabricated sections of fencing, but examine them carefully for the quality of wood (avoid sapwood and wide growth rings), size of lumber, and the number and type of fasteners (staples rather than nails or screws).

Other materials commonly used for fences include prefabricted metal fence kits (tubular aluminum or steel), *plastic lumber* (hollow vinyl shapes molded into fence posts and rails, or boards manufactured from composite materials), plywood (choose exterior grades), or vinyl-covered wire mesh.

When you buy materials, don't forget to pick up some concrete for the fence posts. You need one to two 80-pound sacks (.67 cubic feet each) of concrete mix per post hole (12-inch diameter).

Building the fence

If you have a few weekends, some vacation time, or lots of helpers in the family, you may enjoy building your own fence. The experience offers an excellent opportunity to practice basic carpentry skills. For a basic wood fence, follow these steps:

Laying out post hole locations

Start by laying out the locations for your post hole:

1. **Stretch a string along the fence line (see Chapter 4).**

   Align it with the centers — not the edges — of the post positions.

2. **Establish the post spacing.**

   Posts are typically spaced 5 to 8 feet apart, depending on the size of framing members, weight of the fencing material, and length of prefabricated fence panels, if you use them. If possible, choose a spacing that divides evenly into the total fence length.

   Don't forget to put in posts for the gate (see the "Going for Gates" section, later in this chapter, for more on building a gate). Try to make fence *bays* (sections between posts) equal on either side of the gate. If you end up with an odd-sized bay, get rid of it by readjusting the post spacing or changing the overall fence length. If neither solution works, split the odd-sized bay dimension in half and place the shorter bays at each end of the fence.

3. **Mark the ground.**

   Starting at the uphill end of the fence and holding a tape measure as close to level as possible (rather than laying it on sloping ground), mark the center of each post location with spray paint, a swatch of cloth with a nail through the center, or a pinch of flour. To align the mark with the stringline, hold a *plumb bob* (a string with a weight on the end) against the string or hold a level vertically against it, without deflecting the string.

Installing posts

Use the following instructions, shown in Figure 5-2, to install the posts.

1. **Temporarily move the stringline out of the way.**

2. **Determine post hole size.**

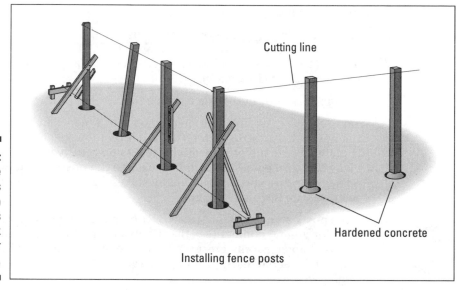

Cutting line

Hardened concrete

Installing fence posts

Figure 5-2:
Use stringlines to align fence posts and mark them for trimming.

Plan 12-inch diameter holes for 4x4 posts set in concrete; 8-inch diameter for posts set in alternating layers of gravel and earth (a technique used in regions with severe winters and firm soils). If you use larger posts, expand the hole accordingly.

The hole depth should be equal to $1/3$ the fence height, plus 6 inches for a layer of gravel at the bottom of the hole. (A 6-foot [72-inch] fence, for example, requires a 30-inch hole — 24 inches for the buried portion of the post, plus 6 inches for gravel). Add another 12 inches (for a hole that's 42 inches deep) for gate posts and corner posts.

3. **Dig holes.**

No way around it, this is hard work. For just a few holes, use a *clamshell digger* (hand tool that resembles a large pair of tongs). For long fences, rent a *power auger* (a gas-powered, hand-held machine with a screw-type blade) or hire an excavator. If you rent an auger, specify an 8-, 12-, or 14-inch diameter blade. Whichever tool you use, have a 6-foot long digging bar handy to dislodge rocks and loosen hard soil. Keep the sides of each hole plumb — don't flare the top of the hole; if anything, flare the bottom to increase stability.

A power auger generates tremendous *torque* (twisting force) and requires two strong people to operate the beast, especially one with a large-diameter blade.

4. **Place 6 inches of gravel or crushed rock in the bottom of each hole.**

5. **Restring lines**.

   Move the stringline position from the post centers to the post edges (either side). For 4x4 posts, for example, move the stringline over 2 inches (1³/₄ inches if you use *surfaced* (that is, planed or smooth) posts, which are 3¹/₂ inches thick).

6. **Set the corner or end posts in place first.**

   Set each one in its hole, burying the bottom 2 inches in the gravel. Align the post with the stringline(s), using a level to make sure that the post is plumb. Brace the post by driving stakes diagonally into the ground along two adjacent sides. Nail the stakes to the post with duplex nails — 8d nails for 1-by stakes; 16d for 2-by stakes, again checking with a level to make sure the post is plumb.

   If the posts aren't pressure-treated with preservatives to a retention level for ground contact (see the "Choosing materials" section, earlier in this chapter), apply preservative to the portion that will be buried by soaking the end of each post in preservative. Use a brush to reach undipped areas.

7. **String a line between the end posts near the top.**

8. **Set the remaining posts in their holes.**

   Align them to both stringlines and brace them, using a level to make sure they're plumb.

9. **Backfill the holes.**

   If you use concrete, mix enough for one or two holes at a time. Shovel the concrete carefully around each post and jab a stick or metal rod into the concrete several times to consolidate it. Using a trowel or shovel, mound the top of the concrete to keep water from settling around the post.

   If you backfill with alternating layers of gravel and soil, pack each layer firmly to a 2- or 3-inch thickness, using a pipe or rod. Mound the top layer of soil to shed water away from the post.

Posts with *mortises* (holes) cut into them to receive rails, or with decorative tops, must all be set to the same level — you can't trim the tops to level them. To do this, install the higher end post first. Attach temporary *cleats* (short pieces of wood that straddle the hole) to opposite sides of the post to keep it from sinking into the hole. Install the other end post at the same level, using a hydrolevel or builder's level to keep them aligned. Brace both posts securely. Then, measure down an equal distance from the top of each post, tack nails at those points, and stretch a line between the nails. Install the remaining posts so that all of the tops are an equal distance above the stringline.

Building the framework

To build a framework for your fence, follow these steps (see Figure 5-3):

1. **Trim the post tops.**

   After the concrete sets, mark and trim the tops of the posts so that they are all level. If the ground is fairly level, simply start with the post at the highest point of the fence. Mark that post where the top rail rests on top of the post. Using a hydrolevel or builder's level, transfer this mark to the other end post. String a *chalkline* (a string coated with chalk) between the two marks and snap the line to transfer chalk marks to the other posts at the same level. Using a square and pencil, extend the mark around the four sides of each post. Cut along these marks.

   If the ground slopes gently, take trial measurements at several posts and refer to your plans to determine the best level for cutting. If the ground slopes steeply, step the fence down the slope by marking only a few posts level with each other and then lowering the marking level a few inches for the next few posts, and so on.

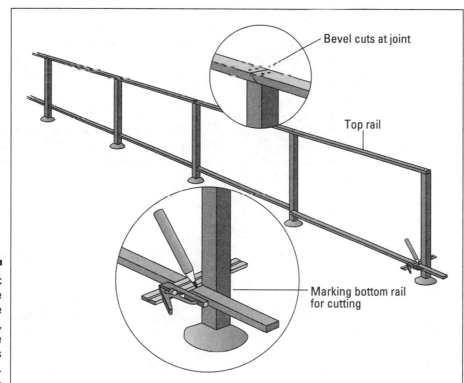

Figure 5-3: After the concrete hardens, attach the fence rails to the posts.

Bevel cuts at joint

Top rail

Marking bottom rail for cutting

Making horizontal cuts with a circular power saw is dangerous. If you don't have experience making such cuts, use a handsaw. If you do have experience, stand on a sturdy stepladder or bench, and wear safety glasses.

2. **Install the top rail.**

   Use 2x4s or 2x6s long enough to connect at least three posts. Take measurements, along a level line, at the *bottoms* of posts (the tops may be out of line). Plan joints over the centers of posts. After cutting each board, secure it to each post with at least two 16d galvanized spiral-shank nails — drill pilot holes for nailing near the ends of boards. You may need to pull post tops into alignment before nailing.

   As boards shrink, joints open up. When joining boards end-to-end, cut the ends at a 30-degree *bevel* (angle, as viewed from the edge — refer to Figure 5-2) so that each board slightly overlaps the previous board. As the joint opens up, the beveled ends appear to touch each other from most viewing angles.

3. **Install bottom rails between the posts.**

   Mark the rail locations on each post by measuring *down* from the top rail (which should be level), not up from the ground. Cut 2x4s to fit between the posts at these marks. Install them by drilling pilot holes and toenailing each end to the post with two 16d galvanized spiral-shank nails.

4. **Install kickboards.**

   To fill the gaps below bottom rails and make the fence stronger, install a 1-by board, set on edge, under each bottom rail, as shown in Figure 5-4. Cut it to fit between the posts. If it's too wide for the gap, excavate some soil or trim the bottom of the board to the same contour as the ground. Toenail it to the posts with 8d galvanized common nails (drill pilot holes first).

Installing the fencing

1. **Install nailers, as needed.**

   If you install boards or panels between the rails, you may need to attach *nailers* (strips of wood) along the bottom of the top rail and top of the bottom rail to nail the fencing to — and perhaps along the posts, as well.

   Avoid a fence design that depends on too many nailers. They create more joints for moisture to get trapped in — which encourages rot — and provide weaker support than the frame itself.

2. **Attach the boards or panels to the framework or nailers.**

   Attach 1-by boards with 8d galvanized box nails. Attach lattice screening with galvanized deck screws.

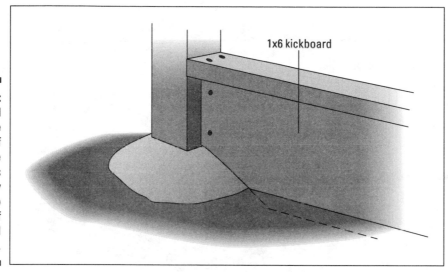

1x6 kickboard

Figure 5-4:
A kickboard secures the bottom of the fence and is relatively easy to replace if the wood rots.

For pickets or other vertical boards with uniform spacing, make a spacer to speed up installation — see Figure 5-5. *Rip* (saw along the board's length) a board to the same width as the required spacing, long enough to extend from top rail to bottom rail. Attach a small cleat to the back side of the spacer, flush with the top edge, as a hanger. After installing each board, hang the spacer beside it, butt the next board against the spacer, and nail the board in place. Use a straightedge or stringline to keep the tops level.

Rent a pneumatic nailer to speed up installation of the fencing. The rental agency provides operating and safety instructions.

3. **Trim the top edge.**

   If you attach boards to the edge of the rails (rather than below the top rail), the tops may not be even (unless you used a straightedge or stringline to keep them level, as with a picket fence). Snap a chalkline along the length of the fence (shown in Figure 5-6), at the finished height, and cut along the line. If you use a power saw, nail a cleat along the fence to guide the saw.

4. **Add decorative trim.**

Applying the finish

Allow the wood to season for a week or two and apply a sealer (for natural color) or water-repellent stain to the fence. If you paint the fence, wait several weeks for the wood to season. Apply white-pigmented shellac to exposed knots to keep resin from bleeding through the paint. Then, prime the fence (use oil-based primer for redwood and cedar; latex for other woods) and finish it with one or two coats of latex paint.

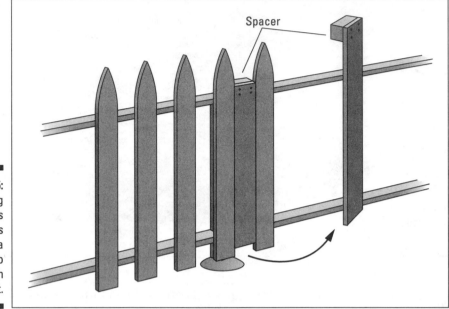

Figure 5-5:
Installing pickets is less tedious if you use a spacer to align each picket.

Spacer

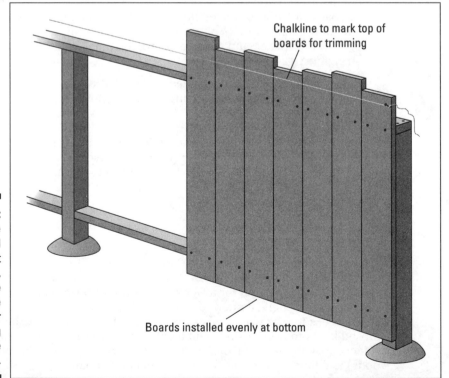

Figure 5-6:
For a simple board fence (not pickets), trim the top of the fence after installing all of the boards.

Chalkline to mark top of boards for trimming

Boards installed evenly at bottom

Working with Walls

Garden walls imply permanence — some seem to have been a part of the landscape forever. You can build low walls (6 to 12 inches high) to establish borders and boundaries. A wall 15 to 18 inches high also serves as a bench. A wall 3 feet high creates a sense of enclosure, and taller walls offer privacy and sound control. As with retaining walls (see Chapter 4), avoid building walls higher than 3 feet by yourself, unless you have experience with masonry.

You have several materials to choose from:

✔ Brick and concrete block, because of their uniform grid patterns, work well in formal gardens that have a strong axis and regular forms.

Concrete block is the most versatile material because the blocks themselves come in plain or decorative formats and several different colors, and because you can cover an ordinary block wall with almost any kind of veneer, from smooth stucco to imitation stone patterns.

For ease of installation, modular materials, especially concrete block, are easy to work with.

✔ Cut stone, which is slightly more rustic but with a modular format, also fits nicely. Stone, although heavy and time-consuming, is fun to work with and is forgiving of mistakes.

✔ For informal gardens, choose fieldstone, irregularly cut stone, or brick, which has a regular grid pattern but earthy texture.

Brick offers more variations in pattern and is easy to lift, but requires considerable working of the joints.

Building a stacked stone wall

To build a *stacked,* or dry, stone wall, follow the same principles as building a stone retaining wall (see Chapter 4):

✔ Before starting the wall, set aside some large flat stones for the top of the wall and several *bondstones* (stones long enough to extend from one side to the other) to place every 4 feet along the middle course. Save the largest stones for the base.

✔ *Batter,* or angle, both sides of the wall in toward the top at a rate of 1 inch for every 2 feet of wall height.

✔ Make the base of the wall approximately 2 feet wide for every 3 feet of wall height.

✔ Build the ends first and work toward the center.

✔ As you build, use small stones to fill cavities and create flat perches for the larger stones.

✔ Interlock the stones as much as possible, and tilt large stones toward the center of the wall.

Building a mortared stone wall

Binding stones together with mortar creates a stable wall and makes it possible to make the sides plumb (straight, not battered), but the wall is vulnerable to ground settlement. To solve this problem, build the wall on a reinforced-concrete base, or footing, and following these steps (see Figure 5-7):

1. **Lay out and dig a trench at least 12 inches deep, or to the frost line, and approximately 4 inches wider than the wall base.**

   Place two lengths of No. 4 ($^1/_2$-inch) rebar in the trench, held off the ground at least 3 inches by stones or *dobies* (small concrete blocks). When splicing rebar end-to-end, overlap the rebar 2 feet, twist tie wire tightly around both pieces.

2. **Fill the trench with concrete, but not to the top, so that the footing is concealed when the wall is complete and soil is placed against it.**

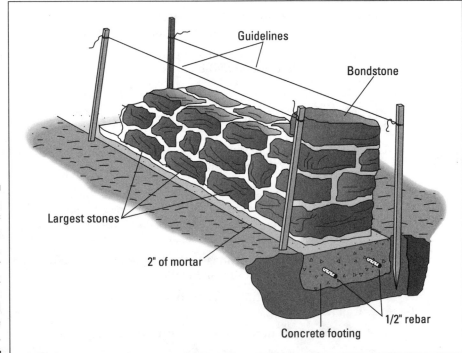

Figure 5-7:
A wall of mortared stone, block, or brick requires a reinforced concrete footing.

Guidelines

Bondstone

Largest stones

2" of mortar

Concrete footing

1/2" rebar

3. After the concrete sets, *dry-fit* (that is, place without using mortar) a few stones at one end of the wall and remove them.

4. Mix a small batch of mortar, place a 2-inch thick layer of it on the footing, and set the bottom stones on the mortar.

5. Place small stones and rubble between the large stones and, using a mortar trowel, throw a layer of mortar over them and the bottom stones.

6. Set the second *course* (layer) of stones over the first.

   As you set each stone. strike spilled mortar off of the wall surface with your trowel.

7. Repeat the process at the other end of the wall.

8. Drive a stake into the ground at each end of the wall and string a guideline between the stakes at the level of the second course.

   Use this line to keep the face of the wall straight and plumb as you lay each course of stones.

9. As you build each course, start at the ends and work toward the center.

   Use the largest stones at the ends. To prevent long vertical joints that have to span several courses, strive to place one stone over two, then two stones over one, staggering the joints.

10. *Rake* (gouge) the joints as you go.

    After the mortar has set for 10 or 15 minutes, scratch away enough mortar from each joint to create an indentation up to $1/2$-inch deep, using a round stick or piece of pipe. Then, remove excess mortar with a soft brush and smooth the mortar, to make the joints stronger, with a *jointing tool* (narrow trowel that fits between the stones) or curved piece of copper tubing.

11. Cap the wall with flat stones and brush off all excess mortar.

12. Cover the wall with a tent of plastic sheeting for five days to allow the mortar to cure without excess evaporation.

Building a brick wall

Bricklaying varies from stacking bricks in a simple, repeating pattern to creating intricate artistic designs. Even with no bricklaying experience, you can build a low garden wall using the following techniques (see Figure 5-8):

1. Plan the brick pattern and layout.

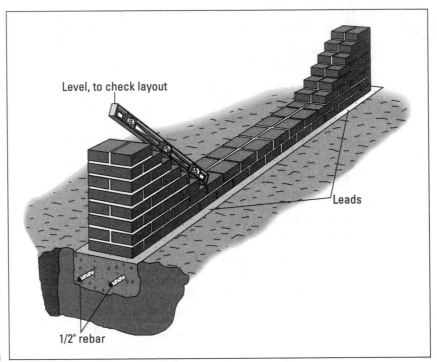

Figure 5-8:
Building a
brick wall.

Level, to check layout

Leads

1/2" rebar

Most garden walls are 16 to 24 inches high and 8 inches — or two *wyeths* (width of one brick) — wide. Lay the bricks end-to-end and flat, offsetting the bricks in each *course* (layer) by half a brick length, so that the vertical joints in alternating courses align. This pattern is called a *running bond*.

2. **Dig a footing trench and install an 8- to 12-inch-wide concrete footing. For walls over 12 inches high, install a vertical rebar, tied to the horizontal rebar, every 24 inches down the center of the wall.**

   See "Building a mortared stone wall," earlier in this chapter.

3. **After the footing hardens, snap a chalkline onto it as a guideline for one edge of the wall.**

4. **Lay out the first course of bricks in a *dry run* (no mortar).**

   Space the bricks $3/8$-inch apart, for mortar joints. Adjust the length of the wall, if necessary, to accommodate full bricks. Then, remove them.

5. **Mix and spread enough mortar at one end of the wall for a row of four or five bricks.**

6. **Set the first brick in place, tapping it to bed it into the mortar.**

Working with mortar

For stone, brick, and block work use a mortar mix of 1 part portland cement, 1 part hydrated lime, and 6 parts sand. You can buy the ingredients in bulk or premixed in 60-pound sacks. If you buy mortar mix, specifiy Type M, which is suitable for ground contact. Mix only enough per batch to use in 30 minutes.

For stone work, add only enough water so that the mortar stays in place without slumping. For bricks, mix a creamier batch that is stiff enough to hold the weight of a brick but moist enough to smooth easily. Color mortar by adding a powdered tinting agent, available at masonry suppliers.

After mixing the mortar in a bucket or wheelbarrow, shovel it onto a piece of plywood close to your work site. Using a pointed brick trowel, slice off a section of mortar; then scoop it off the plywood and "throw" it into place — all in one motion.

7. *Butter* one end of the next brick with mortar (the same way that you butter bread) and shove it into place against the first brick. Scrape off excess mortar with your trowel.

8. **Repeat the process for the next two or three bricks.**

9. **Lay the same number of bricks in the second wyeth, starting with a half brick.**

   Butter one end and the inside edge of each brick before setting it in place.

10. **Throw a row of mortar on top of the first course of bricks.**

    Then, using the point of your trowel, create a *furrow* (indented channel) along the center of the mortar.

11. **Lay the second course of bricks, starting with a half brick on the first wyeth and a full brick on the second wyeth.**

    Using a 4-foot level, check the course to make sure that it's straight and level.

12. **Continue building up one end of the wall with courses, until you have room for only one brick on top.**

    The resulting pyramid-like structure is called a *lead*. Each course steps back a half brick from the previous course, creating an incline. Lay a level or straightedge against this incline to make sure that the bricks are even.

    Every two or three courses, embed *brick ties* (corrugated metal straps) in the mortar at 2-foot intervals to tie the two wyeths together.

13. **Build an identical lead at the other end of the wall.**

14. **After completing both leads, fill in the center area.**

    To keep the bricks aligned, stretch mason's twine between the two leads as you move up each course.

15. **Remove excess mortar and tool the joints as you go.**

    See "Building a mortared stone wall," earlier in this chapter.

16. **Cap the wall with bricks laid across the wall, flat or on edge.**

    To create an overhanging cap, combine a half brick with each full brick.

Building a concrete block wall

Build a block wall the same way as a brick wall, by pouring a concrete footing, doing a dry run, building a lead at each corner, staggering successive courses, and tooling the joints (discussed in the "Building a mortared stone wall" section, earlier in this chapter). One difference is that the hollow units allow you to insert vertical rebar in the footing to reinforce the wall. When setting blocks, place them with the *web* (wider edges) side up.

If you plan to veneer the wall with stone or brick facing, insert wall ties in the mortar of each course, spaced 2 to 3 feet apart, with 1 to 2 inches of tie protruding out of the wall. When the wall mortar cures, trowel mortar onto the face of the wall, embedding the wall ties in it, and adhere the stone or brick to the wet mortar. Another option for veneering a wall is to cover it with stucco, which doesn't require wall ties — consult a contractor for more information on stucco.

Going for Gates

From grandiose to rustic, gates play a prominent role in landscaping and offer rich fodder for the imagination. Even if you're not building a fence or wall, you may want to place a gate in your garden as a decorative focal point.

If you hang a gate on a fence, plan on using larger posts for the gate than for the fence — 6x6s, for example, if the fence posts are 4x4s — and burying them deeper than the fence posts. If your gate features a trellis over it, hang the gate between two of the trellis posts. See the section "Installing posts," earlier in this chapter, for more information.

You have two options for attaching a gate to a stone, brick, or block wall:

✔ Attach a vertical board to the inside face of the wall opening, using lag bolts or similar masonry anchoring devices, and attach the gate to it.

✔ Install two *screw hooks* (L-shaped hinge holders) in the masonry, aligned vertically. Either embed them into fresh mortar as you build the wall — one near the bottom and one near the top of the gate position — or drill holes with a masonry bit and install the hooks with *expansive mortar* (mortar specified for embedding hardware into masonry).

Make the gate opening at least 36 inches wide — 40 to 48 inches is better for moving garden equipment and materials around. If the opening is wider than 48 inches, install double gates.

To build a gate, follow these steps (see Figure 5-9):

1. **Plan the gate width.**

   Measure the width of the opening at the top and bottom of the gate location and reduce these measurements by $^3/_4$ to 1 inch for gate clearance.

2. **Plan the gate height.**

   Allow clearance at the bottom for obstacles. Align the top with the fence or choose a different height to emphasize the gate.

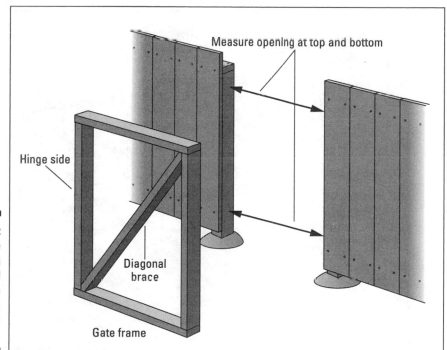

Figure 5-9: Measure the opening at several points when planning the gate frame.

Measure opening at top and bottom

Hinge side

Diagonal brace

Gate frame

3. Build a box frame out of 2x4s.

Cut the top and bottom cross members to the full gate width (width of opening minus 1 inch). Cut each side piece 3 inches shorter than the total height of the frame. Nail, screw, or bolt the cross members to the side pieces (drill *pilot holes,* which are holes a little smaller than the nail or screw, first).

4. Install a diagonal brace.

Lay the frame over a 2x4, set on edge. Align the 2x4 so that it extends from bottom hinge corner to the top latch corner. Square the frame and mark cutting lines on the 2x4 brace by tracing a pencil line against the box frame members. Cut the brace along the lines. Slide the brace into the box frame so that it's flush with the outside face of the frame. Drill pilot holes through the frame and drive nails through them into the brace.

5. Attach fencing or other material to the frame.

Lay the frame down flat with the outside facing up. Lay the fencing material on top of the frame and attach it with nails or screws.

6. Attach hinges to the gate (see Figure 5-10).

Figure 5-10:
Attach hinges to the gate first, and then hang the gate.

Use strap hinges, mounted on the front or back of the gate, or butt hinges, mounted on the side of the gate. Mount them so that the gate swings into your property.

7. **Position the gate and attach the hinges to the gate post.**

   Support the gate temporarily. Drill pilot holes for the hinge screws and attach the hinges.

8. **Add gate hardware (such as a latch, cane bolt, or closer) and a stop.**

   Use a strip of wood for the stop and attach it to the fence post or gate, depending on the gate swing.

Planning Primrose Paths

Garden paths and walks don't necessarily have to take a beeline from Point A to Point B. Base them on where you need to walk, but also allow them to meander slightly to take advantage of views and attractive garden settings. (Avoid low areas with poor drainage and steep inclines, though.) Make paths at least 36 inches wide; two people walking side-by-side require a 48-inch width. For wheelchair use, slope the path no more than 1:12 — 1 inch of rise for every 12 inches of run, measured horizontally — and provide a 5-foot long landing every 30 feet.

For formal, all-weather walks, choose concrete, brick, or flagstone. For informal paths, consider stepping stones, gravel, crushed stone, or wood chips.

Building a gravel or crushed stone path

Gravel and crushed stone, which aren't the same material, create paths with a classic, old-world feeling. The *pea gravel* used for landscaping has rounded edges and is uniform in size. It has the sound and feel of loose pebbles. It drains quickly and stays clean, but it constantly moves underfoot. Most gravel is gray. *Crushed stone,* on the other hand, has sharp edges that enable it to compact into a solid mass. It varies in size. The mixture of small rocks and *fines* (sand and fine particles) compacts into a dense surface that's almost as solid as paving materials. The smaller particles, however, stick to shoes and become messy. Larger-sized particles and stones don't compact as tightly, but are cleaner. Crushed stone varies in color from tan and beige tones to blue and gray tones.

To build a gravel or stone garden path, follow these steps:

1. **Lay out the edges of the path using garden hoses or stringlines.**

   For layout techniques, see Chapter 4.

Figure 5-11:
Formal
brick, less-
formal
stepping
stones, and
informal
gravel are
three
attractive
materials
for
walkways.

2. **Dig between the edges to a depth of 6 to 8 inches (deeper, if your winters are severe).**

3. **Install a border along each side of the path.**

   Set 1x6s or flexible *bender boards* (thin, bendable boards) on edge and nail them to short stakes placed along the outside. You can also buy vinyl edging and install it according to the manufacturer. As another alternative, consider lining the sides of the excavation with bricks, stones, or timbers.

4. **Place 4 to 6 inches of *road base* (crushed rock used for gravel beds) or *class-five gravel* in the bottom of the excavation.**

5. **Using a *flat plate vibrator* (which you can rent), compact the base.**

   Add rock, as necessary.

6. **Fill the rest of the excavation with 2 to 4 inches of pea gravel or crushed rock.**

   If you use crushed rock, build a *crown,* or hump, along the center of the path for drainage, and compact the rock with the flat plate vibrator.

Building a walkway with bricks or pavers

Brick has subtle textures and variable colors that fit into many landscape designs. It is readily available, easy to handle, and has uniform dimensions that make various interlocking patterns possible. You can install bricks in a bed of compacted sand or on a mortar bed over a concrete slab. Although a mortared installation is more durable, bricks laid carefully on a compacted sand base make a very solid walk that's easy to build.

Although some types of brick are referred to as "pavers," the pavers that we refer to in this book are concrete pavers, the modern cousin of brick. Concrete pavers have the same advantages of modular size, compact form, and easy installation, but cost considerably less, are stronger, and have beveled edges that prevent slightly-raised pavers from becoming tripping hazards.

To install bricks or pavers on a sand bed, follow these steps (see Figure 5-12):

1. **Lay out the walk.**

   See the section "Building a gravel or crushed stone path," earlier in this chapter.

2. **Dig to a depth of 9 to 15 inches.**

   See "Building a gravel or crushed stone path," earlier in this chapter.

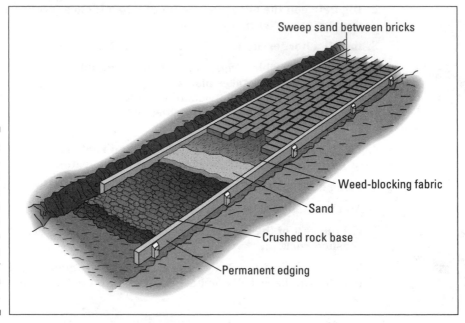

Sweep sand between bricks

Weed-blocking fabric

Sand

Crushed rock base

Permanent edging

Figure 5-12:
A well-compacted base and firm edgings are the keys to installing bricks or pavers on sand.

3. **Moisten the bottom of the area that you just dug out and compact it.**

   Rent a flat plate vibrator (a power compactor) or improvise a tool by tying a heavy wooden block to the bottom of a sledge hammer or pick.

4. **Place 4 to 8 inches of road base or class-five gravel in the excavation and compact it.**

5. **Install edging along the two sides of the walk**

6. **Place 2 to 4 inches of sand over the rock base.**

   Moisten and compact it so that the distance from the top of the sand to the finished level of the walk is equal to the thickness of one brick.

7. **Dampen the sand bed.**

8. **Tie a length of mason's twine to two loose bricks and, using them for anchors, stretch the line parallel with (and one brick's width away from) either edge of the walk.**

   Use this line to guide placement of the first row of bricks, even if they abut the edging.

9. **Install *weed-blocking fabric* over the sand.**

   This material prevents weeds from coming up, but allows rainwater to soak into the ground.

10. **Set the bricks or pavers in place.**

    Gently tap each one with a rubber mallet to snug it into the sand — avoid displacing any sand.

11. **After laying several bricks or pavers, check your work by laying a straightedge or long level over it.**

12. **After all of the units are in place, spread a layer of fine, dry sand over the walk.**

    Sweep it back and forth, working it into the joints. With the excess sand still on the surface, compact the walk with a flat plate vibrator. Keep adding sand, as necessary.

Building a concrete walk

If you build a concrete walk you can finish the concrete in one of several ways for the final surface, or use the concrete as a base for installing other paving materials. To build a basic walk, follow these steps, shown in Figure 5-13:

1. **Lay out the walk and excavate to a depth of 8 to 12 inches.**

   See the section "Building a gravel or crushed stone path," earlier in this chapter.

Figure 5-13:
The most critical steps in building a concrete walk are setting the forms and finishing the surface of the concrete.

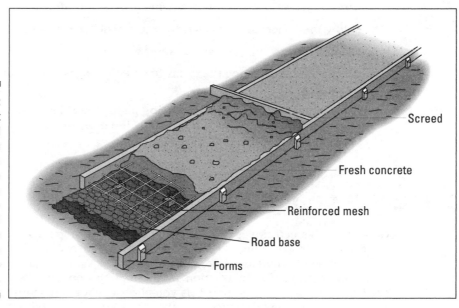

Screed

Fresh concrete

Reinforced mesh

Road base

Forms

2. **Using 2x4s set on edge, build forms along each side of the walk.**

   Set the tops at the finished level of the walk, securing them with stakes. Rather than level the forms from side to side, set one side $^1/_8$-inch lower than the other for drainage. Use two or three thicknesses of flexible bender board as forms for curved walks.

3. **Place 4 to 8 inches of road base or class-five gravel in the excavation and compact it.**

4. **Install reinforcing steel.**

   Use *6-6-10-10 wire reinforcing mesh* (#10 wire on a 6-inch grid, available in 5-, 6-, or 7-foot wide rolls) or #3 ($^3/_8$-inch diameter) rebar, placed on an 18-inch grid and wired together with tie wire. Place 2-inch high *dobies* (concrete blocks) under the steel to keep it centered in the concrete.

5. **Fill the forms with concrete.**

   For information about ordering or mixing concrete, see Chapter 6.

6. **Screed, or strike off, the concrete by dragging a 2x4 over the tops of the forms in a back-and-forth sawing motion.**

7. **Float the concrete (smooth it so that the rocks are fully embedded and the paste floats to the surface) with a wooden or magnesium float.**

8. **Cut grooves across the concrete at 6- to 10-foot intervals, using a *jointer* (trowel-like tool with a ridge centered under the blade).**

9. **Allow the concrete to set slightly and finish the surface.**

   For finishing techniques, see Chapter 6.

   Also run an *edger* along the forms to give the edges of the walk a rounded profile.

10. **Cover the walk with concrete curing paper for at least 24 hours to *cure* (allow it to harden without all of the moisture evaporating) the concrete.**

Stepping in Style

Gardens with steep slopes or multiple levels require steps. You can build informal garden steps out of timbers, sections of railroad tie, or stacked stones. Or, you can build a more formal set of stairs out of concrete, brick, or mortared stone (for information about building wooden stairs for decks see Chapter 6).Whichever materials you choose, your steps must conform to code requirements designed to make stairs safe. If possible, avoid single steps — they are difficult to see and may come as a surprise to the casual stroller. Also, include lighting in your plans (see Chapter 7).

The following requirements are typical of most building codes (verify with your building department):

- Stairs must be at least 36 inches wide.

- The *total rise* (distance from landing to landing, measured vertically) must not exceed 12 feet. For longer climbs, include at least one landing every 12 feet — see Figure 5-14.

Figure 5-14:
Stairs and garden steps must maintain uniform, safe dimensions.

Riser 6"
Tread 14"
Slope ⅛"

Riser 4"
Tread 18"
Slope ⅛"

6"

4'-6'

Main steps

Tread-to-riser rule for steps

- For each step, the *riser* (vertical measurement) must not exceed 7½ inches and the *tread* (horizontal measurement) must be no less than 11 inches deep. The ratio between the two dimensions must be constant — a loose formula for calculating this ratio is: 2 risers + 1 tread = 25-27 inches.

- All riser heights and tread widths within a set of stairs must not vary more than ⅜ inch.

- Stairs with three or more risers require a handrail. Handrails must be a uniform height above all stair treads: 34 to 38 inches as measured vertically from the stair *nosings* (front edges).

- Landings must be as wide as the stairway and at least 36 inches deep.

Calculating step dimensions

Make garden steps as luxurious as possible, with low risers (5½ to 6½ inches), deep treads, and a generous width. To plan your steps, follow these steps:

1. **Measure the vertical rise between landings.**

   Measure from the finished surface of the lower path to the finished surface of the upper path. To do this, set one end of a straightedge on the upper path (or on a support that represents the approximate level of the path). Holding the straightedge level, bridge the step location with it and measure down from the bottom of the straightedge to the surface of the lower path.

2. **Divide this dimension by a trial riser height, such as 6 inches, to determine the number of risers.**

   If the answer is a whole number (not likely), proceed to the next step. If not, round the answer up to the next whole number and divide that number back into the original dimension. The result is your actual riser height. (For example, a total rise of 27 inches, divided by a trial riser height of 6-inches, yields 4.5 risers. By rounding this number up to 5 and dividing it into 27, you get a riser height of 5.4, or $5^3/_8$, inches.)

3. **Calculate the tread *depth* (width, as viewed from the side) by doubling the riser height and subtracting the answer from 26 inches.**

   For example: $5^3/_8$ x 2 = $10^3/_4$ inches. $26 - 10^3/_4 = 15^1/_4$ inches for the tread depth.

4. **Calculate the total run by multiplying the tread depth by the number of treads.**

   The number of treads is one less than the number of risers, so the total run of a set of steps with five risers and a tread depth of $15^1/_4$ inches would be 61 inches.

5. **Test the total run.**

   Holding a tape measure level with the upper path, and using a plumb bob or level to transfer the measurement down to the lower path, measure a distance equal to the total run to see if you have enough space for the steps. If necessary, reduce the total run by shortening the tread depth dimension by 1 inch (remember that the riser-to-tread formula allows a total of 25 to 27 inches), or by reworking the ratio using a higher riser height.

Building steps

Use large building "blocks," such as landscaping timbers, railroad ties, concrete block, or large stones, to make informal garden steps. If a timber or stone is taller than the required riser height, simply bury it in the ground a bit. The techniques for building with block or stone are similar to the following techniques for building with timbers (see Figure 5-15):

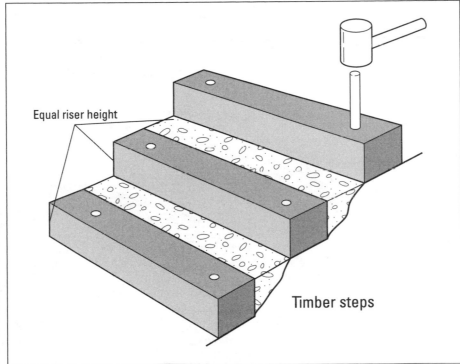

Equal riser height

Timber steps

Figure 5-15:
You can use landscape timbers or sections of old railroad ties to build garden steps.

1. **Cut 6x6 landscaping timbers or used railroad ties into 3-foot sections**.

   Bore two $\frac{1}{2}$-inch diameter holes through each piece, near the ends.

2. **Set the bottom step in place.**

   Excavate and level the ground as necessary. Backfill and level the space behind the step, using gravel, crushed rock, concrete, or compacted soil for the backfill.

3. **Place the next step.**

   Measure back from the front edge of the lower step, at both ends, a distance that's equal to the tread depth (see above). Place the next step so that the front edge is aligned with this dimension. Backfill and level for the next step.

4. **Proceed up the slope.**

   As you build each step, stabilize the timber by driving a 24-inch length of $\frac{1}{2}$-inch rebar through each hole, flush with the top.

   Set each step so that the front edge is $\frac{1}{8}$- to $\frac{1}{4}$-inch lower than the back, for drainage.

5. **For three or more risers, add a handrail along one or both sides of the steps — see Chapter 6 for more information.**

Chapter 6

Building Decks and Patios

. . . .

In This Chapter

▶ Planning and building a deck

▶ Adding stairs and railings

▶ Choosing patio materials

▶ Laying bricks or pavers on a sand bed

▶ Building a concrete patio

. . . .

Home life has shifted to the outdoors. Many families spend as much time cooking, dining, entertaining, playing, and working in their yards as they do in their houses. Having a lovely landscape isn't enough — people want an outdoor living space with all the comforts of home.

The heart of any outdoor living space is a deck or patio, which you will most likely build first. Then, you can let nature provide the ambiance (and nuisances), or you can enhance your deck or patio with such features as an overhead shade structure, built-in seating, a cooking center, and exterior lighting (see Chapter 7).

Building a Deck

Although a deck is a fairly simple structure, building one requires careful planning and workmanship. As a floor system, a deck must support heavy loads. As an outdoor structure, it must endure constant exposure to water and sunlight. These factors alone require that your deck have heavy structural members, strong connections, solid footings, and effective protection from rot. In addition, your deck must fit in with the site, harmonize with your home, and be large enough for whatever activities you plan. (See the color section of this book for examples of well-built decks.) This section, along with the basic construction guidelines in Chapter 4, can help you plan and build a basic deck that meets these challenges. Be sure to read the entire section before beginning your design.

How a deck works

In simplest terms, a deck is a well-organized stack of lumber resting on rot-resistant supports. (See Figure 6-1.) In technical terms, concrete *footings* buried in the ground support *piers,* which support *posts,* which support one or more *beams,* which support *joists* (a *ledger board* connected to the house may also support the joists). The joists support the *decking boards* that you walk on and any *stairs* or *railings* that attach to the deck.

The beams and joists bear a critical relationship to each other. The farther apart the beams, the stronger and/or closer together the joists must be. The posts, footings, and beams bear a similar relationship — the farther apart the posts, the larger the footings and the stronger the beams.

Corrosion-resistant fasteners hold everything together and a *deck finish,* such as a water-repellent preservative, retards deterioration. As with any well-built structure, the deck must be *level,* the posts and railings *plumb* (perfectly vertical), and the corners *square* (exactly 90 degrees — unless the deck design includes different-sized angles).

Getting started

Planning and preparation account for at least 40 percent of a building project's time, starting long before construction begins. For a deck, you must draw up a plan, get any necessary permits, order materials, arrange for delivery and storage, and obtain tools.

Developing a good deck plan

A good deck starts with a good plan. Most decks measure 12 to 16 feet wide and 16 to 24 feet long — approximately 200 to 400 square feet, or the size of a large family room. In choosing a site for your deck, consider how the sun and shade patterns change throughout the day and the seasons. Plan for convenient access to the house, especially the kitchen and other public rooms, and to the garden. Take into account furniture arrangements and traffic flow. You may need to reconfigure the deck's shape or size for more efficient use. Also consider views and privacy. Use a stepladder to make observations from the proposed height of the deck platform. Finally, inspect your deck site for downspouts, buried utility lines, meters, a septic tank, a crawlspace opening, and similar features that may interfere with the deck.

To design the deck itself, outline the platform first. Draw, to scale, an outline of the deck's shape from an aerial perspective. Include the house walls — with window and door locations — and other existing features that affect the deck.

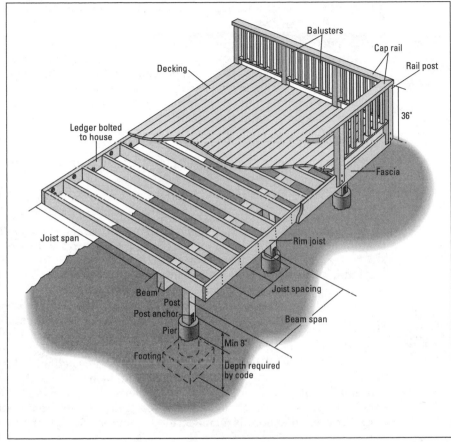

Figure 6-1:
The basic structural system of a deck consists of footings, piers, posts, ledger board, beam, joists, decking, and railing posts.

Next, plot the direction of the decking boards, joists, beams, and ledger board (refer to Figure 6-1) for the shortest joist spans and most convenient footing locations. Typically, decking runs parallel with the house wall or along the longer deck dimension. To calculate the size and spacing of the joists and beams, consult joist span and beam span tables in *Decks & Patios For Dummies* by Robert Beckstrom (IDG Books Worldwide, Inc.) or use the following recommendations.

✔ **Decking.** Use 2x6 boards, which safely span 24 inches no matter what species or grade.

✔ **Joists.** Plan 2x8 joists, spaced 24 inches *on center* (measured center-to-center or from one side of a joist to the same side of the adjacent joist). 2x8 joists of construction grade lumber, such as No. 2 pine, "standard & better" Douglas fir, or "construction heart" redwood, can span from $8^1/_2$ to 10 feet safely, depending on the species of wood. For longer spans, use larger joists or space the 2x8s closer together.

- **Ledger.** Choose a ledger board one size larger than the joists (a 2x10 or 3x8 for 2x8 joists).

- **Beams.** Place the first beam 9 feet from the ledger, and place subsequent beams 8 feet apart. The joists can extend 2 to 3 feet beyond the outside beam. This span is called a *cantilever*. The size of beam depends on the spacing between posts. A 4x8 beam, for example, spaced 9 feet from adjacent beams, can span up to 6 feet. If the posts are farther apart, use a larger beam.

- **Posts.** Use 4x4s for posts shorter than 6 feet; larger sizes for taller posts.

- **Piers and footings.** Plan footing locations so that each one supports approximately 50 square feet of deck area.

Choosing decking material

Lumber varies widely in durability, strength, appearance, availability, and cost. Choose pressure-treated lumber for the structural members, to ensure strength and durability. If larger beam sizes aren't available, choose untreated lumber and apply a preservative/sealer on-site.

You have a wider choice for the decking boards, including redwood, cedar, pressure-treated pine or Douglas fir, tropical hardwoods, and nonwood alternatives made from plastics and other recycled materials. Pressure-treated pine, stained in reddish or brown tones, makes an economical choice that's widely available. If you buy redwood or cedar decking, avoid lumber that may contain sapwood by using all heart grades. Also look for a low number of growth rings (less than 10 per inch, as viewed in cross-section from the end of the board). For longevity and low maintenance, consider nonwood boards manufactured from recycled plastic and sawdust.

Besides lumber, you need to purchase concrete for the footings and piers, *rebar* (steel reinforcing bars for concrete; use 1/2-inch diameter), connecting hardware, and deck finish.

Prepping the site, installing the ledger, and laying out the area

Prepare the deck site by removing weeds and grading the soil to slope away from the house. If necessary, install drainage lines to prevent water from puddling under the deck (see Chapter 4). If you're attaching the deck to your house, make any alterations or repairs, such as removing a porch or repainting an area covered by the deck, at this time.

If you're installing a new window, wait until after you build the deck to do so. The deck provides a convenient platform for completing the exterior part of the installation.

If your deck is going to cover an existing patio that slopes away from the house by at least a quarter inch per foot, leave the patio in place and break holes through it where the footings for the deck go. The patio enhances drainage, inhibits weeds, provides a convenient storage platform, and keeps the area under the deck clear. If the patio doesn't slope correctly, break it up and remove the concrete — if you don't, puddles may accumulate against the house foundation because of the shade from the deck.

Lay out the deck using the techniques described in Chapter 4. If you attach your deck to the house, simplify the layout by installing the ledger board first. It makes a convenient batterboard, especially for multiple rows of footings, which require intermediate stringlines between the perimeter lines.

Before attaching a ledger, check the affected section of the house carefully. You don't want to cut or nail into a water pipe, electrical line, heating duct, and so on. Also make sure that the lag screws holding the ledger board will penetrate into the house framing, not just the siding.

Installing the ledger

To install the ledger, prepare the wall following these steps:

1. **Draw a level line along the wall for the top of the ledger (2¹/₂ inches below floor level if the decking boards are 2-by lumber; 1¹/₂ inches for ⁵/₄-inch decking boards).**

   You can mark a long, level line in any of the following three ways:

   • Having a person help you, hold a long straightedge with a level on it against the house and scribe the line.

   • Link a series of marks that you make by using a long level.

   • Using a hydrolevel or builder's level, make two end marks that are level with each other and then snap a chalkline between them.

If the siding is stucco, plywood, or board siding that makes full contact with the *sheathing* (plywood or similar panels between the studs and siding) behind it, proceed to the steps for installing the ledger board.

If the siding is vinyl, aluminum, shingles, or wood lap siding that doesn't make full contact with the sheathing behind it, proceed to the next step.

2. **Remove a section of siding where you intend to install the ledger.**

3. **Cover the exposed sheathing with a piece of metal *flashing* (aluminum or galvanized sheet metal).**

   Tuck the flashing under the siding board above it, smooth the flashing flat against the sheathing, and bend the bottom to lap over the siding below it. Bend the loose ends the same way and lap them over the adjacent siding an inch or so. Seal the exposed flaps with caulking and nail them tight.

Installing the ledger board

To install the ledger board, follow these steps:

1. **Cut the board to length.**

2. **Mark locations on the board for drilling ⁵/₈-inch diameter holes for ¹/₂-inch diameter lag screws.**

   Place two holes within 6 inches of each end and a pair of holes every 16 to 32 inches. Make sure there are no obstructions in the wall to interfere with hole locations and that the holes don't interfere with the joist layout (see the section, "Framing the deck," later in this chapter).

3. **Position the ledger against the wall, keeping the top aligned with your guideline.**

   Tack it in place using 16d duplex nails, or prop it up with braces.

4. **Using a pencil, mark the hole locations on the wall.**

5. **Take down the ledger and drill pilot holes into the wall for the lag screws.**

   If you need to drill through metal flashing and the flashing is aluminum, use a hole saw. If the flashing is galvanized steel, use a metal-cutting bit and lubricate it with a few drops of oil as you drill.

6. **Prepare the ledger for attachment.**

   Prop the ledger into an upright position and thread all of the lag screws through their washers and the ledger holes. Use *malleable* (thick iron) washers. On the back side of the ledger, place a spacer over each screw. Use aluminum or plastic spacers specifically designed for this function or a group of five or six cut washers. (The spacers create a gap that prevents moisture from being trapped between the ledger and house wall.)

7. **Attach the ledger.**

   With a helper, carefully lift the ledger into place and start the lag screws in their holes. Slowly tighten them in a random sequence until the ledger is snug and level.

After installing the ledger, complete the layout by building batterboards and stringing lines for the perimeter of the deck and any rows of intermediate footings. See Figure 6-2 (and check out Chapter 4 for more information about layout).

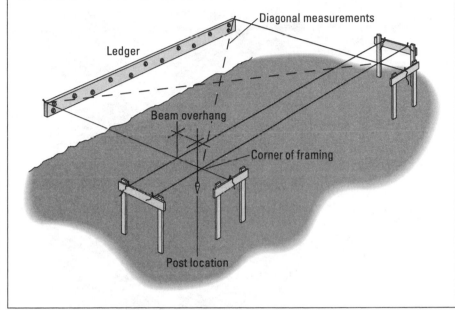

Figure 6-2:
For a deck layout, attach stringlines directly to the ledger board.

Starting with footings and piers

Dig holes for the footings to the depth required by your local building code, which is typically below the frost line in areas with severe winters, or at least 12 inches below grade (18 inches on slopes). Dig the holes using a posthole digger, hand auger, or power auger. Keep the sides straight and the bottom level. Flare or enlarge the bottom of each hole enough to provide at least 2 square feet of bearing surface for the footing (an 18x18-inch square, or 20-inch-diameter circle).

To build forms for the concrete, follow these steps (see Figure 6-3):

1. **For each hole, cut a length of 8- or 12-inch diameter forming tube that's 4 inches shorter than the hole depth.**

2. **Center the tube under the stringlines and suspend it so that the top extends 8 inches above grade.**

3. **Lay a 2x4 across the hole on each side of the forming tube and, using deck screws and a power screwdriver, secure the tube to both 2x4s.**

   Center the tube again and secure the 2x4s in position by driving a stake next to each end and attaching it to the 2x4 with screws.

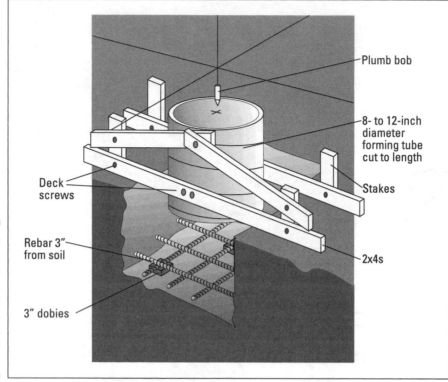

Figure 6-3:
Concrete
will be
placed in
the hole and
forming
tube for this
footing and
pier.

Plumb bob

8- to 12-inch
diameter
forming tube
cut to length

Deck
screws

Stakes

Rebar 3"
from soil

2x4s

3" dobies

4. **For additional bracing, run 1x4s diagonally from the stakes to the upper part of the tube; secure them by using deck screws.**

5. **Cut a length of rebar for each pier the same length as the tube and set it aside for the concrete pour.**

After the building inspector okays your forms and footing holes, order or mix the concrete (see "Building a concrete slab patio," later in this chapter). Place just enough concrete in the bottom of each hole to fill the bottom 1 inch of forming tube. Using a stick or rod, jab the concrete to consolidate it. After the concrete sets for a few minutes, fill the rest of the tube, settling the concrete by jabbing it and tapping the sides of the form with a hammer. Using a scrap of wood, strike off the concrete to level the top. Then push the rebar down into the center of the pier until it's buried 1 to 3 inches below the top. Using the string lines and a plumb bob to guide you, set the post anchors into the wet concrete. Make sure they are plumb and level. Allow the concrete to cure for 5 days before removing the forms.

Installing posts, beams, and joists

After the concrete hardens, install the posts by following these steps:

1. **Rough-cut the two outer posts slightly long and set them in the post anchors or brackets, plumb them with a level, and temporarily brace them with stakes.**

2. **Using a hydrolevel, builder's level, or a long straightedge and carpenter's level, mark each post at the same level as the top of the ledger board.**

3. **Measure down from this mark the depth of the joist material ($7^1/_4$ inches for 2x8s) plus the depth of the beam, and mark the post.**

4. **Using a square, scribe a line around each post at this mark.**

5. **Remove each post, trim off the top at the cutting line, and reattach it to the post anchor.**

     For maximum rot prevention, soak all of the cut ends in wood preservative for eight hours before reattaching the posts to the post anchors.

6. **String a tight line between the tops of these outer posts and use it to mark the intermediate posts for cutting.**

7. **Cut and install the other posts.**

8. **After installing all the posts, brace each one temporarily with diagonal braces.**

Before installing each beam, cut it to the same length as the ledger and treat the cut end with preservative. For long spans, cut beams to length so that splices occur over posts. Attach connecting brackets, such as post caps, to the tops of the posts. Then, set the beam(s) in place. Measure along the beam and mark the precise locations for the post tops. Using a sledge hammer, knock the posts (not the beam) into alignment. Check to make sure they're plumb and fasten the connectors to the beam with 16d galvanized joist hanger nails or common nails.

To install the joists, follow these steps:

1. **Starting at either end of the ledger board, draw a vertical line $1^1/_2$ inches from the end, using a square to keep the line accurate.**

    If you don't plan to cover the end joist with a fascia board, trim the ledger along this line so that you can cover the end of the ledger with the first joist (do the same at the other end).

2. **Continue to the other end of the ledger, making similar lines every 24 inches (or at whatever joist spacing you're using).**

   Mark an X on the side of each line where the joist goes.

3. **Mark the same joist layout on the beam, making sure that you start from the same end.**

4. **Attach joist hangers to the ledger.**

   Using a scrap of joist lumber as a gauge, set the joist hangers so that the tops are flush with the top of the ledger. Nail only one side of each hanger to the ledger, aligning it with the layout line. Use 16d galvanized joist hanger nails.

5. **Attach the first joist to the ledger.**

   Rest it on the beam and slide the other end into the joist hanger. Leave $^1/_8$ to $^1/_4$ inch of clearance at the end of the joist, squeeze the joist hanger closed, and nail the loose side to the ledger. Then nail the hanger to the joist, holding a sledge hammer against the opposite side of the joist that you nail to keep the board from splitting.

6. **Attach the joist to the beam by toenailing three 8d galvanized common nails or by securing the joist with a metal rafter tie or hurricane tie.**

7. **Install the rest of the joists, securing both ends of each joist before installing the next one.**

8. **Trim the free ends of the joists.**

   Holding a chalkline between the outer joists, snap a cutting line across the tops of all the joists. Mark a cutting line along one side of each joist where the chalkline crosses it. Cut along the marks.

9. **Attach a rim joist (also called a *header*) to the ends of the trimmed joists.**

   Mark the joist layout on the back of the rim joist and, working from one end to the other, attach the header to each joist with 16d galvanized spiral-shank nails or 3-inch deck screws (drill pilot holes for the end joists).

   Make sure that you attach the rim joist on the same day that you install the joists, or they may warp. Also, apply preservative to the cut ends of all boards before you install them.

10. **Install blocking between the joists along the beam.**

    Snap a chalkline across the joists. Measure each joist bay and cut a 2x8 block for it. Tap it into place between the joists and nail it with four 16d nails at each end. Stagger the blocks on each side of the chalkline to facilitate nailing.

Laying decking boards

Before laying the decking boards, apply sealer to the joists, especially the tops. You should also apply a coat of finish (sealer or sealer/preservative, depending on type of lumber) to the decking boards if you have sufficient room to lay them out in a shaded, well-ventilated area. Otherwise, apply finish to the bottom sides, after laying them out, before you attach them. To install the boards, follow these steps:

1. **Sort through the stack of lumber and select the best boards for prominent locations, such as in front of doorways and stairs, and along the outer edge of the deck.**

   Likewise, select the worst boards for hidden locations.

2. **Starting along the house wall, lay out the decking boards loosely over the joists.**

   Be careful walking near the ends of boards until they are fastened to the joists.

3. **Fasten the first board.**

   First, tip it on edge and snap a chalkline across the joists, measuring out from the wall the width of one board plus $^3/_8$ inch. Align the outer edge of the board along this line. Fasten with two *deck screws* (3-inch galvanized screws installed with a power screwdriver), two 12d galvanized common nails, or a *deck clip* (hidden fastening device) at each joist. Drill pilot holes for deck screws or nails at the ends of the board.

4. **Fasten the remaining boards.**

   Maintain a $^1/_{16}$- to $^3/_{16}$-inch gap between boards. Straighten bowed boards by driving a chisel into the joist and using it to pry the board into alignment.

   If the boards are shorter than the deck, join them end-to-end over joists. Stagger the joints at least 3 joists apart from each other.

5. **Trim the ends of the boards.**

   Snap a chalkline along the edge of the deck, either flush with the outside edge of the joist (if you're adding a fascia board) or $^1/_2$ inch beyond the joist. Cut along the chalkline.

6. **Attach the fascia.**

   Use 1-by or 2-by lumber one size wider than the joist size (a 1x10, for example, for 2x8 joists). Apply preservative and sealer to the joists and back of the fascia (not to the *front* of the fascia). Cut the fascia boards at 45 degrees for mitered joints at the corners. Attach them by driving screws through the back of the joists into the fascia, every 6 inches along the top and 12 inches along the bottom.

Adding stairs

Deck stairs consist of two or more stringers and treads attached between them (see Figure 6-4). The width of the treads and height of the risers are critical measurements and must be consistent.

For information about stair requirements and calculating dimensions, see Chapter 5. Use the following techniques for building deck stairs:

1. **Choose 2x12s for the stringers, 4 feet longer than the total stair run**.

2. **Lay out the first stringer, using a framing square.**

   See Figure 6-5. First, use tape to mark the riser dimension on the *tongue* (short leg) of the square and the tread dimension on the *blade* (long leg). For each step, align these marks with the top edge of the stringer and trace along the lower edge of the square. Move the square to the next position and trace again, until you have enough risers.

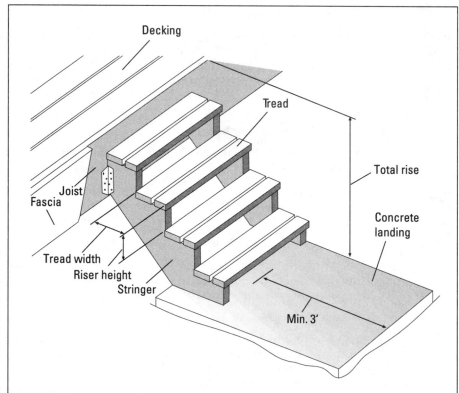

Figure 6-4: The basic dimensions and components that you use for planning stairs.

Figure 6-5:
Building
stairs and
railings
requires
precise
measure-
ments and
careful
carpentry.

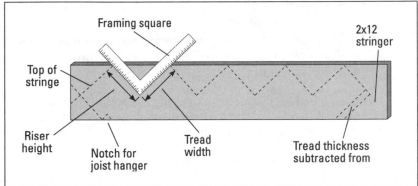

3. **Cut out the stringer.**

   Mark a cutting line for the bottom step by subtracting the thickness of
   the tread material (1¹/₂ inches, for example, for 2-by boards) from the
   bottom riser. If you're using a circular power saw to cut out the steps,
   stop the saw before you reach the corners and finish each cut with a
   handsaw.

4. **Test the stringer by setting it in place.**

   The bottom should rest flat on a concrete landing or a wooden cleat
   bolted to a concrete footing. Use a level to make sure that the treads
   are level and the risers plumb. Note any necessary adjustments and cut
   out a new stringer.

5. **Trace the first stringer onto a second 2x12 and cut it out.**

6. **Install both stringers.**

   Secure them to the deck joist with joist hangers. Secure them to the
   landing by bolting 2x4 cleats to the landing along the inside edge of
   each stringer. Drive deck screws through the stringers into the cleats.

7. **Install the treads, starting at the bottom.**

   Align the front edge of each tread so that it overhangs the stringer
   cutouts by 1 to 1¹/₂ inches.

Stairs with three or more risers require a handrail on each open side of the
stairway.

 ✔ Handrails must be *grippable* — that is, a continuous portion of the
    handrail must be 1¹/₄ to 2 inches wide so that you can easily grip it,
    with at least 1¹/₂ inches of clearance above and behind the rail and a
    maximum projection out from any wall of 3¹/₂ inches.

 ✔ The ends of handrails must not be exposed (they're sleeve-catchers)
    and they must terminate in a post or wall.

LANDSCAPE LINGO

 ✔ Handrails must be uniform height above all stair treads: 34 to 38 inches as measured vertically from the stair nosings.

 ✔ Handrails for any dropoffs over 30 inches must include childproof *screening* (that is, a 4-inch sphere can't pass through it) between the handrail and stairs.

To install a handrail, attach posts at the top and bottom of the stair stringer and every 4 to 6 feet in between (see "Adding railings" later in this chapter). Attach a string from the bottom post to the top post that's parallel with the stringer and at a uniformly consistent height of 34 to 38 inches above the tread nosings. Mark where the string intersects each post and attach the handrail at these marks.

Adding railings

Decks higher than 30 inches require railings, which must adhere to very strict safety standards. Most codes require that the rails be 36 inches high (42 inches in some areas), have closely-spaced members (called a *screening*) that prevent a 4-inch sphere from passing through, and be strong enough to resist a *lateral force* (sideways pressure) of 200 pounds per square foot. Most railing designs consist of posts, horizontal rails, and some type of screening.

Use the following techniques to build railings:

1. **Bolt the railing posts to the outside of the joists.**

   Use 4x4s and space them evenly, 4 to 6 feet apart. For a more finished appearance, cut a $1^{1}/_{2}$-inch-wide notch out of the bottom of each post so that it overlaps the decking, and bevel the bottom of the post "tail" at a 30-degree angle. Bolt each post with two $^{1}/_{2}$-inch diameter carriage bolts (see Figure 6-6).

2. **Mark and cut pairs of 2x4 rails (horizontal supports) to fit between the posts.**

   Set the bottom rails 4 inches above the decking. For *balusters* (vertical slats), set the rails on edge and flush with the inside face of the posts. For wiring screening attached to the outside face of the framing, set the rails flat.

3. **Attach the rails to the posts by drilling pilot holes and driving two 3-inch galvanized deck screws at an angle through the face of each post and into the rail.**

4. **Drive additional nails at an angle up through each end of the rail and into the post and then down through each end of the rail and into the post.**

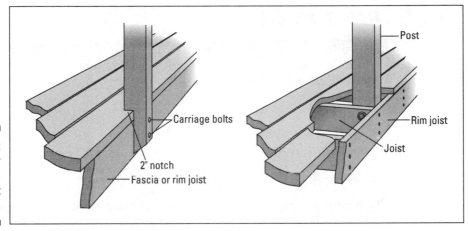

Figure 6-6:
Detail for
bolting a
railing post
to the deck.

5. **Install a 2x6 cap rail on top of the 2x4 top rails.**

   Use miter joints at the corners and attach the cap rail by driving deck
   screws up through the top rails at an angle.

6. **Attach the screening to the top and bottom rails.**

Finishing your deck

For finishing touches, spread gravel or mulch under the deck — after
putting down weed control fabric — or attach lattice panels to the deck
posts so that the area under the deck is concealed. Dress up the railing and
post edges using a router with a round-over bit (which produces a rounded
edge) or other decorative bit.

For the finish itself, apply a water-repellent preservative or a semitransparent stain that's specifically designed for deck surfaces (not for general
outdoor use, including masonry). Other products, such as paint or solid
stains, make attractive finishes but are more difficult to apply and maintain.

Before applying the finish, test it on a hidden part of the deck or some scrap
wood. Choose a sunny day on which the air temperature is between 40° and
90°, but try to avoid working in direct sunlight. Apply the product according
to manufacturer's recommendations. Using a brush or pad increases penetration, but avoid overapplying the finish because an excess can lead to
filming. For stains, coat the full length of each board to avoid overlap marks
and puddle stains.

Building a Patio

Patios offer more design options than decks, but even with those options, patios are, in some ways, simpler to design and build than decks. The four basic building steps are:

- ✔ Planning the size and shape of your patio
- ✔ Choosing the paving material
- ✔ Constructing the base
- ✔ Install the paving

The techniques vary primarily with the type of paving you install — constructing the base is similar for most materials.

Designing the patio and selecting materials

As with decks (see the section "Getting started," earlier in this chapter), the size and shape of a patio reflect the uses you intend for it and the available space to fit it in. More than decks, patios lend themselves to curves, freeform shapes, and flowing transitions into paths and walks. (See the color section of this book for ideas on patio shapes and uses.) Patios can be slightly larger than decks because, being at ground level, they aren't as prominent a structure. However, any large expanse of paving is monotonous, so break it up with tree wells, planters, benches, fountains, low walls, borders, and similar features. Minimize the impact even more by softening the edges of the patio with plants (see Part III for more on plantings).

The major planning decision for a patio is choosing what material to use for the surface. In evaluating your choices, consider the following factors:

- ✔ **Color:** Terra cotta and brick colors complement greenery but have strong red or orange tones that seem artificial or overwhelming in some settings. Very light and very dark colors call attention to themselves and accentuate the patio. Mid-tones blend with their surroundings. Bold colors create interesting accents and contrasts. Color also affects the capability of the patio to absorb or reflect sunlight, which can be a factor in exposed locations.

- ✔ **Texture:** Smooth surfaces tend to be monotonous and may become slippery. Excessively bumpy surfaces create the risk of people tripping, and may make furniture wobble.

- ✔ **Scale and proportion:** For small patios, choose finely-textured paving, such as brick, tile, or small stones. For large patios, choose flagstone, large pavers, or concrete.

- ✔ **Durability:** Brick and stones that absorb moisture, such as sandstone, are vulnerable to frost damage and moss. Materials set on a sand base endure unstable ground quite well.

- ✔ **Drainage:** Solid paving sheds water, while paving that's set on sand absorbs it.

- ✔ **Availability:** Most stone and brick is distributed within a small geographic region, although choices are abundant within most regions. Consider ease of transportation and storage. All masonry materials are heavy, but have different handling characteristics. Pallets of flagstone are difficult to handle. Bricks and concrete pavers stack easily and are fairly easy to move.

- ✔ **Ease of installation:** The easiest installations are of brick or pavers on a sand base. Concrete is easy to place but requires skillful handling and finishing. Bricks are easy to lift and handle, but require great patience to set in patterns.

- ✔ **Cost:** In pricing materials, verify the unit of measurement (cubic yard for concrete, square foot for tile or cut stone, weight for stone, and unit for brick or pavers). Generally, concrete is the least expensive material; flagstone the most expensive. As you price various materials, factor in the delivery cost.

Materials for a patio include the following choices:

- ✔ **Concrete:** Concrete is a relatively inexpensive choice that offers durability, a uniformly smooth surface, and a wide range of finishes — from smooth grays to colorful textures. Over the last few years, embossing techniques have revolutionized concrete finishing. If you associate concrete with drab slabs, consider surfaces that resemble huge slabs of natural stone or realistic patterns of cut stone, colored with permanent stains in warm earth tones. Other finishes include exposed aggregate and *broomed finishes* (a finish created by dragging a concrete-finishing broom across the fresh concrete), which create subtle patterns of straight or wavy lines.

- ✔ **Brick:** Brick that is suitable for patios includes *common* brick (also referred to as *standard* or *building* brick) and *paving* brick.

  For common brick, choose type *SW* (severe weathering) for areas with subzero tempera tures, and SW or *MW* (moderate weathering) for areas where temperatures frequently dip below freezing but seldom below zero. Avoid type *NW* (nonweathering) for patios.

Paving brick, designed for mortarless installations, is half the thickness of common brick and has straight, even sides. Be wary of using used bricks if you have extreme weather conditions — old bricks absorb moisture too easily. Bricks vary in color and texture, depending on the manufacturing method and source of clay. They also vary in size, but always have modular dimensions that enable them to fit into different patterns. The basic module is 4 x 8 x $2^1/2$ inches. Actual dimensions vary to take the mortar joints into account, ranging from $3^1/2$ to $3^3/4$ inches, for example, for the 4-inch dimension. Paving brick is usually a full 4x8 inches wide.

✔ **Pavers:** A younger cousin of brick, modular pavers have swept the patio scene as the ideal paving material for do-it-yourself installations. They're cheaper and more durable than brick but lack the rich variations of color and texture, although manufacturers are continually striving to improve their appearance. Shapes vary from mock bricks to hexagon and herringbone patterns. Some patterns require two different shapes of paver. Thickness varies — choose between $1^1/2$ and $2^1/2$ inches. Install pavers over a sand bed. Most paver designs have rounded edges to prevent sharp transitions between pavers, because they settle and move at different rates.

✔ **Stone:** Basalt, bluestone, granite, limestone, sandstone, and slate are common types of stone for paving. You can buy stone cut into regular or modular shapes, much like tile, or in random sizes and shapes, which require fitting together like a jigsaw puzzle. If you live in an area with cold winters, avoid sandstone and limestone, which absorb water and crack when they freeze. Some stones, such as granite, become very slippery when wet. The best stone is rough enough for good traction but smooth enough for tables and chairs. Install stone on a concrete slab or over a sand base (which requires thicker stones).

✔ **Borders:** Patio materials that you install on a sand bed require a permanent edge to hold them in place. Even a patio that you install on a mortar bed or concrete slab may look better with some kind of border. Materials for permanent borders include bricks laid flat or on end, stones, a concrete curb, wood timbers, 2-by lumber set on edge, and concealed plastic edging held in place with spikes. See Figure 6-7.

To estimate the quantity of materials you need, start with the overall dimensions of your patio and compute the total area. If the patio is a simple geometric shape, such as a rectangle, multiply the length times the width. If the patio is free-form, draw it to scale on graph paper and count the squares that it covers. Then, convert the surface area into the amount of each material that you need, starting with the paving.

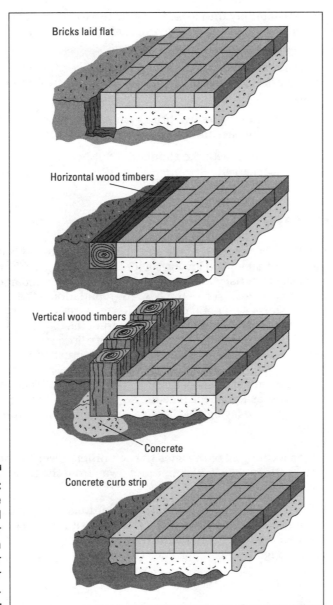

Bricks laid flat

Horizontal wood timbers

Vertical wood timbers

Concrete

Concrete curb strip

Figure 6-7:
You have
several
options for
creating a
border
around your
patio.

- For concrete, multiply the surface area by the thickness of the slab, which is usually 4 to 6 inches (use fractions of a foot) for a concrete slab.

- For base materials (see the "Building the base" section, later in this chapter), figure 4 to 8 inches. Then, convert the answer to cubic yards by dividing by 27.

- If the paving is brick, figure five bricks per square foot. If it's dimensioned stone, simply use the square footage.

- For flagstone, consult with the supplier about how many tons you need, based on the total area.

Building the base

Patio construction is simple: Dig a hole and fill it with a patio. This image emphasizes the fact that a patio involves a lot more than the surface. No matter what paving material you choose, the most important component of your patio is what you don't see — the *base* (or foundation). The process of building the base starts with preparing the site and assessing slope and drainage conditions. Then, lay out the patio's perimeter, digging a hole to the correct depth, installing whatever drainage or utility lines may be necessary, building a border, and laying down a bed of gravel or crushed rock.

To lay out the base, build batterboards and string lines between them. Use the same techniques as for a deck (see the section "Prepping the site, installing the ledger, and laying out the area," earlier in this chapter), with two differences:

- Rather than leveling all of the lines to each other, lower the outer line so that the patio slopes $^1/_8$ inch per foot away from the house for drainage.

- In addition to the perimeter lines, string additional lines five feet apart to create a grid of lines crisscrossing the patio site. These intermediate lines allow you to take depth measurements throughout the patio as you dig (although they're a nuisance to navigate around).

To complete the base, follow these steps:

1. **Excavate the soil within the patio perimeter to a depth of 8 to 12 inches, depending on the severity of winter temperatures.**

   To gauge the depth as you dig, measure down from the grid of string lines.

2. **Install 4 to 8 inches of crushed rock or class-five gravel and compact it with a vibrating plate compactor.**

3. **Install the edging material.**

4. **For a sand base, lay a pair of temporary 2x4 screed guides, 3 feet apart, between opposite borders, and dump sand between them — see Figure 6-8.**

   Screed the sand smooth (see Figure 6-8) so that the surface is the same distance below the border as the thickness of the paving material plus $1/2$ inch. Repeat the process across the entire patio. Remove the screed guides and fill the voids with sand. Wet the sand bed and compact it with a flat plate vibrator. If you install paving directly on the sand, lay weed-blocking fabric over the sand bed.

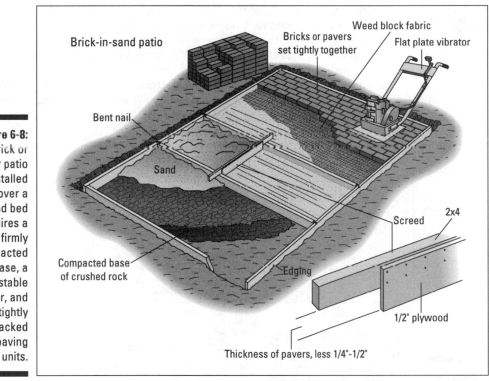

Figure 6-8:
A brick or paver patio installed over a sand bed requires a firmly compacted base, a stable border, and tightly packed paving units.

Installing the paving

The patio surfaces that most homeowners undertake on their own are brick or pavers laid on a sand bed (the easiest installation), and a concrete slab. Even if you're not comfortable building your own concrete patio, the information in this section helps you work with professionals — for example, building the forms and having a professional concrete finisher handle the pouring and finishing.

Installing brick or pavers on a sand bed

To install bricks or pavers over a sand bed, follow these steps (refer to Figure 6-8):

1. **Choose a pattern.**

   Bricks offer a variety of time-honored patterns, shown in Figure 6-9. The easiest to lay, called *jack-on-jack,* is bricks lined up next to each other in even rows. Staggering each row so that the joints fall at the midpoint of bricks in the adjacent rows creates a pattern called *running bond.* Other patterns, such as *basketweaves* and *herringbones,* involve placing bricks at right angles to each other. Avoid patterns that require cutting lots of bricks in half or into other shapes. Jack-on-jack, running bond, and basketweave patterns require minimal cutting.

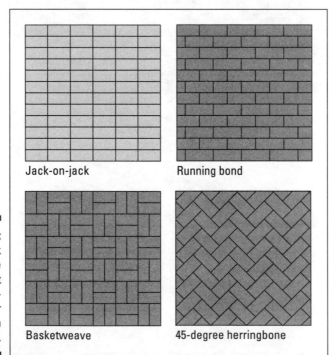

Figure 6-9: These brick patterns are designs that any do-it-yourselfer can duplicate.

Jack-on-jack

Running bond

Basketweave

45-degree herringbone

Pavers may or may not have as wide a choice of pattern options, depending on which shape you choose. If your pavers require two different shapes to complete the pattern, be sure you have enough of both shapes.

2. **Dampen the sand bed.**

3. **Install weed-blocking fabric over the sand.**

   It sinks slightly as you install the pavers.

4. **Tie a length of mason's twine (nylon string line) to two loose bricks or pavers and, using them for anchors, stretch the line parallel with (and one brick's width away from) the starting edge.**

   Move the line over and use it as a guide as you lay each row of bricks.

5. **Set each brick or paver in place without sliding it.**

   Tap it lightly with a rubber mallet to snug it into the sand — avoid displacing any sand. The paver should protrude above the edging $1/4$ to $1/2$ inch for compaction later on.

6. **After laying several bricks or pavers, check your work by laying a level or straightedge over it.**

   Reset bricks or pavers as necessary to align them.

   As you work your way across the patio, place 2-foot square pieces of plywood on the bricks or pavers to kneel on, to distribute your weight.

   To cut concrete pavers, rent a paving stone cutter. You can also buy a masonry cutoff blade for your circular power saw. Clamp the paver in a bench vice or portable work table and cut with the power saw. Cut bricks with the same tools, or use a *brick set* (wide chisel) to whack a brick in half — after scoring a cutting line around the brick by tapping the brick set lightly. Figure 6-10 shows several options.

7. **After all the bricks or pavers are in place, compact the patio.**

   Spread a layer of fine sand over the patio and then sweep it back and forth into the cracks. With the excess sand still on the surface, go over the patio with a vibrating plate compactor, which you can rent. Sweep again, as necessary, to force sand into the joints and compact the paving tightly. Sweep away the excess sand and hose off the patio for a final cleanup.

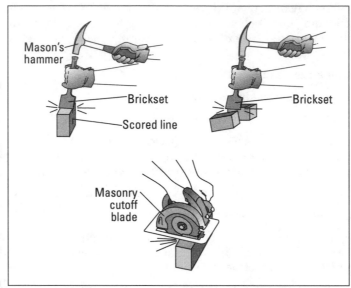

Figure 6-10: Cut bricks with a brickset and hammer, or with a power saw that has a masonry cutoff blade.

Placing a concrete slab patio

The actual placing of concrete — technically, it's *placed*, not poured, although using the word *pour* is customary — isn't as important an event, in spite of the high drama, as what happens before and after the pour. If you focus on preparing the base, building the forms, setting the reinforcing steel, estimating the volume of concrete that you need, getting enough help, getting the necessary tools for finishing the surface, and giving the concrete sufficient time to cure correctly, you should find that handling tons of wet concrete is no more stressful than playing in the mud. Unless you plan to finish the surface with a simple broom finish, however (as described in the following list in Step 12), have a professional do the final finish work. Follow these steps for the preparation and the pour (see Figure 6-11):

1. **Install a base of crushed rock or gravel. (See the section "Building the Base," earlier in this chapter.)**

2. **Build 2x4 forms around the patio perimeter.**

   Set them on edge and hold them in place with steel or wooden stakes every 3 to 4 feet, adjusting the boards so that the tops are exactly at the finished height of the patio.

   If the patio is adjacent to the house foundation, install a strip of expansion joint material (available at concrete and masonry suppliers) against the foundation to absorb pressure from the patio as it expands during hot weather.

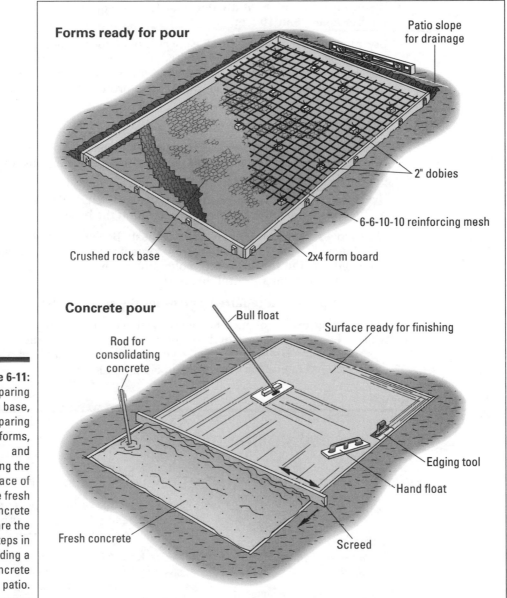

Forms ready for pour

Patio slope for drainage

2" dobies

6-6-10-10 reinforcing mesh

Crushed rock base

2x4 form board

Concrete pour

Bull float

Rod for consolidating concrete

Surface ready for finishing

Edging tool

Hand float

Fresh concrete

Screed

Figure 6-11:
Preparing the base, preparing the forms, and finishing the surface of the fresh concrete are the steps in building a concrete patio.

3. **If you install permanent divider boards in the patio, place them no further apart than 10 feet.**

   Use pressure-treated or a durable species of lumber, sealed with a water-repellent preservative. Drive 16d galvanized nails part way into the sides of each board, every 16 inches, for the concrete to grip. Cover the tops of the boards with masking tape to protect them from concrete stains.

4. **Dampen the gravel base to compact it.**

5. **Place *welded-wire reinforcing mesh* (mesh consisting of 6x6-inch squares formed by 10-gauge wire running in both directions) over the base.**

   Overlap edges by at least 6 inches, and place 2-inch *dobies* (small concrete blocks) under the mesh to raise it off the base.

   Wear gloves when handling reinforcing mesh. Be very careful when unrolling it — it can recoil with terrific force if you don't straighten it out as you go. Cut the mesh with bolt cutters, a hacksaw, or a circular power saw with a metal cutoff blade.

6. **Get an inspection, if required, and order the concrete delivery.**

   Calculate the exact volume of concrete you need by multiplying the width × length × thickness of the slab (measured in feet or fractions of a foot). Divide the result by 27 to give you the number of cubic yards, which is how concrete is ordered. Add 5 percent for waste.

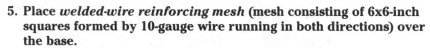

Loading up on concrete

Not all concrete is the same. Mixes vary in cement content, aggregate size (maximum size of rocks in the sand/gravel mix), water-to-cement ratio, *slump* (or consistency, from soupy to stiff), and additives. When ordering, tell the company what you're using the concrete for. If you're asked for additional information, specify the following:

✔ **Cement content:** Six sacks (the number of 90-pound sacks of cement per yard).

✔ **Aggregate size:** Maximum ³/₄ inch; ³/₈ inch if the concrete is pumped through a 3-inch hose instead of a 4-inch hose.

✔ **Water/cement ratio:** Specify a ratio of 1:2 (.5) or ask for a recommendation.

✔ **Slump:** 4 inches (the number of inches that fresh concrete in a 12-inch-high cylinder slumps after you remove the cylinder).

✔ **Additives:** None (unless very unusual conditions require an accelerator for cold weather, retardant for hot weather, or plasticizer for low water to cement ratio — consult with the delivery company).

7. **Place concrete in the forms, starting in one corner.**

   Have a helper place the fresh concrete up and down with a rod (refer to Figure 6-11) or shovel to consolidate it and fill any voids in the mix. Pile the concrete just slightly higher than the forms.

8. **After filling the forms, strike off the concrete by dragging a *screed* (2x4 or 2x6 long enough to span the patio) across it in a back-and-forth sawing motion.**

9. **After placing and screeding all of the concrete, and before water collects on the surface, smooth the concrete further by using a wood or magnesium *float,* which resembles a flat trowel (a *bull float* has a very long handle).**

10. **After floating the slab, run the blade of a brick trowel between the slab and forms to smooth the hidden edge of the slab.**

11. **Using an *edger* (small hand trowel with a curved lip along one edge), glide back and forth along the edges of the slab to round them and smooth 2 or 3 inches of concrete surface.**

12. **Using a 1-inch *groover* (similar tool with a ridge on the bottom), cut *control joints* into the concrete every 10 feet.**

    Control joints (or grooves) help to confine cracking of the concrete, which is inevitable. To keep the joints straight, snap a chalkline on the concrete or lay a straightedge on it. Use knee boards to keep your knees and feet off the concrete as you run the groover back and forth.

13. **After the concrete becomes a bit firm, steel-trowel the surface very smooth, being careful not to leave any trowel marks or ridges. Then re-edge the slab and re-cut the joints.**

14. **Have lunch and wait for the concrete to harden enough so that, when you touch it, you barely leave an impression.**

15. **To apply a basic non-skid *broom finish,* drag a soft, wet, concrete-finishing broom with fine nylon bristles gently over the concrete, in straight lines or a wavy pattern.**

Chapter 7

Creating an Outdoor Room

. . . .

In This Chapter

▶ Putting together a raised bed

▶ Getting comfortable with a built-in bench or planter

▶ Planning a cooking center

▶ Installing low-voltage lighting

▶ Getting covered by a trellis, arbor, or shade structure

▶ Using a shed for storage

▶ Constructing a garden pond

. . . .

You can turn decks and patios into exciting living spaces with shade covers, built-in seating, planters, cooking centers, lighting systems, and numerous other amenities. These features combine to create an outdoor room, with its own floor, walls, ceiling, and furnishings.

✔ Your deck or patio, of course, provides the "floor."

✔ The "walls" may vary from house walls or fences to low barriers such as planters or benches. The open side of a patio or deck may have a loosely-defined "wall" consisting of nothing more than a simple transition to a lawn or other surface, perhaps framed by a pair of planters.

✔ For the "ceiling," a canopy of tree branches, an overhead shade structure, or a few patio umbrellas relieve the immensity of the wide-open sky.

✔ Your choice of furnishings ranges from portable furniture to built-in amenities for cooking, dining, or lounging.

This chapter also presents a few construction projects for the garden — projects that help you create a miniature world of your own where you can tend plants and enjoy quiet moments away from the hectic pace of life.

Building a Raised Bed

Raised beds relieve the tedium of bending over to plant, weed, and care for your vegetables and flowers. They also offer a way to terrace a sloping yard or solve soil problems, such as excess clay or rocks. You can even gopher-proof your raised beds to control those pesky varmints. Figure 7-1 shows some examples.

Figure 7-1:
Three types
of raised
beds.

Although a raised bed is nothing more than a large, bottomless box, the most appealing designs include a wide enough edge around the top for sitting or setting things on. Raised beds vary in height from 8 to 18 inches, depending on the material you use. Make the beds no wider than 5 feet, so that you can reach the interior areas. They can be any length you want, from 5 to 20 feet — a 12-foot-long bed makes a convenient size. Plan 30 inches of space between beds for wheelbarrows and easy access. Use gravel, bark chips, or bricks for the pathways, and install weed-blocking fabric under the walkway material first.

Landscape timbers, stacked log-cabin-style, make a sturdy bed that's easy to build. Stack 6x6 timbers two or three high. Check the first course (layer) with a level before adding the second two courses. Drill ¹/₂-inch diameter holes through each timber, aligning the holes over each other. Drive ¹/₂-inch *rebar* (rod used for concrete reinforcement) into the holes after you stack the timbers to lock them in place.

You can also make raised beds from brick, stone, or dimensioned lumber. For a brick or stone bed, see Chapter 5.

For a lumber bed, use 2-by boards, such as a single 2x12 or a pair of stacked 2x8s. For a bed measuring 5 feet wide by 12 feet long, for example, you would need two 12-foot lengths and two 5-foot (or one 10-foot) lengths of lumber for each layer. Use heartwood lumber of a durable species. To build a lumber bed, do the following:

1. **Drive 4x4 stakes into the ground at the four corner locations and every 4 feet along the long sides.**

   Use stringlines to keep them aligned and a level to keep them plumb (check out Chapter 4 for more information).

2. **Cut the side pieces to length and place them around the outside of the 4x4s to make a box.**

3. **After you level each piece, clamp it to the 4x4s, drill ⁵/₈-inch diameter holes through the lumber and stakes, and bolt them together with ¹/₂-inch carriage bolts.**

   If you stack boards, overlap the corners, log cabin style.

4. **After you attach all of the side pieces, trim the 4x4s flush with the tops of the sides.**

   For a seat, install 2x8s around the top of the box. If necessary, reinforce the 2x8s by attaching a 2x4 cap piece around the top of the box.

5. **Cut the ends at 45 degrees for *miter joints* (joints with no end grain showing).**

6. **Position the 2x8s on the 4x4s and the top edge of the side pieces, and attach them with 3-inch galvanized deck screws.**

To keep burrowing animals, such as gophers, out of your box, cut wire mesh netting to fit in the bottom of the box. Secure it to the sides with poultry-netting staples before filling the box with soil.

Providing a Built-in Bench

A built-in bench is like a magnet, making a deck or patio instantly inviting. The easiest way to provide a bench is to buy an attractive ready-made bench that you can set anywhere in your landscape. If you wish to build your own, you can design a simple bench with no back or blend a bench into a railing or planter and use those as the "back" of the bench.

See the color photo section, near the center of this book, for bench ideas.

✔ For basic dimensions, the seat should be 15 to 18 inches high and at least 15 inches deep.

✔ If you add a back, it should be at least 12 inches high and lean back at an angle of 20 to 30 degrees from vertical.

✔ If the bench is part of a deck railing, extend the back 36 inches above the *seat* (not just the deck) and observe the screening requirement (see Chapter 6), including the area below the bench seat.

An elegant, low bench

A classic design for a deck bench of any length is to make the seat out of 2x2s, 2x4s, or 2x6s (or a combination) running lengthwise and trim the edge with a fascia of 1x4s or 2x4s (see Figure 7-2).

1. **To prevent nail heads or screw heads from showing on the top surface, construct the bench seat face-down by laying out the long boards and attaching 2x4 *cleats* (short boards) to them every 3 to 4 feet with deck screws.**

   Leave a $^1/_4$-inch gap between the seat boards.

2. **Taper the bottom edges of the cleats at each end so that the ends are 2 inches deep, instead of $3^1/_2$ inches, to conceal them behind the *fascia* (edge board).**

3. **Attach the cleats by using 3-inch deck screws driven down through them into the seat boards (after first drilling countersink holes, of the same diameter as the screw heads, $1^3/_4$ inches into the cleats so that the screws will reach the seat boards).**

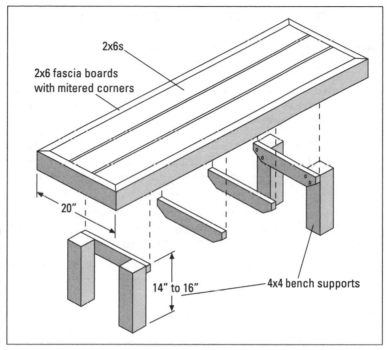

2x6s

2x6 fascia boards
with mitered corners

20"

14" to 16"

4x4 bench supports

Figure 7-2:
The basic
garden
bench is
easy to
build.

4. **After assembling the seat, attach legs to the cleats.**

   Cut the legs out of 2x8 or 2x10 lumber, 14 to 16 inches long, or cut pairs of 4x4s to the same length.

5. **Attach the legs to the cleats by using $3^1/_2$-inch carriage bolts and use a framing square to align the legs.**

6. **Turn the bench back upright, set it in place, and attach it to the decking by driving deck screws through the legs into the deck boards or by using angle brackets that you screw to the deck and then into the legs.**

   To conceal angle brackets, screw all of them down to the deck first and then set the bench in place with the legs on top of the lower flanges.

   If you're building a new deck, attach the bench legs to the deck joists and/or beams prior to installing the deck boards, to increase stability.

7. **To complete the bench, install 1x4 or 2x4 fascia boards around the seat.**

   Cut the corners at 45 degrees to make *miter joints* (boards joined with angled, rather than square, ends) and attach them by driving screws into them from the back, not from the face. Smooth all the edges by using a plane and sandpaper.

Variations on the basic bench

You can adapt the basic bench for different effects in several ways. Here are just a few:

- ✔ To give the bench a more substantial look, replace the legs with simple boxes measuring 12 inches square. The boxes can also be planters, as shown in Figure 7-3.

- ✔ To give the bench more delicate details, don't attach a fascia to the edge of the seat boards. Instead, use a router with a round-over bit and go around the top edge of the seat boards to give them a more refined profile.

- ✔ Add a decorative edge to 1x4 stock and attach it *below* the seat boards (rather than to the edges, as you do with a fascia). You need to add some cleats and blocking to which to attach the decorative trim.

- ✔ Dress up the cleats and legs by cutting them into decorative shapes with s-curves or similar classic profiles.

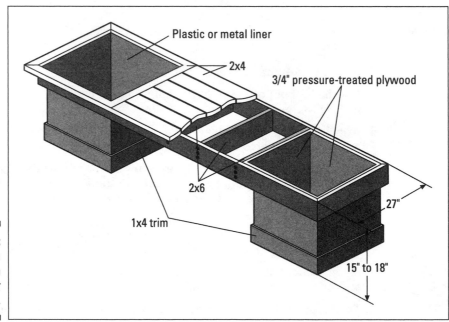

Figure 7-3:
Enhance a bench with planter boxes.

Plastic or metal liner

2x4

3/4" pressure-treated plywood

2x6

1x4 trim

27"

15" to 18"

Masonry benches

Although you can build a freestanding bench out of brick, stone, or concrete block, it tends to look like a lost pile of masonry unless you integrate it with a garden wall, steps, fountain, or similar feature. Portions of a low garden wall can easily be modified into benches if you plan the dimensions carefully. Make the seats 15 to 18 inches high, 15 inches deep, and at least 48 inches wide for two people to sit comfortably.

Buying or Building a Planter

Although you can buy attractive planters made out of wood, fiberglass, acrylics, ceramics, metal, and other materials at garden centers and other outlets, building wooden planters of your own has some advantages: You can design planters to match the dimensions and details of your deck or landscape, you can build larger planters than are available for sale, and you can incorporate planters into a deck as built-ins.

If you build planters for a deck, keep in mind that large planters are heavy. A planter 2 feet high, 2 feet wide, and 6 feet long holds almost a ton of moist soil — too heavy for a deck without reinforcement. If possible, place such planters within openings in the deck and support them on a concrete or gravel bed on the ground. Another option for large planters is to build a wooden enclosure with a shallow shelf and place container plants on the shelf, leaving most of the wooden planter empty.

Building a wooden planter

✔ Construct planters out of redwood, cedar, or preservative-treated wood (including plywood) and use corrosion-resistant screws or bolts. If you plan to put edible plants in the planter, use naturally-durable species of wood, rather than treated wood.

✔ Because a box full of moist soil exerts considerable pressure against the sides, reinforce corners by bolting the side boards to vertical 4x4s (2x2s for small planters) that you place inside the corners.

✔ If necessary, reinforce the corners more by lapping the alternating boards, log-cabin fashion, or by attaching a band of 2x4s or other trim boards around the top of the box and bolting them together at the corners. Drill $^3/_4$-inch drain holes in the bottom of the box and cover them with window screen.

Building a masonry planter

Masonry planters, placed around the edge of a patio, within a patio, or elsewhere in the garden, add an elegant touch to your landscape. They can also double as dividers, benches, and — on slopes — retaining walls. Brick, stone, and concrete blocks covered with a veneer are all attractive materials for these planters. You can incorporate them into benches or low walls for even greater effect.

To build a masonry planter, form and pour a concrete base with openings in the center for drainage directly into the soil. (See Chapter 6 for more information about working with concrete.) An easy way to provide such drainage is to set short lengths of plastic pipe, such as two-inch-diameter PVC (plastic) pipe, vertically within the planter area before pouring concrete for the footing. Simply insert them into the gravel base and then trim the tops flush with the finished concrete surface.

You can also build a box form that's the same size as the interior dimensions of the planter and pour concrete around it — something like a doughnut — and then lay the brick, stone, or concrete blocks on the reinforced concrete ring.

Planning a Cooking Center

For most people, outdoor living means outdoor cooking. Preparing food over an open flame appeals to ancient instincts and the latest grilling craze alike. (Get a copy of *Grilling For Dummies,* by Marie Rama and John Mariani [IDG Books Worldwide, Inc.] to find out more about grilling equipment and get some great recipes for grilled food.) An outdoor cooking center also allows you to entertain guests on your deck or patio. It can be as simple as a table and portable grill, or as elaborate as a gourmet kitchen. Even if your kitchen is only steps away from your deck or patio, consider having an outdoor grill.

For remote locations, such as a poolside patio, consider a mini-kitchen, complete with sink, grill, counters, cabinets, and a refrigerator, as shown in Figure 7-4. Protect it from rain and snow with an overhead structure (see the "Attaching an Overhead Shade Structure" section, later in this chapter) and plan at least one wall behind it — or at least provide weatherproof enclosures for the cabinets and appliances. Use tile or similar durable materials for countertops. Plan the location of plumbing, electrical wiring, and gas lines carefully before you build the patio or deck.

Figure 7-4:
A complete cooking center includes a grill, sink, storage cabinets, and ample counter space so that more than one cook can stir up some grub.

Keep the following safety tips in mind:

- ✔ When locating a grill or barbecue, plan it away from traffic areas and downwind from windows and doors.

- ✔ Don't place the grill inside an unvented enclosure or under low-hanging tree branches.

- ✔ Avoid placing a charcoal grill on a deck unless the grill has at least two feet of clearance all around and the deck surface is protected by bricks or similar fireproof materials.

- ✔ Although they can stand alone, gas grills are more attractive and easier to use if you set them into a permanent enclosure with countertops close at hand.

To create a complete cooking center, you can adapt kitchen cabinets for outdoor use.

- ✔ Avoid cabinets constructed out of particleboard, which absorbs moisture easily, or those covered with laminates.

- ✔ Old plywood cabinets, especially with painted finishes, work well.

- ✔ Repaint all surfaces, inside and out. First, wash them with *trisodium phosphate* (TSP) or a similar cleaning product. Then, roughen the surfaces by using sandpaper, vacuum the surfaces, and wipe them with a tack cloth to remove all dust. Prime the cabinets with a white-pigmented shellac. After the shellac dries, use a sprayer or foam roller to apply a finish coat of high-quality, oil-based exterior enamel. After the enamel dries, sand the cabinets lightly and remove dust with a tack cloth. Then, apply a second coat of enamel.

✔ To discourage mildew, drill two $1/2$- or 2-inch vent holes in the back of each cabinet. Insert louvered vent plugs (available for exterior walls) of the same diameter as the holes, to keep out insects and rain.

✔ Provide additional insect protection by attaching self-sticking weatherstripping tape (available at hardware stores) to the inside edges of the cabinet doors and drawer fronts, and tight-fitting latches to the doors.

Installing Lighting

If you think that lighting your deck or patio means putting up a few flood-lights, you're in the dark about outdoor design! Today's decks and patios bring high fashion into their lighting schemes. This trend doesn't mean high expense, thanks to affordable low-voltage outdoor lighting. But it does mean sensible, strategic use of many different light fixtures — most of them simple in design.

At the bare minimum, plan lighting for doorways, stairs, and main traffic areas, and whatever else your local building codes may require. Placing fixtures close to the ground illuminates stairs, paths, and plants in soft pools of light. For interesting effects, use strings of minilights to accentuate trees and outline deck railings. Use 120-volt (standard house voltage) lights for doorways and cooking areas. Also consider using *photo-voltaic* (solar-powered) lights in locations where they will receive abundant sun and a limited amount of light is all you need.

Use the following guidelines to help you plan your lighting:

✔ **Light your yard, not the neighborhood.** Avoid lights that shine onto your neighbors' property. In fact, try to place all lights so that nobody can see the light bulb — only the results. You can't enjoy even the most exquisite patio or deck with a light glaring into your eyes.

✔ **Light up your lifestyle.** Identify your lighting needs. Some lighting is for traffic and movement; some is for activities, such as cooking or eating; some is to create moods, or ambiance; and some is for decoration.

✔ **Hide ugly fixtures.** Many outdoor lighting fixtures are works of art and should be on display, but you don't need to rely completely on these money-eaters. Use lots of plain, ordinary fixtures, but just hide them.

✔ **Step into the light.** Light all stairs and traffic paths. To light stairs, set a fixture close enough to illuminate all the steps or install an in-wall fixture into the riser of each step. To light traffic paths, place lights high and direct them straight down or place several lights close to the ground to illuminate areas along the path, spilling light onto the pathway.

✔ **Light for work.** Use higher-intensity lighting for task areas, such as a cooking center or game area. Just as for paths, place several lights in trees or overhead structures and aim them straight down. Don't illuminate eating areas with harsh lighting. Use low-intensity lights or, if necessary, candles.

✔ **Trip the light fantastic.** Create special lighting effects. Place two or three lights, aimed downward, high in a tree to create interesting shadows from branches and leaves. Light other trees or plants along walls from below, using *well lights* set into the ground or low floodlights. Conceal the light source behind plants or rocks.

✔ **Avoid overlighting.** You don't need to illuminate the entire outdoor landscape or to light every feature or point of use with its own light. Plan light schemes so that pools of light spill over into other areas. Instead of lining a path with lights that shine directly onto it, for example, light the garden areas along one side of the path enough to illuminate the path, too.

✔ **Avoid underlighting.** A common mistake is to illuminate a deck or patio beautifully, but not light the rest of the yard. Rather than surround your deck with darkness, create variety and security by *uplighting* (aiming light fixtures upward) a few trees and bathing distant flower beds in soft light.

✔ **Don't undertake a wiring project yourself** (except low-voltage lights) unless you have experience with electrical wiring and have obtained the necessary permit.

Low-voltage lighting systems consist of light fixtures, cable (or wire), and a transformer, which you plug into a standard 120-volt receptacle (refer to Figure 7-5). Because the wire between the transformer and light fixtures carries low-voltage current, you don't need to bury it or enclose it in conduit (although you may want to conceal it). Simply run it along the ground, up tree trunks, under deck railings, or wherever needed, securing it by using staples or clips. Avoid suspending wires overhead.

Low-voltage fixtures produce a fairly low level of light (three to five *foot-candles,* in the lingo), which is desirable for most outdoor lighting needs. Adequate lighting, however, requires many fixtures, for example:

✔ Eight to ten for an average deck

✔ Two to three for a short run of stairs

✔ Three per tree for effective downlighting

✔ One for every 6 to 8 feet of pathway

Because transformers have a limit to the number of fixtures they can power and the distance the wire can run, divide the lighting load into several circuits of six to ten lights each (depending on the size of bulbs and transformer — consult the manufacturer's specifications). No run should be longer than 100 feet.

To install the system, follow these steps:

1. **Start by mounting the transformers.**

   Mount each transformer next to an electrical outlet, which must have *ground-fault circuit-interrupter* (GFCI) protection (unless it's indoors, away from a concrete floor or water faucet). Transformers have weatherproof cases that enable you to locate them outdoors, but try to find a protected place. Although your choice of locations is limited by available outlets, locate each transformer as close to the lights it powers as possible. A central location, where you can place all the transformers, is ideal because you can change settings for the whole system easily.

2. **Install the lights.**

   Some lights have plastic or metal stakes for support, which you simply drive into the ground. Some have brackets that you can attach to posts, branches, walls, and other structures. Set well lights into holes in the ground. (Don't backfill yet.)

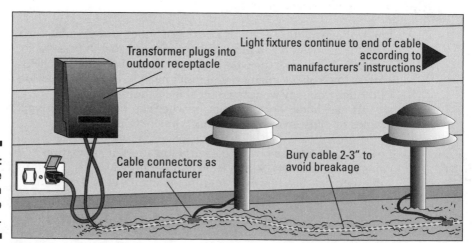

Figure 7-5: Low-voltage lighting is a cinch to install.

Transformer plugs into outdoor receptacle

Light fixtures continue to end of cable according to manufacturers' instructions

Cable connectors as per manufacturer

Bury cable 2-3" to avoid breakage

Recessed fixtures require cutting a hole into the stair riser, post, railing, or other surface in which you place each one. These in-wall lights come in several sizes, but the most versatile fit into the same-sized opening as a standard light switch box, 2 inches by 4 inches. If you install recessed lights in masonry, install the boxes and run wire as you build the wall or steps.

3. **Run the cable.**

   After installing all of the light fixtures, run the cable. Make sure that you use cable that's compatible with the transformer and light fixtures. Attach one end to the terminals on the transformer. Then, run it to the nearest light fixture, fastening it or burying it as necessary. Most fixtures have a clamp, which looks something like a clamshell, that you lay the cable in and close tightly over the cable. The clamp has metal prongs that penetrate the insulation of the cable to make contact with the copper core. You don't need to strip or cut the cable. Simply enclose it in the clamp and continue running it to the next fixtures.

4. **After hooking up all the lights, plug in the transformer, turn it on manually to test the system, and set the timer.**

Getting to Know Trellises and Arbors

Trellises and arbors bring order to the garden. (The terms are often used interchangeably, but in this book, a *trellis* is a vertical frame for supporting plants and an *arbor* is an overhead structure.) They not only provide a framework for plants to grow on, but they frame your plants and can provide a dramatic focal point themselves.

You can buy ready-made trellises at nurseries and home centers or fashion your own from small-dimensioned lumber, bamboo, or wire mesh (green or black vinyl-coated wire mesh, galvanized wire mesh, or steel-reinforcing mesh left to rust naturally). Most trellises have a basic square or rectangular shape, much like a picture frame, or a vase shape that mirrors the spreading foliage of many plants. If you make a trellis, like the one shown in Figure 7-6, space cross members 6 to 12 inches apart and attach them securely to each other at all joints using screws, nails, or tie wire. Mount trellises on fences or walls, or make a free-standing trellis by joining two vertical trellises at right angles to each other. Support your trellis with stakes driven into the ground and tied to the bottom rungs of the trellis.

An arbor, shown in Figure 7-6, is more substantial than a trellis and offers many design variations, from an archway to a criss-crossing framework. Build a small arbor over a gate, bench, or path to add a dramatic focal point to your landscape, and support it with a single post or a pair of legs on each side. When planning your arbor, keep in mind that the standard lumber sizes that are most readily available are not well-proportioned: the ubiquitous 2x4, for example, is more awkward than graceful at most lengths; a 2x3 has more appealing proportions; and a 3x4, which must be custom-milled, has the same proportions as the classical golden mean (a 5:7 ratio).

Figure 7-6:
An arbor (left) or a trellis (right) adds a beautiful focal point to your landscape.

Attaching an Overhead Shade Structure

An overhead shade structure (also called an *overhead*) can enhance your outdoor living in many ways. They provide shade, define spaces, provide an arbor for plants, and delight the eye. As you think about an overhead for your deck or patio, consider the following design issues:

✔ **Freestanding or attached to the house?** For an attached structure, the height of the house's roof overhang determines some of your design options. If the overhang is at least nine feet above the patio or deck surface, you can probably tuck a patio roof under the eave. Otherwise, plan to attach the overhead to the house roof itself or build a freestanding structure that clears the roof eave.

✔ **Made in the shade:** To provide minimal shade (in areas where overheating isn't a problem), plan a structure without any *canopy* (slats or solid covering) above the rafters or a canopy consisting of very few slats. For more shade, space slats no farther apart than their depth. If the slats are 2x4s, for example, space them 3½ to 4 inches apart. If you orient the slats east to west, they provide shade all day, except during early morning and late afternoon hours. If you orient them north-south, they admit the sun at noon but provide shade in the late afternoon. For maximum shade, build a solid roof — to avoid heat buildup, plan the roof with a vented ridge or similar openings. A good compromise between an open structure and a solid roof is to plant vines, such as grapes, clematis, or wisteria, that fill out the canopy during the summer and drop their leaves in the fall.

✔ **Scale and proportion:** Plan the overhead structure so that it's large enough for comfortable seating under it (at least 10 feet square) and high enough to leave approximately 8 feet of clearance. Balance the overhead with other vertical elements in the landscape, such as trees or the house itself, to keep it from overwhelming the patio or deck. As you plan individual components, such as posts and beams, consider the overall scale. A 4x8 beam, for example, may be strong enough to span between posts, but a 6x12 beam may be a more appropriate size, visually.

✔ **Choose your canopy:** The *canopy,* or screening, that goes on top of the rafters may be lattice, *lath* (flat, skinny strips of wood), 2x3s or 2x4s set on edge, fabric, shade cloth, woven reeds, clear plastic, or a similar material. If the rafters provide sufficient shade or the overhead is only a decorative structure with no practical function, you don't need to install a canopy.

✔ **What about views?** An overhead structure affects views. It blocks certain views, especially of the sky, but it can also frame views of the horizon for a pleasing effect. Use stepladders, poles, and other devices to mock up the location of your overhead to make sure that it doesn't obstruct desirable views.

✔ **Overall look:** By varying the size of structural members and the finished details, you can make an overhead structure appear light and airy or massive and dominant, refined and elegant or rustic and comfortable. Fix in your mind which of these attributes blend best with the architecture of your home, your patio, or your deck and plan the structure's color, size, details, and shape to correspond. Each element of the overhead contributes to the overall look.

- If your home and landscape have a formal style, keep the design symmetrical and choose elegant details.

- If your home has traditional architecture, plan an overhead with a Victorian or other well-defined motif by adding a "gingerbread" of intricate scrollwork or lattice and finishing it with white or richly colored paint.

- If your home and landscape are rustic, plan posts of natural timbers and a canopy of poles and branches, reminiscent of a Southwestern ramada.

- For other effects, use classical columns or massive stucco-covered pillars instead of posts, or a canopy of brightly colored fabric instead of wooden slats.

✔ **Structural rigidity:** Although a patio roof seems like a much simpler structure than other roof systems, it must be designed to withstand the same loads and stresses.

- The *footings* (foundation) must be adequate to support the weight of the entire structure, plus any snow loads.

- The structure must attach securely to the footings.

- The individual beams, rafters, and lattice members must be large enough and strong enough for the spans.

- The structure must be rigid enough to withstand lateral forces. This requires strong connections between all members and, if necessary, knee braces or similar diagonal bracing.

✔ **Durability:** As does any outdoor structure, an overhead must resist deterioration caused by constant exposure to sun, rain, snow, and other elements. All connections must be corrosion-resistant. Wood members must be at least 8 inches above ground, unless they're treated with a preservative specified for ground contact. Wood members must also be well-secured to resist warping and cracking and should be treated with a preservative and sealer.

To calculate the size and spacing of the joists and beams, consult joist span and beam span tables, available in *Decks & Patios For Dummies* by Robert Beckstrom (IDG Books Worldwide, Inc.).

Utilizing a Storage Shed

A shed for storing tools and corralling clutter in the garden enhances not only your gardening pleasure, but it frees up storage space in the garage, on the patio, in the basement, or wherever you store gardening supplies. A storage shed also provides a rationale for an inviting path or two and the suggestion of a secret destination that adds an element of charm or whimsy to your garden. (See the color photo section near the middle of this book for more shed ideas.)

You don't have to build the Taj Mahal to gain such benefits. You should, however, invest enough time and effort to create a shed that is tidy, durable, water tight, and attractive. Fresh paint and real shingles may be enough to dress up your shed, or you can attach a trellis to one or two sides, paint a *trompe l'oeil* (fake) window or similar foil on the outside, or conceal the shed completely behind a fence or lattice screen. If you place your shed in the open, soften the impact by parking it under a tree, if possible, or place large shrubs around it to blend it into the natural scenery.

Shed designs vary from utilitarian boxes to replicas of distinctive architectural styles, such as a log cabin, Swiss chalet, Japanese tea house, or Greek temple. A typical do-it-yourself shed usually measures 8 feet wide, 6 feet deep, and 7 feet tall (6 feet, 8 inches inside) at the peak — plenty of space for a lawnmower, rotary tiller, wheelbarrow, dozens of implements, and other gardening supplies. See your local building-supply store for plans and materials.

Building a Garden Pond

There is something irresistibly appealing about water in the landscape. Whether you tuck a tiny pond into a corner of your garden or plant a larger pond right in the middle of things, the sight (and sound) of water has a dramatic calming effect and quickly becomes the focal point of your garden. Waterproof membranes and pond liners make building a garden pond as easy as digging a hole. Check your local zoning laws to see if your pond requires the same kind of safety barrier as a swimming pool — typically, childproof fencing that's at least 42 inches high around the entire area. See the color section near the middle of this book for more pond shapes and dimensions.

To build a pond, follow these steps:

1. **Plan the dimensions of your pond.**

   An oval or kidney shape up to 9 feet long by 5 feet wide is adequate for most gardens. Plan a depth of $1^1/2$ to 3 feet, with a 9-inch wide plant shelf, 9 inches deep, around the perimeter.

2. **Lay out the pond, using a garden hose and chalk or flour to mark the ground.**

3. **Excavate the hole.**

   Use a straightedge and level to keep the bottom and perimeter of the excavation level. Slope the sides approximately 20 degrees to minimize cave-ins.

4. **Grade around the hole so that the rim is 2 inches higher than the surrounding grade, to prevent ground water from draining into the pond.**

5. **Place 2 inches of sand on the bottom and shelves of the hole and dampen the sand.**

6. **Install a pond liner.**

   Lay a PVC (polyvinyl chloride) pond liner loosely over the excavation and, beginning at the center of the hole, smooth and press the material against the ground. As you move outward from the center, fold or tuck the material to take up slack.

7. **Weight the edge of the liner with stones.**

8. **Fill the pond with water slowly as you adjust the liner to fit.**

9. **When the pond is full, trim the liner 12 inches away from the edge of the pond.**

   Conceal the flap of liner around the edge of the pond with stones, bricks, or other masonry.

10. **Install a submersible circulating pump in one end of the pond.**

    Provide a ground-fault circuit interrupter (GFCI) outlet near the location, for plugging in the pump. You can find numerous pump and filter packages for garden ponds, which are easy to install, at home and garden centers. For a waterfall, build a waterproofed rock outcropping at the edge of the pond, attach tubing to the outlet of the pump, and run it to the top of the rock outcropping.

11. **Place aquatic plants in containers on the shelf and bottom of the pond.**

    To control algae, stock the pond with fish, striving for a balance between the plants and fish.

12. **Landscape around the pond, placing plants near the edge to give the pond a natural appearance and provide shade for the fish.**

Part III
The Planting o' the Green

In this part . . .

When you're landscaping your home, no question is more important than "Which plants should I use?" Even though landscaping involves planning decks, paths, patios, and other hardscape, when most people think about landscaping, they think about plants. And rightfully so — plants provide the beauty that changes a plain building into a lush home that melts perfectly into its surroundings.

This part discusses trees, shrubs, vines, all types of flowers, and lawn grasses to help you decide which ones fit your landscape needs. We know that you want beautiful plants, so we give you wonderful choices of flowers, fall foliage color, berries, and more. But choosing plants isn't just about beauty, it's also about function. Which tree keeps your house cool in summer? Which shrubs screen out that bad view? Which flowers combines for the longest season of color? This part covers all of that.

Choosing plants is also about adaptation. Not all plants grow in every climate. You want ones that adapt well to your area, are easy to care for, and will live for a long time. And they better not get too big. This part provides that information.

And after you choose your plants, we even show you how to plant them properly.

Chapter 8

Barking Up the Right Tree

*N*o home or neighborhood should be without trees. They bring a home into scale with the surrounding wide open landscape and give a neighborhood a sense of identity. (What makes the difference between a new neighborhood and one that's 30 years old? The trees!) Trees provide protection from the elements by buffering strong winds and blocking hot summer sun. In crowded neighborhoods, trees can provide privacy, screening you from your neighbors or from unpleasant views.

But more than anything else, trees offer beauty — beauty in flowers held high among the branches, in the leafy green canopy, in colorful berries and seedpods dangling among the limbs, in dazzling hues created by their autumn leaves. Take a look at Figure 8-1 for a breathtaking example. Trees are even beautiful in winter, when the texture of their bark and the silhouette of their branches adds structure and form to the landscape. Trees are beautiful in their diversity, as well — after all, without trees, where will the birds perch or the squirrels dash?

Choosing the Perfect Tree

People who work with trees like to say that the perfect tree doesn't exist — and they're right. As with people, every tree's personality has its good and bad aspects. Before you plant one, try to find out everything you can about the tree, both the good and the bad. Most trees get big and live a long time (possibly longer than you!), so if you make a mistake and plant the wrong one in the wrong place, the result may be a costly removal or replacement. (Removing it may even be dangerous to people and property.)

Figure 8-1:
Large trees
form the
perfect
deep green
backdrop to
a formal
landscape.

Before committing to any new tree for your landscape, ask the following questions:

- ✔ How fast does it grow?

- ✔ How tall and wide will it eventually get?

- ✔ Is it adapted to your climate and the sun, soil, and water conditions at the proposed planting site?

- ✔ Does the tree tend to have problems — invasive roots (that can lift concrete and destroy your lawn), weak limbs (that can fall on your house), insects or diseases (that can kill the tree)?

- ✔ Does the tree need any special maintenance, such as pruning?

- ✔ How messy is it? Does it drop excessive amounts of flowers, fruits, or leaves?

Releafing the world

To help get trees planted in the public areas of your community or in forests damaged by fire or abuse, contact Global ReLeaf. For $10, this organization plants ten trees in your name and returns a personalized certificate. Call 800-873-5323 to order. For more information, write P.O. Box 2000, Washington, DC, or call 202-667-3300.

A local nursery is a good place to find out how a tree performs in your area; so are city or county parks departments. Your county cooperative extension office can help you with information about trees, and parks and university campuses often have fine plantings to study. Botanical gardens and arboretums are especially good places to observe a wide variety of trees.

Consider some details before purchasing

After you decide on the kind of tree that you need in terms of size, shape, *adaptation* (whether or not it will grow well in your area), and maintenance, you have a wealth of ornamental characteristics to choose from. Here are some points to consider:

- ✔ **Seasonal color.** Many trees, including flowering fruit trees, bloom in early spring. Others bloom later in spring, and some, like crape myrtles, in midsummer. And you can choose almost any flower color.

   By planting trees such as liquidambars (discussed in the "Ten great shade trees" section, further on in this chapter), you can have stunning autumn color even in warm-winter climates. And these trees offer a whole palette of leaf colors to choose from.

- ✔ **Colorful fruit.** Trees such as crab apples and hawthorns follow their blooms with colorful fruit, which can (if the birds don't eat it) hang on the tree into winter, after the leaves have fallen.

   Don't overlook trees that produce edible fruit when you're making your choices. Many fruit and nut trees are also good-looking landscape plants and have the added bonus of bringing food to the table.

- ✔ **Attractive bark.** The white bark of birch trees is familiar to most people, but many other trees have handsome peeling or colorful bark.

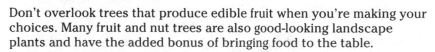

Finding a healthy tree at the nursery

Before you go shopping, check out these tips for buying a healthy tree:

- Avoid trees that have been in a nursery container too long or are unhealthy and growing poorly — they'll probably be disappointing after they're in the ground.

  Examine the top of the rootball. Avoid trees that have large, *circling roots* (roots that go round and round at the outside edge of the pot) near the surface — that's a sure sign that the tree has been in the container too long.

- Avoid trees that are the smallest or largest of a group. Select ones that are well-proportioned, with foliage and branches evenly spaced along the trunk. Select a tree without closely spaced, criss-crossing branches or tight *crotches* (the crotch is the angle formed where a branch joins the trunk).

- Select trees that can stand on their own without being tightly tied to a stake (tightly tied stakes can be like crutches, preventing a tree from developing a strong trunk).

- Ideally, pick a tree with a trunk that is evenly tapered from bottom to top.

- Look for healthy, even-colored leaves.

- Pick a tree that's free of insects and disease — avoid ones with chewed or misshapen leaves, goop oozing from the trunk, or dead branches.

Getting cool with trees

In this fast-paced world of concrete, asphalt, and hazy sky, trees are the great equalizers. They shade your street and cool your neighborhood, they absorb dust and air pollution, and their roots hold the soil in place and prevent erosion.

Providing cooling shade is one of a tree's greatest assets, especially in regions where summers are hot and dry. If you plant *deciduous* trees on the warmest side of your house (usually the south or west side, but the east side can also be warm), the shade that they provide keeps your house cooler in summer and reduces your air-conditioning expenses. The best shade trees spread wide and tall enough to shade a one- or two-storied home, but you can

effectively shade a patio or deck with smaller trees, especially if you plant several. You can also use smaller trees to shade windows as a way to prevent the sun from shining through and quickly warming the house.

Of course, you don't have to worry about overcooling in winter: Trees lose their leaves — right when you need them to — so the warm sun is able to get through, thus reducing heating costs.

You can save energy by planting trees as windbreaks. Planted close together and at right angles to the prevailing wind, dense-growing trees can reduce the chilling effects of winter winds and will lower heating bills.

Discovering Some Favorite Trees

With so many good trees to choose from, we think you may need some advice on the best ones. We divide the following suggestions according to common landscape uses — shade trees, small garden and patio trees, and evergreen trees that are valuable for their winter appeal and screening capabilities — with each list arranged alphabetically according to botanical name, but listing the common name first. Consider combining all of them into your landscape, as shown in Figure 8-2.

Trees can also be divided into two main groups: *deciduous* and *evergreen*. Evergreen trees include *conifers,* such as pine and fir, and *broadleaf evergreens,* such as the southern magnolia. Unlike deciduous trees, which drop their leaves in autumn, evergreen trees retain their leaves throughout the winter. To make your final choice, check out the Appendix, which is full of other resources, or consult the experts at your local nursery.

Figure 8-2:
Deciduous trees provide shade and privacy in this well-organized backyard.

To find out which zone you're living in, check out Chapter 12.

Ten great shade trees

The ideal shade tree is between 25 and 50 feet high. For most homes this is the appropriate size to partially shade the roof, but not get too big so the tree becomes a liability. However, different size lots and homes may call for different-sized trees, so not all of the trees listed have the perfect size and shape.

The best shade tree is also deciduous, so that sun can warm the house in winter. (Besides the trees in this section, you can also effectively use any of the deciduous trees listed in the "Ten small garden and patio trees" section.) In southern climates, where winters can be quite warm, you may be able to use some evergreen trees as shade trees.

Look for shade trees with a spreading canopy (the leafy top portion of the tree).

- **Maples.** *Acer* species. The maples are a large group that includes many trees known primarily for their wonderful autumn color. Most are hardy to at least Zone 5 (–20°F). Sugar maples and Norway maples (*A. saccharum* and *A. platanoides*) are hardy to Zone 3 (–40°F). Many of them grow over 70 feet high.

  Most maples perform poorly in areas with mild winters or hot, dry summers, including large, upright species like the red maple, *A. rubrum*, which can reach up to 50 feet high, and some very useful smaller types, like the spreading Japanese maple, *A. palmatum* (discussed in the "Ten small garden and patio trees" section).

- **Silk tree.** *Albizia julibrissin*. Tough, airy trees with finely cut, fernlike leaves and pink powder puff-like flowers in summer. Wide spreading shape is ideal for shade, but seed pods and falling leaves can be messy. Grows quickly to 40 to 50 feet high. Hardy into Zone 6. 'Charlotte' and 'Tyron' varieties are resistant to wilt disease, common in the southern and western United States.

- **Red horse chestnut.** *Aesculus carnea*. Large roundish leaves and huge spikes of pink to reddish flower spikes top this bold textured tree. Grows up to 50 feet high and about 30 feet wide, casting dense shade. Roots can be invasive. Leaf edges turn brown in hot summer climates.

- **European white birch.** *Betula pendula*. Loved for its papery white bark, multiple trunks, and yellow autumn color. Hardy to Zone 3 (–40°F), but not well adapted to areas with hot, dry summers or to areas where birch borers are prevalent. Call your extension office or local nursery to find out about birch borers.

- **Russian olive.** *Elaeagnus angustifolia.* Tough tree with narrow, silvery leaves. Fragrant — but not showy — spring flowers. Small, yellow fruit. Excellent hedge, shade tree, or screen in dry, windy situations. Grows 30 to 35 feet. Hardy to Zone 2 (–50°F).

- **Ash.** *Fraxinus* species. Mostly large, spreading-to-upright trees, many reaching well over 50 feet high, with divided leaves. They're good, fast-growing, tough shade trees that can thrive under a variety of conditions. Most are hardy to at least Zone 4 (–30°F). Many have excellent autumn color. Anthracnose and borers can be problems.

  Our favorite ash is the Raywood ash, *Fraxinum angustifolia (F. oxycarpa)*. It's a full-sized (30 to 40 feet), but not huge tree, and its leaves turn a striking purple color in autumn.

- **Thornless honey locust.** *Gleditsia triacanthos inermis.* Finely cut foliage casts a wonderful shade from this adaptable tree. Leaves turn yellow before dropping in autumn; leave little mess. Grows 40 to 60 feet high with a spreading habit. Has some pest problems in parts of the western and southern United States (check with your nursery). Hardy into Zone 4 (-30° F). Several varieties to choose from including 'Sunburst' with yellow foliage and 'Rubylace' with purplish leaves.

- **Liquidambar.** *Liquidambar styraciflua.* Tall (40 to 50 feet and higher), narrowly upright trees prized for their bright autumn colors, in shades of yellow, orange, red, and purple. Some are multicolored. Named varieties differ in their autumn colors. They also have interesting seedpods, which can be messy. Hardy to Zone 5 (–20°F).

- **Chinese pistache.** *Pistacia chinensis.* A wonderful, spreading shade tree with stunning yellow, orange, or red autumn color. Grows 30 to 35 feet high, has divided leaves, and is hardy to Zone 6 (–10°F). Drought tolerant.

- **Aristocrat pear.** *Pyrus calleryana* 'Aristocrat'. Upright oval tree (30 to 40 feet high) with white spring flowers. Shiny green leaves turn bright orange, red to purple in cold-winter climates. Other good varieties include 'Capital', 'Cleveland Select', 'Earlyred', 'Redspire', and 'Whitehouse'. Also well-suited to small landscapes. Hardy to Zone 5 (–20°F).

- **Oaks.** *Quercus.* A large family of varied evergreen and deciduous trees, many of them very large and only suitable for open areas. Some deciduous types have good autumn color. Natives — such as the red oak, *Q. rubra,* in the eastern United States, the English oak, *Q. robur*, throughout western Europe, the cork oak, *Q. suber,* of northern Africa and southern Europe — are often good choices. However, many species are widely adapted.

Ten small garden and patio trees

The following well-behaved, smaller trees (usually 15 to 30 feet high) are especially suitable around patios or in small gardens where larger trees won't fit.

✔ **Japanese maple.** *Acer palmatum.* The Japanese maple is one of the most popular small trees (ranging from 5 to 25 feet high, depending on the variety). It comes in dramatic weeping forms with finely cut leaves and bright autumn color, mostly in shades of red, orange, and yellow. Some varieties, like 'Bloodgood', have purplish leaves during the entire growing season. In hot, dry-summer areas, Japanese maples are best planted in partial shade. Most are hardy into Zone 5 (–20° F).

✔ **Redbud.** *Cercis* species. Most popular is the eastern redbud, *C. canadensis,* which reaches 20 to 30 feet high and spreads almost as wide. It is hardy to Zone 4 (–30°F). 'Alba' has white flowers; 'Forest Pansy' has maroon foliage.

The western redbud, *C. occidentalis,* is a multi-trunked, small (12 to 15 feet), drought-tolerant tree particularly well adapted to dry-summer areas. It is hardy to Zone 8 (10°F).

✔ **Flowering dogwood.** *Cornus florida.* Key attributes are deep-red autumn color and large white or pink midspring flowers followed by bright-red fruit. An excellent small (20 to 30 feet) tree that's hardy to Zone 5 (–20°F). Not well adapted to hot, dry climates but can be grown successfully in partial shade. Anthracnose and borers can be serious problems. Hybrids 'Aurora', 'Galaxy', 'Constellation', and 'Stellar Pink' are less prone to anthracnose disease.

✔ **Hawthorns.** *Crataegus* species. These small trees (most are 20 to 25 feet high) offer a long season of color: white, pink, or red flowers in midspring, bright-orange-to-red berries in autumn and winter, and usually orange-to-red autumn leaf color. Most are hardy to at least Zone 5 (–20°F). Fireblight can be a serious problem.

✔ **Crape myrtle.** *Lagerstroemia indica.* Beautiful, summer-blooming, small trees (usually 10 to 20 feet high but can also be grown as a multi-trunked shrub), hardy to Zone 7 (0°F). Flowers are huge, crinkly, and crepelike, in shades of white, pink, red, and purple. Crape myrtles also have shiny, peeling brown bark and orange-red autumn color. Grow best in areas with hot, dry summers. Elsewhere, plant mildew-resistant varieties, which usually have Native American names, such as 'Cherokee' and 'Catawba'. Dwarf varieties are available, as well.

✔ **Goldenrain tree.** *Koelreuteria paniculata.* A well-behaved, round-headed tree with divided leaves and large, bright-yellow flower clusters in summer. Unusual, papery, Japanese lantern-like fruit follow the flowers. Grows 25 to 35 feet high and grows well in many different climates. Hardy to Zone 5.

✔ **Magnolia.** *Magnolia* species. The deciduous magnolias bloom stunningly on bare branches in early spring. Flowers are huge, often more than 10 inches across, and come in shades of white, pink, and purple. Some of the flowers are bi-colored. Leaves are large and leathery. Trees usually grow 15 to 25 feet high, are often multi-trunked, and are hardy to at least Zone 6 (–10°F). One of the best is the saucer magnolia, *M. soulangiana,* a multi-trunked tree that bears large, cup-shaped flowers, usually white on the inside, purplish on the outsides.

The southern magnolia, *Magnolia grandiflora,* bears fragrant, white summers flower that are huge — up to 12 inches across — and held among bold, deep green leaves. One of the all-time favorite evergreen trees for mild-winter climates. The species gets large, upwards of 80 feet high. Dwarf varieties, such as 'Saint Mary', grow a quarter to a third as high and are perfect for small landscapes. Hardy to Zone 7 (0°F).

✔ **Flowering crab apples.** *Malus* species. Crab apples differ from apples in that they have fruit less than 2 inches in diameter. You have many species and varieties to choose from, ranging in tree size and shape. Spring flowers come in white, pink, or red and are followed by colorful red, orange, or yellow edible fruit that often hangs on the bare branches into winter. Most are hardy to at least Zone 5 (–20°F) and grow best where winters are cold. Flowering crab apples are subject to severe diseases, including fire blight, powdery mildew, and scab. Ask for disease-resistant varieties such as 'Dolga', Japanese flowering crab apple (*M. floribunda*), 'Pink Spires', 'Royalty', Sargent crab apple (*M. sargentii*), 'Snowdrift', and *M. zumi calocarpa*.

✔ **Flowering fruit.** *Prunus* species. A large family of trees that bloom in early spring that includes flowering cherries and plums. Flowers are usually fragrant and come in shades of white, pink, or red. Most are hardy to at least Zone 5 (–20°F) and range in height from 15 to 20 feet. Favorite fruitless types include Kwanzan flowering cherry, *P. serrulata* 'Kwanzan', with drooping clusters of double pink flowers. Another favorite is Krauter's Vesuvius purple-leaf plum, *P. cerasifera* 'Krauter Vesuvius', which has pink flowers and bronzy-purple leaves.

✔ **Evergreen pear.** *Pyrus kawakamii.* This tree adapts well to landscapes, because of its mature height and root system. Leaves are shiny and bright green. White flowers come in spring. Hardy into Zone 8 (10°F), but will drop its leaves (which often turn a beautiful red before falling) in coldest areas. Grows 15 to 25 feet high with a wide-spreading canopy. Fireblight may be a problem.

A few evergreen trees

We divide evergreens into two groups: *conifers* and *broadleaf* evergreens. (The broadleaf group consists of all the varieties listed after "conifers.")

LANDSCAPE LINGO

✔ **Conifers.** The pines, junipers, spruces, firs, hemlocks, and cedars are a diverse group of evergreens, most with needlelike leaves. They are widely grown throughout the world and are especially valuable for year-round greenery and as windbreaks and screens. Most are large trees (some get over 100 feet) and need room to grow, but many dwarf forms are available. Conifers are often similar in their overall pyramidal appearance, but foliage density, color, and texture varies. *Adaptation* (in which climates they can be grown) also varies. Check with a local nursery for species that are adapted to your climate.

✔ **Camphor.** *Cinnamomum camphora.* Dense-foliaged tree with light green, aromatic leaves. Grows 40 to 50 feet high with a round head. Hardy to Zone 8 (10°F). Withstands drought. Has aggressive surface roots.

Try any of these five unique trees

Here are five very special trees that are a little harder to find than some of the others listed in this chapter. But the outstanding color from flowers or foliage makes them worth a little extra effort.

✔ **Serviceberry.** *Amelanchier species.* There are serveral species of this outstanding small tree. They offer a long season of color through spring flowers, edible berries, and glowing yellow, orange, or red fall color. They are hardy to at least Zone 4 and prefer acid soils. Serviceberries usually grown as multi-trunk trees and rarely reach over 15 to 20 feet high.

✔ **Katsura tree.** *Cercidiphyllum japonicum.* Tiny reddish pink spring flowers, handsome, heart-shaped leaves that turn glowing yellow or red in autumn, and a beautifully-shaped canopy more than justify growing this excellent deciduous tree. Slow growing to 40 to 50 feet, katsura tree prefers ample water and protection from hot sun and strong wind. Hardy to Zone 5.

✔ **Coral tree.** *Erythrina species.* Several species of distinctive flowering trees for mild winter climates (most are hardy to Zone 9). Bold leaves are held on muscular, spreading branches; drop briefly in winter to spring. Huge clusters of shocking red or orange blossoms appear at various times of year depending on the species. Height ranges from 15 to 40 feet.

✔ **Silver bell.** *Halesia carolina.* A stunning North American native that prefers shady conditions and acid soil. White, bell-shaped, spring flowers are followed by interesting seed pods that last into fall and winter. Roundish leaves turn yellow in fall. Usually grows 25 to 35 feet with multiple trunks. Hardy to Zone 5.

✔ **Japanese snowbell.** *Styrax japonicus.* Glorious in flower and foliage, the Japanese snowbell adorns its horizontal branches with beautiful white, fragrant, bell-shaped flowers in spring. The roundish leaves turn red or yellow in fall. Grows 25 to 30 feet high. Doesn't do well where summers are hot and dry. Hardy to Zone 5.

✔ **Eucalyptus.** *Eucalyptus* species. Large group of fast-growing, drought-tolerant plants native to Australia. Most valued in dry-summer and mild-winter climates; few can be grown north of Zone 8 (10°F). Some are too large for home landscapes, and you may have trouble growing other plants beneath them. All have heavily aromatic leaves. Many have very colorful flowers and interesting seed capsules. Lower-growing species include Nichol's willow-leaf peppermint, *E. nicholii*. It grows to about 40 feet high, but with weeping branchlets that droop like those of a willow tree. Interestingly, leaves are peppermint-scented. Another is the coolibah, *E. microtheca*, also reaching about 40 feet high, with one trunk or several, and "willowy" blue foliage.

✔ **Oaks.** *Quercus.* Evergreen oaks come in many species, most of which get quite large and spreading. Widely adapted species include the southern live oak, *Q virginiana*, which grows 40 to 60 feet high, is wide spreading, and is hardy to Zone 7 (0F). Another one is the holly oak, *Q. ilex*, which reaches 20 to 35 feet high and is hardy to Zone 8 (10F). The coast live oak, *Q. agrifolia*, is a California native that is widely planted in that state.

Tree Planting Guide

Proper planting ensures that your trees get off to a good start and thrive for years to come. Newly-planted trees need special attention (especially with watering) until they can stretch their roots out into the surrounding soil and fend for themselves.

Does the size you buy matter?

You may wonder whether to buy a small tree and wait several years for it to grow to its full size or purchase a larger, more mature tree.

✔ Buying larger trees gives you immediate impact in your landscape, but they are much more expensive and can be difficult to plant. Larger balled-and-burlapped trees or container grown trees are very heavy and may require a crew of several strong people, maybe even some heavy equipment, in order to plant them.

✔ Smaller, container-grown trees are easy to handle and can be planted any time the weather is mild. And to be honest, because younger trees have been in containers less time, they usually start growing faster after they're in the ground. Within a few years, small trees can often catch up with the size of larger trees that were planted at the same time.

Contact your city or county planning or parks department before planting trees along your street. The officials there may have a list of suitable street trees and a city street tree plan for your street. If you plant something not on their list or in their plan, they may make you remove it.

Trees are sold three different ways. Here's how to plant each one:

- **Bare-root trees.** Deciduous trees are available for planting during the dormant season (winter) without soil on their roots. Bare-root trees look kind of like an old witch's broom, but with a trunk and roots instead of a handle and straw. They're lightweight and easy to handle — the most economical way to purchase trees. Watch out for roots that are damaged, soft, broken, or mushy — prune those damaged roots back, as necessary.

- **Balled-and-burlapped trees.** These trees are dug and sold during the dormant season with the *rootball* (the mass of soil and roots) intact and wrapped in burlap. Check for major cracks or breaks in the rootball and make sure the trunk doesn't rock or move in the soil ball.

- **Container-grown trees.** These trees, sold in large plastic or clay pots, are easy to handle and available year-round. Check for circling or densely matted roots, signs that the tree has been in the pot too long and may not grow well after it's in the ground.

After purchasing your tree, follow these steps for planting it:

1. **Dig a hole.**

   The hole should be deep enough to accommodate the roots (use a stick to determine depth) and two to three times as wide as the rootball.

2. **Slant the walls of the hole outward and loosen them with a shovel or garden fork to allow easy root penetration.**

   Don't bother to *amend* (improve) the soil that you use to refill the hole after you plant the tree — the roots may have a tough time growing beyond the amended area if you do. If your soil is especially poor (mucky clay or gravel) though, work compost or organic matter such as composted fir bark into the backfill soil. You can also build a raised bed (covered in Chapter 7) that can provide a more expansive rooting area.

3. **Insert the tree into the hole.**

   - **Bare-root trees.** These can come one of two ways — with a single, thick *taproot* that extends directly down from the trunk or a fibrous, branched-root system. Tap-rooted trees are placed in the hole so the trees *nursery soil line* (you'll see a color change from light to dark along the trunk) is even with the surface of the soil and the hole is filled. For fibrous rooted trees, set the base of the roots on a cone of soil in the middle of the hole, adjusting the cone height so that the plant's nursery soil line is even with the surrounding soil. Spread the roots in different directions and then refill the hole. You can see how this is done in Chapter 9.

- **Container-grown trees.** Loosen any roots that have become tangled inside the pot by spraying off the soil from the outer inch or two of the rootball. Cut off roots that are broken or permanently damaged.

- **Balled-and-burlapped trees.** Remove the burlap, nails, and any twine or wire used for wrapping after setting the ball in place in the hole (very gently so the rootball doesn't break). If you don't do this, the burlap, nails, and twine may interfere with future growth or strangle the trunk. Burlap is supposed to break down quickly in the soil, but we prefer to take the burlap off of the rootball to make sure that it doesn't get in the way of root growth. If you can't get it all off, use a sharp knife to cut off everything except what is directly beneath the ball. Refill the hole.

4. **Water the tree well by letting a hose trickle into the planting area until the soil is soaked deeply.**

   To help direct irrigation and rainwater to new roots, create a soil watering basin at least 4 to 6 inches high just outside the rootball. Refer to Figure 8-3.

   Continue to water the tree any time that the soil begins to dry out during the next six months to a year — even longer where summers are hot and dry.

5. **Stake and mulch.**

   To stake the tree, drive two tree stakes in the soil beyond the roots. Attach tree ties to the tree at the lowest point at which the tree stays upright. Tie loosely so the trunk can move in the wind and gain trunk strength. See Figure 8-3.

   A tree with a strong trunk stands on its own without staking. However, if the tree was staked in the nursery or if you are planting in a windy location, proper staking will help support the tree during its first years in the ground. After that, stakes must be removed.

In heavy, mucky, clay soils, or rocky soils that are not well-suited to planting, set the plant higher in the soil, digging the hole only $1/2$ to $2/3$ of the depth of the rootball. Then set the plant inside the hole. Refill the hole and use good landscape soil to build up a raised planting bed around the top of the ball.

Don't try this at home!

The following list points out some things that you should *not* do — for practical and aesthetic reasons — when planting a tree.

🖉 **Plant a tree that's too big at maturity.** Some trees can get huge — more than 100 feet tall and almost as wide. These belong in parks and open spaces where they can spread out. But even smaller trees can be too big for a planting site, eventually crowding houses or shading an entire yard. For example, horse chestnut and weeping willow will overwhelm a small landscape in only a few years. Choose something that's in scale with your house and won't become crowded and cramped-looking at maturity, with branches that overhang the house and walkways.

Don't plant trees where they'll grow into power lines or utilities. Pruning such trees is dangerous and costly and results in misshapen trees. And fallen limbs may cause power outages.

🖉 **Plant a messy tree in the wrong place.** All trees shed some leaves at one time or another, but certain species are messier than others. Don't plant trees that drop wet fruit or excessive flowers near patios or sidewalks. They will not only make a mess but can also make the surface slippery, causing a passerby to fall.

🖉 **Plant too many fast-growing trees.** Fast-growing trees are valuable for providing quick shade, but they are often also weak-wooded and short-lived. Consider planting a mixture of slow- and fast-growing types and then removing the less desirable trees when the slower ones reach acceptable size.

🖉 **Plant too close to buildings.** Even smaller trees should be planted at least 5 to 10 feet away from the side of a house or building. Larger trees should be even farther away. Otherwise, the trees don't have room to spread and develop their natural shape. Also, aggressive roots can damage the foundation; falling limbs can damage the house.

🖉 **Plant too close to paving.** Some trees are notorious for having shallow roots that, as they grow, buckle sidewalks and raise patios. Actually, almost any tree, especially larger species, will cause problems if planted too close to paving. Leave at least 3 or 4 feet between the trunk and the paving. If you live where trees require watering, apply water slowly and for long periods so it can soak deeply into the soil. This practice encourages roots to grow deep and not near the surface.

Figure 8-3:
A properly planted tree with strong stakes and watering basin.

WIND

Chapter 9

Landscaping with Shrubs and Vines

*B*ecause they are both versatile and hardworking, shrubs can work wonders in your landscape. They tie the landscape together, bringing unity to all the different elements — from tall trees to low-growing ground covers. Simply put, shrubs bring together the voices of many different plants and landscape features and turn them into the song of a well-planned landscape — Figure 9-1 shows an example. Vines are equally as versatile, able to fit into the narrowest places and provide shade by sprawling over the largest arbor or trellis. We start this chapter with shrubs and then wind our way down to the vines.

Finding Out about Shrubs

The term "shrub" covers a wide variety of plants. Shrubs can be deciduous or evergreen, and they provide a variety of ornamental qualities, from seasonal flowers to colorful fruit to dazzling autumn foliage color. But of equal importance is the diversity of foliage texture and color that shrubs offer — from bold and dramatic to soft and diminutive. Shrubs are always visible, whether or not they're in bloom, so be sure to consider the foliage, color, texture, and form of the plant when selecting shrubs and deciding how to use them.

Figure 9-1:
A garden
filled with
flowering
shrubs,
perennials,
and vines.

Technically, a *shrub* is a woody plant that branches from its base. But that's actually too simple a definition. Shrubs can range from very low-growing, spreading plants that are ideal ground covers (see Chapter 11 for shrubs that are also ground covers) to tall, billowy plants that you can prune into small, multi-trunked trees. In general, shrubs cover themselves with foliage from top to bottom. Try to pigeonhole all shrubs into an absolute size range and you run into many exceptions, but for our purposes, most shrubs fall into the 1- to 15-foot range.

Looking at design considerations

Shrubs serve so many functions in landscapes that categorizing them is useful to better understand them. As you consider your landscape design, use the following categories to understand how to best use shrubs.

- **Foundation plantings.** Traditionally, one of the most common uses of smaller evergreen shrubs is to plant them around the base of a house to conceal the foundation and soften the transition between the lawn and the building. This use of shrubs also gives the landscape winter appeal.

  Using too many of one species of plant leads to monotony and an unnatural look. Try mixing groups of plants with different sizes (the sizes that the shrubs will eventually grow to) and textures. And don't plant too close to your house. Bring the plantings out some distance to gain a smoother transition, to give the shrubs growing room, and to keep the branches of the shrubs from rubbing against the house.

- **Unifiers.** Repeating small groupings of plants (groups of three, five, seven and on up — in odd numbers — tend to look best) in different parts of a landscape ties everything together and gives the yard a feeling of order and purpose. Similarly, shrubs work well when planted among shorter-lived perennials in border plantings. Because shrubs are usually larger and more substantial, they provide a foundation for the more extravagant perennials and a structure for the landscape when the perennials are dormant. In other words, shrubs provide consistent beauty and unity even when everything isn't looking its best. For more about perennial plants, see Chapter 10.

- **Backgrounds and barriers.** Shrubs can be the perfect backdrop for flower beds. A consistent, deep green background is one of the best ways to highlight blooming plants. If you want to keep pets (or people) out of a certain area, plant a line of thorny Pyracantha or barberries. They'll get the "point."

- **Accent plantings.** Some shrubs, such as azaleas and rhododendrons, are spectacular bloomers. Others have stunning berries or autumn color. Just a plant or two in a special place can light up a whole yard. And don't forget the foliage — a bold hydrangea with diversely colored leaves can make a stunning statement among plants with smaller leaves, like azaleas.

As you're selecting shrubs for your landscape, be sure to note the season of the shrub's peak interest. For example, many shrubs produce flowers in early spring, but others — such as several of the hollies — are showy in winter, particularly against a backdrop of snow. By mixing shrubs with different seasons of peak interest, you can be sure to have plants worth admiring in your landscape any time of the year.

✔ **Hedges, screens, and ground covers.** Many shrubs, usually ones with smaller leaves, can be planted close together and maintained as hedges and screens. Some, including boxwoods and euonymus, can be clipped regularly into the rigid shape of a formal hedge to give a landscape a very organized look. (See Figure 9-2 for how to prune a hedge.) Many others can be left to grow more naturally, creating screens for privacy. Many *prostrate* (low-growing) shrubs make excellent ground covers. For more information, see Chapter 11.

Figure 9-2:
Keep formal hedges full-foliaged by lightly tapering the sides so that the whole hedge receives light.

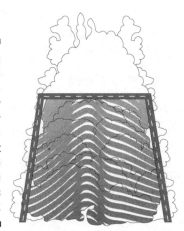

Organizing shrubs by height

In mixed plantings of different shrubs, or when shrubs are mixed with other plants, such as flowering perennials, the mature height of the shrub determines where it should be placed in the overall planting. Remember this landscaping axiom: lower growers in front, medium sized plants in the middle, talls in back. That way, nothing gets blocked out and you can see all the plants. Height will also determine which shrubs you use as hedges and screens. In the "Discovering our favorite shrubs" section that follows this one, we organize shrubs by botanical name, but with the common name listed first. In Table 9-1, we group them by common name and by size; small (1 to 5 feet high), medium (6 to 10 feet high), and large (over 10 feet high).

You can find many shrubs listed in two or more categories. That's because many types of shrubs include species or varieties of varying heights. Use this list to get you to the right type of shrubs, then read on to find the one that grows to an appropriate height. You should also know that mature heights of plants are — at best — only generalizations. Plants often grow taller in areas with long, warm growing seasons than they do in areas with short summers.

Color jumpstarts your landscape.

6 This hillside garden comes alive with color.

7 Mounds of color, surrounding a half-hidden gazebo, unify this landscape.

8 Colorful jasmine adds privacy to this residence.

9 Use layers of color and texture — from ferns to shrubs to colorful rhododendrons and azaleas to flowering dogwood.

Pathways can be constructed of many different materials.

(Previous page)

1 A strip of grass through thickly-planted perennials, shrubs, and trees creates an inexpensive pathway.

2 A fieldstone walkway gives your landscape an informal look.

3 Use concrete to create a durable pathway.

4 A brick and mortar path lends a formal look.

5 Take advantage of crushed pebbles — an inexpensive option — so that surrounding plants can take center stage.

15

11

13

9

12

10

14

Use color in your landscape the way you do in your wardrobe.

10 Make use of perennials and reseeding annuals as colorful ground cover.

11 Soft colors harmonize with this classic brick residence.

12 Construct a window box to add color to your home.

13 Use a single color throughout an otherwise green landscape for a sophisticated look.

14 Colorful bulbs announce the beginning of spring.

15 Utilize color sparingly around a beautiful view.

A simple bench

captures your imagination.

16 A teak bench creates a quiet hideaway.

17 Two white, wooden benches form a conversation spot.

18 A wooden bench and arched trellis combine in a romantic setting.

19 A stone bench, which needs little maintenance, invites you to relax.

20 A whitewashed wooden bench makes even the smallest outdoor spaces inviting.

17

18

20

19

21

22

23

24

25

26

Add a deck to your landscape for an outdoor retreat.

21 Lush greenery blends this deck into the landscape.

22 Even on a small lot, a deck extends outdoor living space.

23 Decking links a peaceful pond to the rest of the landscape.

Decks comes in all shapes and sizes.

24 Accentuate a simple deck with color, like these bright-red Adirondack chairs.

25 Make the most of a sloping lot with a towering deck and shade structure.

26 Create an outdoor retreat with a built-in hot tub.

27

28

29

A patio is your outdoor living room.

27 This private patio follows a graceful curve.

28 Patio and pond combine in a quiet, peaceful setting.

29 This patio and extra-wide walkway blend seamlessly.

Ponds and pools are lush landscape additions.

30 Brick adds a formal touch to this lily pond.

31 Create your own private, outdoor waterfall.

32 An outdoor pool invites family fun.

30

32

31

34

35

36

33

Outdoor structures

add liveliness to your landscape.

33 Fabricate a shed to store your lawnmower, potting soil, and garden tools.

34 This shed unobtrusively blends with the architecture of the home and neighborhood.

35 Surround your shed with greenery growing on lattice.

36 What child wouldn't love this outdoor playhouse?

37 A tiny dollhouse offers a private retreat for a child.

38 Transform your yard with a safe, durable play structure.

39 A gazebo, nested among greenery, is a welcome spot for unwinding.

37

39

38

Table 9-1	Common Shrubs and Their Sizes	
Small *(1 to 5 feet high)*	*Medium* *(6 to 10 feet high)*	*Tall* *(over 10 feet high)*
Glossy abelia	Glossy abelia	Cotoneaster
Barberry	Barberry	Euonymus
Boxwood	Butterfly bush	Holly
Camellia	Camellia	Juniper
Rockrose	Flowering quince	Oleander
Gardenia	Cotoneaster	Photinia
Holly	Euonymus	Indian hawthorn
Juniper	Forsythia	Rhododendron
Heavenly bamboo	Hydrangea	Flowering fruit
Bush cinquefoil	Holly	Lilac
Hydrangea	Juniper	Viburnum
Indian hawthorn	Oleander	
Azalea	Photinia	
Rose	Mugho pine	
Spiraea	Tobira	
	Flowering fruit	
	Firethorn	
	Indian hawthorn	
	Rhododendron	
	Rose	
	Spiraea	
	Lilac	
	Viburnum	

Discovering some favorite shrubs

This section lists the shrubs that we consider to be foolproof, arranged alphabetically according to botanical name, but listing the common name first. All are widely available and most are *broadly adapted* (they can grow in many different climates). Regarding specific soil needs, please refer to Chapter 12 to see how to adjust soil as needed for certain plants and for more information about hardiness zones.

- ✔ **Glossy abelia.** *Abelia grandiflora.* Evergreen. Handsome, arching plant with bright green, glossy foliage. New growth is bronzy-red. Leaves turn reddish purple in winter. Small, fragrant, white flowers in summer. Loses its leaves in colder areas. Can be grown as a hedge. 'Edward Goucher' and 'Sherwoodi' are smaller versions, reaching 3 to 5 feet high. Plant in full sun or light shade. Hardy to Zone 6.

- ✔ **Barberries.** *Berberis* species. Evergreen and deciduous shrubs known for their thorny stems, red berries, and tough constitution. Some have showy yellow flowers and colorful foliage. Upright-growing barberries make excellent hedges and barriers. The deciduous Japanese barberry, *B. thunbergii,* is generally 4 to 6 feet high with arching stems. However, you have many varieties from which to choose, varying in height and foliage color. Most have good autumn color. 'Atropurpurea' has reddish-purple foliage during the growing season. It is hardy to Zone 4. Evergreen barberries include *B. mentorensis,* a compact, dense plant growing 6 to 7 feet high, that's hardy to Zone 6. Most barberries can grow in sun or partial shade and thrive under a variety of growing conditions.

- ✔ **Butterfly bush.** *Buddleia davidii.* Deciduous. Much loved, summer flowering shrub with long, arching clusters of lightly fragrant flowers which attract butterflies. Most varieties bloom in shades of purple, but you can often find selections with pink or white flowers. Grows very fast, reaching up to 10 feet high in areas with long summers. Cut back severely in winter to keep the plant compact and attractive. Plant in full sun. Hardy to Zone 5.

- ✔ **Boxwoods.** *Buxus* species. Evergreen. The boxwood is one of the finest plants for a tightly clipped, formal hedge. Small, dark green leaves densely cover the branches. The Japanese boxwood, *B. microphylla japonica,* is one of the most popular types. Unpruned, it grows about 4 to 6 feet high. 'Winter Gem' and 'Green Beauty' are two varieties that stay bright green all winter. Others pick up a brownish tinge. Grow in full sun to partial shade. Hardy to Zone 5. The English boxwood, *B. sempervirens,* is the classic boxwood of the mid-South. Many named varieties are available. It is hardy to Zone 6.

- ✔ **Camellias.** *Camellia* species. Evergreen. With its glossy, deep green leaves and perfectly formed flowers, it is one of the finest shrubs for shady conditions. Flowers come in shades of red, pink, and white, with some bicolors. Most types bloom in winter and early spring.

  - The Japanese camellia, *C. japonica,* is the most commonly grown camellia, usually reaching 6 to 12 feet high. Many varieties are available, varying by color and flower form. Most are hardy into Zone 8.

- Sasanqua camellia, *C. sasanqua,* has smaller leaves and earlier flowers (often in autumn). These shrubs range from small shrubs to more spreading, vine-like plants. Hardy to Zone 8.

- New varieties are more cold hardy, to Zone 6a. These shrubs are hybrids of the Japanese camellia and *C. oleifera.* Named varieties include 'Winter's Beauty', 'Winter's Interlude', 'Winter's Star', and 'Winter's Waterlily'.

Flowering quince. *Chaenomeles.* Deciduous. Among the first shrubs to bloom in early spring, flowering quince are tough, reliable plants that never let you down. The flowers are born on bare stems in shades of mostly red and pink, but may also be white. Plants range in size and shape depending on variety, but generally grow 5 to 10 feet high, are upright and have thorny branches. They can be clipped as a hedge and usually look best with regular pruning. Plant in full sun. Hardy to Zone 4.

Rockroses. *Cistus* species. Evergreen. Particularly well adapted to dry summer climates, such as in the western United States, rockroses are tough, colorful plants that can get by on little water. You can find several species and hybrids available, most growing between 3 and 6 feet high and blooming in late spring to early summer. The round, silky blooms are 1 to 2 inches wide, come in shades of white, red, and pink, and are often spotted or marked. Foliage is gray-green. Plant in full sun. Hardy to Zone 8.

Cotoneaster. *Cotoneaster* species. Evergreen and deciduous. You can choose from many types, ranging from low-growing ground covers to tall, upright shrubs. (See Chapter 11 for more on ground covers.) Most share a profusion of white spring flowers followed by red berries and are tough, widely adapted plants. Deciduous kinds often have good autumn color. Taller types include the evergreen Parney cotoneaster, *C. lacteus,* which reaches about 8 feet high and equally as wide, and *C. watereri,* which reaches up to 20 feet high with arching stems. Deciduous *C. divaricatus* has stiff, arching branches to 6 feet high and bears a heavy crop of berries. Most cotoneasters are hardy to Zone 5 or 6. Plant in full sun. Fireblight can be a problem.

Euonymus. *Euonymus* species. Evergreen and deciduous. Euonymus are workhorse foliage plants. Deciduous kinds, such as winged euonymus, *E. alata,* are hardy to Zone 4 and are grown for their convenient size and shape and their stunning red autumn color. The European spindle tree, *E. europaea,* grows to about 20 feet high and produces attractive red berries in autumn.

Evergreen euonymus, such as *E. japonica* and *E. fortunei,* are hardy to Zones 5 to 7, depending on the variety. Varieties with colored leaves, like 'Silver King' (white with green) and 'Aureo-variegata' (yellow with green), are very popular. They range in height from 6 to 20 feet and make fine hedges. Plant euonymus in sun or light shade. *E. japonica* is often troubled by powdery mildew.

✔ **Forsythia.** *Forsythia intermedia.* Deciduous. One of the earliest bloomers, the bright yellow flowers on bare forsythia branches announce the coming of spring. Plants are upright to spreading, generally 6 to 10 feet high. Many varieties are available, differing in the shade of yellow, from pale to bright yellow. Plant in full sun. Prune after bloom. Hardy to Zone 3.

✔ **Gardenia.** *Gardenia jasminoides.* Evergreen. Intensely fragrant, pure-white summer flowers and beautiful deep green leaves make gardenias a favorite shrub wherever they can be grown. Plants usually grow 3 to 6 feet high and must have acid soil and consistent moisture. Plant in full sun in cool climates, partial shade in warmer areas. 'Mystery' is a popular, large-flowered variety. Hardy to Zone 8.

✔ **Hydrangea.** *Hydrangea* species. Deciduous. The big, bold leaves and huge summer flowers of these unique plants put on a great show in shady landscapes. The bigleaf hydrangea, *H. macrophylla,* is most commonly grown. Flower clusters are up to a foot across and are light to deep blue in acid soil, pink to red in alkaline soil. Plants usually grow 4 to 8 feet high and must be pruned heavily to encourage compactness and heavy bloom. Several varieties, including 'Silver Variegated Mariesii' and 'Tricolor' have leaves marked with silver and white. Hardy to Zone 7.

✔ **Hollies.** *Ilex* species. The most commonly grown hollies are evergreen plants known for their bright-red berries and clean-looking, spiny, often multicolored leaves. Many make excellent hedges. The most familiar holly is the English holly, *Ilex aquifolium.* It generally grows 15 to 25 feet high but can get larger. Varieties such as 'Argenteo-marginata', with leaves of diverse shades of white, make excellent accents. Other popular types include the compact 'Burfordii' and 'Dazzler', varieties of *I. cornuta.* They grow 8 to 10 feet high. 'Carissa' reaches only 3 to 4 feet high but spreads twice as wide. 'Nellie Stevens' is a hybrid that grows at least 15 feet high. Plant hollies in full sun. Most are hardy to at least Zone 5.

✔ **Junipers.** *Juniperus* species. Evergreen. The low- and wide-spreading growth pattern of most junipers makes them most useful as ground covers (see Chapter 11). However, you can find many more upright, shrubby types, including forms of the Chinese juniper, *J. chinensis,* such as 'Hetzzi' and 'Torulosa'. Look also for very columnar varieties, like 'Wintergreen' and 'Spartan'. Plant in full sun. Hardiness varies; most can be grown into at least Zone 5.

✔ **Heavenly bamboo.** *Nandina domestica.* Evergreen. Light and airy in appearance, heavenly bamboo has divided leaves and straight, erect stems of a small bamboo. However, it is much more ornamental. New growth is bronzy red when the plant is grown in full sun. The entire plant turns red in chilly winter areas. White spring flowers are followed by bright red berries. Grows 6 to 8 feet high, but many dwarf forms are available. Hardy to Zone 6.

✔ **Oleander.** *Nerium oleander.* Evergreen. Oleander is a tough plant that puts on an incredibly long show of color throughout summer and into autumn. The flowers are born in large clusters in shades of white, pink, and red. The plants are low maintenance and thrive in hot summers. Oleanders are densely foliaged and generally grow 10 to 20 feet high but can be kept lower with annual pruning. You can also choose dwarf varieties. Plant in full sun. Hardy to Zone 8.

All parts — leaves, stems, flowers, and seeds — of all types of oleander are toxic.

✔ **Photinia.** *Photinia* species. Mostly evergreen. Several species of useful shrubs that show bronzy-red new growth in spring followed shortly by clusters of small, white flowers and often black or red berries. *P. fraseri,* which reaches 10 to 15 feet high, is popular because of its resistance to powdery mildew, but it does not have berries. Japanese photinia, *P. glabra,* is slightly lower growing and has red berries that gradually turn black. Plant photinias in full sun. They are hardy to Zone 6.

✔ **Mugho pine.** *Pinus mugo mugo.* Evergreen. A neat, compact pine that rarely exceeds 4 to 8 feet in height (don't confuse it with *pinus mugo* — that's just one *mugo* — which gets quite a bit taller). Easy to care for as a specimen or in group plantings. Plant in full sun. Hardy to Zone 3.

✔ **Bush cinquefoil.** *Potentilla fruticosa.* Deciduous. Particularly valuable in cold-winter climates, bush cinquefoil is a handsome little shrub with bright green, ferny foliage and colorful wild-roselike blossoms. Plants bloom from late spring into autumn in shades of red, yellow, orange, and white. Yellow varieties, such as 'Katherine Dykes', are most popular. Ranges in height from just under 2 feet up to 5 feet. Plant in full sun. Hardy to Zone 3.

✔ **Tobira.** *Pittosporum tobira.* Evergreen. A handsome, well-behaved shrub with glossy deep green leaves and clusters of white, fragrant spring flowers. The species is rounded and can reach over 10 feet high but can easily be kept lower with pruning. The 'Wheeler's Dwarf' variety grows into a neat, mound shaped plant that grows to only 2 to 4 feet high. 'Variegata' has light gray-green leaves edged with white. It grows 5 to 10 feet high. Plant in full sun to light shade. Hardy to Zone 8.

✔ **Flowering fruit.** *Prunus* species. Evergreen or deciduous. You can find many valuable shrubs in the large family of plants, which includes some of our most popular fruit, such as peaches and plums. Carolina cherry laurel, (*P. caroliniana),* English laurel (*P. laurocerasus),* and Portugal laurel (*P. lusitanica*) are evergreen with white spring flowers, handsome foliage and tall stature (20 feet high or more). The evergreen types are useful as tall screens but their smaller varieties are more appropriate for most landscapes. For example, 'Bright 'n' Tight' is dwarf form of Carolina cherry laurel that reaches about 10 feet high. 'Zabelliana' is a fine leafed form only 6 feet high. 'Otto Luyken' is a small version of English laurel growing only 6 feet high. Evergreen flowering fruit are generally hardy to Zone 8 and grow best in full sun.

The purple-leafed sand cherry, *P. cistena* is a very hardy deciduous flowering fruit with white spring flowers, purple foliage, and small edible plums. It grows about 10 feet high and is hardy to Zone 3. Plant in full sun.

✔ **Firethorn.** *Pyracantha* species. Evergreen. Colorful and dependable, firethorn come in a wide range of forms, from low-growing ground covers to upright, spreading shrubs. (See Chapter 11 for the scoop on ground covers.) All firethorn shrubs cover themselves with clusters of small, fragrant, white flowers in spring followed by showy, orange-to-red berries lasting into autumn and winter. Branches are sharply thorned. Popular types include the very hardy *P. coccinea* 'Lalandei', which grows 8 to 10 feet high and has red berries. Fireblight can be a serious problem; hybrids 'Mojave' and 'Teton' are fireblight-resistant. They grow about 12 feet high, with orange-red and yellow-orange berries, respectively. Plant firethorn in full sun. Most are hardy to Zone 5 or 6.

✔ **Indian hawthorn.** *Rhaphiolepis indica.* Evergreen. Chances are, you can't go wrong with Indian hawthorn. Compact and carefree, the plants bloom profusely from late winter into spring. The pink-to-white flowers are followed by blackish-blue berries. New growth is tinged bronze. Plants generally grow 3 to 6 feet high. 'Majestic Beauty' is taller, growing up to 15 feet high, and has large leaves. Plant Indian hawthorn in full sun. Hardy to Zone 7.

✔ **Azaleas and rhododendrons.** *Rhododendron* species. Evergreen and deciduous. Huge family of much-loved flowering shrubs. You can find many types to choose from, but all grow best in acid soil.

• Azaleas are generally lower-growing, compact plants that cover themselves with brightly colored spring flowers in shades of pink, red, orange, yellow, purple, and white. Some are bi-colored. Favorite evergreen types include Belgian Indicas, Kurumes, and Southern Indicas. Deciduous kinds, many of which have bright yellow, orange, or red fall color, include Knap Hill-Exbury Hybrids, Mollis Hybrids, and the very hardy Northern Lights Hybrids.

• Rhododendrons are usually taller with larger flower clusters. They come in basically the same color range as azaleas, but aren't as well adapted to hot-summer climates.

Most azaleas and rhododendrons prefer moist, shady conditions and soil rich in organic matter. Some can take full sun. Hardiness varies. Rhododendrons include some of the most cold-hardy evergreen shrubs, a few of which tolerate winters in Zone 4. Deciduous azaleas share the rhododendron's cold tolerance. The Northern Lights series is also hardy to Zone 4. Evergreen azaleas are much less tolerant of cold. Belgian Indicas are hardy to Zone 9, and Kurumes to Zone 8.

✔ **Roses.** *Rosa* species. Deciduous. Many roses are outstanding landscape shrubs, but you have to choose varieties carefully. A rose suited for landscaping should exhibit good disease resistance, bloom over a long period (heavily in spring, on and off in summer, heavy again in fall), have an attractive compact habit, and be well adapted to the climate that you live in. With those criteria met, roses are exceptionally colorful landscape plants, useful as hedges, edgings, barriers and even as ground covers. Here are some of our favorite landscape roses, organized by class. For more information, check out *Roses For Dummies* by Lance Walheim and the Editors of the National Gardening Association (IDG Books Worldwide, Inc.).

- *Floribundas* are free-blooming, shrub-like roses with large clusters of flowers. They usually grow 3 to 5 feet high and can be used as informal hedges, mixed in perennial borders or planted in masses. Favorite varieties include 'Iceberg,' with white flowers, 'Europeana' with deep red blooms, and 'Sexy Rexy' with rose-pink flowers.

- *Shrubs* are a catch-all group of roses that includes many diverse plants, including ones that can be used as ground covers (see Chapter 11 for more on that). Height can range from 18 inches to over 10 feet high, but most are in the 4 to 6 foot range. They tend to be tough, durable plants. 'Bonica' has warm pink blooms on an arching plant, 'Carefree Beauty' large pink blooms, 'All That Jazz' has bright poppy orange flowers, 'Watermelon Ice' is a low growing shrub with lavender pink flowers, 'Carefree Wonder' has pink blooms with white centers. Also in the shrub category are some very hardy roses bred specifically for areas with very cold winters. The Morden (varieties have Morden in the name) and Explorers (named after explorers) are hardy to –25°F. Repeat blooming varieties of *Rosa rugosa* are hardy to –30°F and can also thrive in coastal conditions under the constant assault of salty winds. Many rugosas have good-looking, crinkled leaves and bright red hips (seed pods).

- *Miniature* roses grow 6 inches to 30 inches high. They have small leaves and small flowers (less than 2 inches wide) but are very useful as edgings, small informal hedges, or mixed in with flowering perennials. Favorite varieties include 'Magic Carousel' with red flowers edged in white, 'Black Jade' with red blooms, and 'Gourmet Popcorn' which has white flowers with yellow centers.

- *Climbers* are vigorous-growing roses that can be trained to a wall, fence, or trellis. For more information, see the "Using Vines for Your Landscape" section, later in this chapter.

- *Hybrid* teas are the most popular type of rose, loved for their beautifully formed flowers. However, their open habit and common disease problems make them less useful as landscape shrubs. They grow better in groups of other hybrid teas in a more classic rose garden setting.

- *Old garden roses* are the grandparents of modern roses. They are a very diverse group of plants, many of which only bloom once or get huge (some can swallow your house). However, if you do some homework, you can use old roses effectively in your landscape. But I would get *Roses For Dummies* before trying.

Most roses are hardy into Zone 5 or 6, depending on type. But even in those zones, roses need winter protection — soil or organic matter piled 6 to 8 inches over their *crown* (where the branches grow from the trunk) in winter. This extra precaution limits their practicality as landscape shrubs. In cold climates, plant hardy varieties like those described in the "Shrubs" bullet point, earlier in this list. Even those varieties may be killed to the ground in winter, but they return and bloom the following spring. Plant roses in full sun.

✔ **Spiraea.** *Spiraea* species. Deciduous. You have many types of spiraeas to choose from. Many are mounding, fountainlike shrubs with an abundance of tiny, white flowers in mid-spring to late spring. Included among these is the bridal wreath spiraea, *S. vanhouttei,* which grows about 6 feet high and at least 8 feet wide. Its small, dark green leaves turn red in autumn. Other spiraeas, like *S. bumalda* 'Anthony Waterer', have clusters of pink-to-red blooms later in summer. 'Anthony Waterer' has upright stems reaching about 4 feet high. Plant spiraeas in full sun. Hardiness varies, but most grow in Zones 4 and 5.

✔ **Common lilac.** *Syringa vulgaris.* Deciduous. Wonderfully fragrant clusters of spring flowers make lilacs a favorite wherever they grow. Most bloom in shades of lavender and purple, but some are white or rosy pink. Plants usually grow 8 to 15 feet high and have dark green leaves. Plant in full sun. Lilacs grow best where winters are cold; they're hardy to Zone 3. The newer Descanso Hybrids will flower where winters are milder.

✔ **Viburnum.** *Viburnum* species. The viburnums represent a large family of evergreen and deciduous shrubs that are wonderful additions to the landscape. They offer great variety of form and function, and their ornamental characteristics include colorful flowers, brightly colored berries, and, often, autumn color. Favorite evergreen types include the neat-growing *V. tinus,* which grows 10 to 12 feet high and has pink-to-white spring flowers followed by metallic-blue berries. The variety 'Variegatum' has leaves colored with white and creamy yellow. 'Compactum' is lower growing than is typical for the species. All make good unpruned hedges and are hardy to Zone 7.

Choices among deciduous types include the Korean spice viburnum, *V. carlesii,* which has very fragrant clusters of white flowers in spring followed by blue-black berries. Leaves turn red in autumn. Plants grow about 8 feet high, spreading just about as wide. The horizontal-branching *V. plicatum* is also distinctive, with rows of white spring flowers and red autumn color. It grows about 15 feet high. Deciduous viburnums are generally hardy to at least Zone 5. Plant viburnums in full sun or partial shade.

Colorful shrubs

If its color you're after, you can plant shrubs that provide it in abundance through a combination of flowers, fruit, and fall color. In other words, the following are shrubs that provide more than one season of color:

- **Barberry:** flowers, fruit, fall color, colorful foliage
- **Cotoneaster:** flowers, fruit, fall color
- **Euonymus:** fruit, fall color, colorful foliage
- **Hydrangea:** flowers, colorful foliage
- **Holly:** berries, colorful foliage
- **Heavenly bamboo:** flowers, fruit, colorful foliage
- **Photinia:** flowers, colorful foliage
- **Tobira:** flowers, colorful foliage
- **Flowering fruit:** flowers, colorful foliage
- **Firethorn:** flowers, fruit
- **Azalea:** flowers, fall color
- **Roses:** flowers, fruit
- **Spiraea:** flowers, fall color
- **Viburnum:** flowers, fall color, fruit, colorful foliage

Drought-tolerant shrubs

Many of the shrubs listed in this section, such as junipers, cotoneaster, oleander rockrose, and Indian hawthorn, can withstand periods of drought that are common in dry summer areas like parts of the southwestern United States. For more information and additional plants, consult your local water district or the *Sunset Western Garden Book* (see the appendix for more information).

- Manzanitia, *Arctostaphylos* species. Varied group of plants native to western states. Includes trees, shrubs, and ground covers. Handsome shiny bark, small pink to white flowers. Range in height from low growing ground covers (only a foot or two high) to tall shrubs that are over 15 feet high.

- Cassia, *Cassia* species. Australian natives particularly well-adapted to desert climates. Attractive foliage with brilliant yellow flowers. Range in height from small shrubs to tall trees that are over 25 feet high.

- Wild lilac, *Ceanothus* species. Evergreen shrubs and ground covers with dark green foliage and mostly blue spring flowers. Native to western states. Range in height from low-growing shrubs just a few feet high to taller shrubs 15 to 20 feet high.

- Hop bush, *Dodonea viscosa.* Tough, fast growing, evergreen shrub with narrow leaves. Grows 12 to 15 feet high. Makes a good screen. 'Purpurea' has bronzy green leaves.

- Toyon, *Heteromeles arbutifolia.* Native to California. Evergreen with shiny dark green leaves, white flowers and bright red berries. Grows 15 to 25 feet high.

- Lavender, *Lavendula* species. Attractive, tough family of evergreen herbs with fragrant blue flowers and gray-green leaves. Most grow between 2 and 4 feet high.

- Mahonia, *Mahonia* species. Evergreen with spiny leaves and yellow flowers. Good in the shade. Grows 5 to 12 feet high.

- Rosemary, *Rosmarinus* species. Upright to spreading, evergreen herbs with blue, white, or pink flowers and aromatic foliage. Some varieties are excellent ground covers, but most reach 2 to 3 feet high.

- Germander, *Teucrium* species. Evergreen shrubs with colorful flowers and attractive foliage. Most reach 2 to 4 feet high.

Evergreen shrubs

Many kinds of dwarf conifers (needled evergreens) are available and useful as landscape shrubs. Here's a list of our favorites:

- **Firs.** *Abies* species. *A. koreana* is not truly miniature, but it's so slow growing that it's regarded as such. *A. koreana* 'Aurea' grows to 6 $\frac{1}{2}$ feet tall, has green needles with silvery undersides, and sports appealing bluish cones. *A. nordmanniana* 'Golden Spreader' is compact and irregularly shaped. Grows to 20 inches. Hardy to Zone 5.

- **Cedars.** *Cedrus* species. *C. deodara* 'Compacta' forms a 30-inch mound of weeping, green-gold foliage. Hardy to Zone 7.

- **Cypresses.** *Chamaecyparis* species. *C. lawsoniana* 'Ellwoodii' is pillar-shaped and grows to 30 inches high, with blue-green leaves. *C. lawsoniana* 'Minima Aurea' is bushy and golden yellow; grows to 24 inches high. Both are hardy to Zone 6.

- **Junipers.** *Juniperus* species. *J. communis* 'Compressa' is columnar, grows to 18 inches high; has blue-green foliage. Hardy to Zone 3.

- **Spruces.** *Picea* species. *P. glauca* 'Conica' is a neat, conical shrub with bright-green needles; grows to 4 feet. Hardy to Zone 3.

- **Pines.** *Pinus* species. *P. strobus* 'Nana' grows 3 to 4 feet high with dense, blue-green needles. Hardy to Zone 3.

- **Red Cedars.** *Platycladus* species. *P. orientalis* 'Aureus' is a vivid golden green; round and grows to 30 inches. Hardy to Zone 5.

- **Yews.** *Taxus* species. *T. cuspidata* 'Nana' grows to 3 feet high and wide; has dark green foliage. Hardy to Zone 5.

Caring for evergreen shrubs

Broadleaf evergreen shrubs are likely to be less tolerant of intense cold than deciduous shrubs. To protect the evergreens, be sure to do the following:

✔ Plant them in wind-sheltered locations.

✔ Protect them with a burlap wind screen (see Chapter 12) or spray with an *antidesiccant* (a lacquerlike material that won't damage leaves but slows evaporation of water from them, thus reducing winter injury).

Selecting high-quality shrubs

Like trees, shrubs are large and long-lived plants, so select ones that can thrive in your region and at your specific site. Consider the advice offered in Chapter 12 regarding climate, hardiness, and quantity of light or shade.

No matter what the condition of the soil in your landscape, so many shrubs are available that you are sure to find several that will thrive. However, if you make even modest improvements in your soil, such as improving the drainage of heavy soils or the moisture retention of sandy soils, adjusting pH, or increasing the fertility of poor soils, the number of shrubs that can grow well increases dramatically. (You can read more about improving your soil in Chapter 12.)

As with trees (see Chapter 8), you can buy shrubs in containers, as bareroot plants, or balled-and-burlapped, but the vast majority of shrubs that are sold in the U.S. are in containers. Check for quality as follows:

✔ Examine the container-grown shrub carefully to be sure it is not damaged. Avoid plants with broken branches or chewed foliage — a sure sign of bugs.

✔ Slide the rootball out — this is easy if the shrub is in a plastic pot — and look for young, white roots — these are essential for efficient uptake of water and nutrients.

Older, darker roots function primarily to stabilize the plant.

Planting shrubs

Shrubs grown in containers are planted the same way container-grown trees are planted, as discussed in Chapter 8. Plant bareroot shrubs as follows:

1. **Set the base of the roots on a cone of soil in the middle of the hole. (See Figure 9-3.)**

   Adjust the cone height so that the plant sits slightly higher (1 to 2 inches) than it was originally planted in the nursery (you can see a change in color from light to dark along the trunk which tells you where the original soil line was. Lay a stick across the top of the hole to check planting depth.) Spread the roots in different directions and then refill the hole.

Figure 9-3: For bare-root shrubs, set the plant on a cone of soil in the middle of the hole.

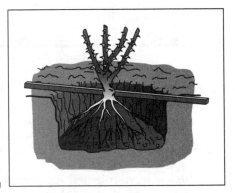

2. **Build a soil basin and water deeply, as shown in Figure 9-4.**

3. **Apply an organic mulch 2 to 3 inches deep, mounding the soil over the shrub if planting roses, as shown in Figure 9-5.**

Figure 9-4: Soil basin directs water to roots.

Figure 9-5: Mounding soil over a bare-root rose

Using Vines for Your Landscape

Vines are constantly on the move. Usually very vigorous, these plants sprawl over, twine around, climb up, or attach to whatever gets in their way. They're also very useful plants for landscapers. As long as you keep them within bounds and under control, they can be used as ground covers (covered extensively in Chapter 11), as a covering for a fence or blank wall (fences are discussed in Chapter 5), or as shading on an arbor or trellis (see Chapter 7) to cool a patio or deck (described in Chapter 6).

Like other plant groups (trees, shrubs, and so on), vines offer a variety of ornamental characteristics, including seasonal flower color, bright berries, and autumn color. Because most grow vertically, you can use them in tight spots where few other plants would fit. And they are versatile — they can create privacy, provide shade, and conceal unattractive landscape features.

Keep vines where they should be

Clinging vines, such as English ivy and Virginia creeper, can attach so firmly to walls and fences that getting them off without damaging the structure becomes almost impossible. And sometimes the attaching parts of the plant work their way into cracks and crevices. As they enlarge and grow, they can lift shingles and damage even the sturdiest materials, such as concrete and brick.

Letting a vine attach directly to the walls of your house usually isn't a good idea, unless the house is made of brick, stone, or aluminum siding. And even then you can have problems. Instead, build a trellis a few feet away from the side of the house and let it support the vine. That way, you can also paint the wall (behind the trellis) if you need to.

Provide sturdy support

As vines grow, the branches enlarge and the plant gets heavier. If the supports aren't strong enough, they can buckle under the weight. Build supports that are sturdy and long lasting. Two-inch galvanized pipe and pressure-treated 4x4 lumber are both good choices. (See Chapter 7 for more on supports.)

Vines need to grow on something, either another plant or a trellis you provide. Before deciding what kind of support to provide for your favorite climbers, you need to know exactly how the climbers will hold on. Vines are grouped into several types, according to the way they climb, as shown in Figure 9-6.

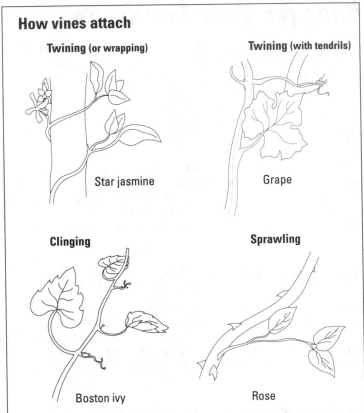

How vines attach

Twining (or wrapping)

Star jasmine

Twining (with tendrils)

Grape

Clinging

Boston ivy

Sprawling

Rose

Figure 9-6:
Ways that
vines
attach.

  ✔ **Clinging vines.** Examples are English ivy and Boston ivy. These vines
    have specialized growths — like little suction cups or claws — along
    their stems that can hook onto any surface they touch.

  ✔ **Sprawling vines.** An example is a climbing rose. These vines are often
    vigorous, spreading plants. In order for them to climb, they need to be
    tied to a trellis or support.

  ✔ **Twining vines.** These vines come in two types. Some, like star jasmine,
    wrap around anything that falls in their way. Others, like grapes, have
    small, twining *tendrils* at the bases of their leaves. The tendrils grab and
    wrap around anything they can reach.

You have many ways to support a vine, from arbors to lath trellises to wires
strung between secure anchors. The important thing is to plan the supporting device in advance, make it strong, and design it to fit the growth habit of
the vine. (Chapter 7 can help you do this.)

✔ Probably the simplest way to support a vine is to let it climb up and ramble through a companion tree or shrub — the way many vines grow in nature. This display can be enchanting in a landscape if the two plants are good companions. Moderate growers, like clematis, happily associate with large shrubs. Vigorous growers, such as ivy, are best kept out of trees.

Don't let any type of vine climb into the tops of trees. The health of the tree is almost always compromised by the vigorous vine.

✔ Heavy fences or the walls of outbuildings are another place to plant climbers, and these supports require little work from you. A chain-link fence can be transformed from an eyesore to a wall of color with a handsome climbing rose or Virginia creeper. In winter, the leaves drop from deciduous plants, but the eyesore will still look better than without the vine.

✔ The classic structure for any vine is an arbor. The simplest of these may be a pair of posts with a timber or arch spanning the top. You train the vine to grow up the posts and over the arch. (See Figure 9-7 for an example.) You can use a series of these arches to make a shady outdoor tunnel or to cover an entire patio. Attach wire to the posts to help the young vine find its way to the top. (See Chapter 7 for more about arbors and trellises.)

Pruning for healthy vines

Pruning prevents vines from getting out of control, becoming too heavy, or growing into places that you don't want them. Prune heavily to keep the vine healthy and attractive.

✔ Winter is a traditional time for pruning, but you can prune in any season to keep a rampant vine in check.

✔ Prune flowering vines like wisteria immediately after the plants drop their blooms.

✔ The best time to do your major pruning of vigorous-growing fruiting plants, such as grapes and kiwi, is during their dormant season (winter).

Taking a peek at some favorite vines

You can choose from dozens of vines to adorn the sides of buildings or fences as well as ramble through your shrubs and trees. If your space is limited, look for kinds that offer more than one "pleasure," usually those with handsome foliage as well as beautiful flowers or delectable fruit. Some vines provide handsome bark on artistically twisting branches in winter, and others offer superb autumn color.

Figure 9-7:
Evergreen
jasmine is a
fragrant
cover for
this entry
arch.

Plant encyclopedias are a good place to start digging deeper into the world
of vines. You can also find a good selection of vines at botanical gardens and
quality nurseries. Meanwhile, here are a few of our favorites, arranged
alphabetically according to botanical name, but listing the common name
first. (For more on hardiness zones, see Chapter 12.)

✔ **Bougainvillea.** *Bougainvillea* species. Evergreen or partially deciduous.
Bougainvilleas are one of the most spectacular flowering vines. Stunning flowers in electric shades of purple, red, pink, orange, yellow, and
white cover the plant all summer and beyond. Leaves are an attractive
bright green. Plants are shrubby and must be tied to a sturdy trellis or
arbor and given room to grow. Plant in full sun or, in the hottest climates, partial shade. Plant carefully, being sure not to disturb the roots.
Needs only a little water after it's established. Can be grown in mild-
winter areas with light frosts (Zones 10 and 11) or protected areas in
Zone 9.

✔ **Clematis.** *Clematis* species. Mostly deciduous. A diverse family of eye-catching flowering vines, with hundreds of selections available. Large-flowered hybrids, with summer blooms up to 10 inches across in shades of white, pink, red, blue, and purple, are most popular. Delicate plants can twine more than 10 to 15 feet high. Plant where the roots are cool and shaded but where the top can grow into full sun. For example, set the plant at the base of a large shrub and let it ramble through to the sunny top. Or plant it anywhere and cover the roots with a thick mulch. Hardy to Zone 5.

✔ **Evergreen clematis.** *C. aramandi.* Bears masses of fragrant white flowers in early spring and has handsome, shiny, dark green leaves. It grows under similar conditions as other clematis but quickly reaches 20 feet high and is hardy to only Zone 8.

✔ **Creeping fig.** *Ficus pumila.* Evergreen. A vigorous, compact-foliage vine that tightly adheres to any surface it touches. Good-looking, small, heart-shaped leaves. Best grown on stone or masonry. Plant in sun or shade. Hardy to Zone 8.

✔ **English ivy.** *Hedera helix.* Evergreen. Fast-growing, tenacious, and adaptable, English ivy comes in many varieties differing in foliage size, shape, and color. The species has deep green, heart-shaped leaves and is very vigorous. Clings with small aerial rootlets and takes over open areas in a minute — you have to keep your eyes on this one! It will damage all but the hardest surfaces and climb over anything. 'Hahn's Self-Branching' is a small-leaved type with more restrained growth. 'Baltica', with leaves that are a mixture of white and green, is one of many varieties with colorful, variegated leaves. Plant in sun or shade. Generally hardy to Zone 5, although hardiness of some varieties varies.

✔ **Chinese jasmine.** *Jasminum polyanthum.* Evergreen. The wonderfully fragrant flowers of Chinese jasmine perfume the air for months in spring. The small blooms are borne in clusters, white on the face, pink on the back. The twining stems hold bright green, divided leaves and are fast growing to 20 feet high. Good choice to cover a fence, trellis, or arbor. Prefers partial shade. Hardy to Zone 8.

✔ **Virginia creeper and Boston ivy.** *Parthenocissus* species. Deciduous. Two vines grown for their dramatic red and gold autumn color. Virginia creeper, *P. quinquefolia,* has leaves divided into 5 leaflets. Boston ivy, *P. tricuspidata,* has glossy, three-lobed leaves. Both climb vigorously, clinging to any surface with their small adhesive discs. Plant in sun or shade. Hardy to Zone 4.

✔ **Climbing roses.** *Rosa* species. Many types of vigorous-growing roses can be used as vines, however, they need to be tied to sturdy supports like fences, trellises, arbors, or posts to remain upright. Favorite varieties include 'Altissimo' with single (just 5 petals) deep red flowers, 'Improved Blaze' with large clusters of red flowers, 'America' with fragrant coral pink blooms, and ' White Dawn' with white flowers. Height varies by variety –some are very vigorous. Prune annually to promote flowering and keep in bounds. Winter protection usually necessary in Zone 5 and colder areas. Plant in full sun. For more information, see *Roses For Dummies* by Lance Walheim and the Editors of the National Gardening Association.

✔ **Star jasmine.** *Trachelospermum jasminoides.* Evergreen. One of the most attractive and well-behaved vines for mild climates. Showy clusters of fragrant white flowers almost obscure the shiny, dark green foliage in late spring to summer. Twining stems reach up to 20 feet high — they're not invasive but need support. Great for climbing through lattice or on fences. Plant in full sun or light shade. Hardy to Zone 8.

✔ **Grapes.** *Vitis* species. Deciduous. The sprawling grapevine is one of the best choices for covering an arbor or trellis. Besides gnarled trunks, good-looking leaves, and autumn color, you also get edible fruit. Hardy from Zone 3 to Zone 9, depending on the type of grape.

✔ **Chinese wisteria.** *Wisteria sinensis.* Deciduous. Purely elegant — that's about the best way to describe one of the finest vines you can grow. Beautiful, large (often over 12 inches long), dangling clusters of fragrant purple blooms hang among bright green, divided leaves in spring. The twisting, twining shoots will keep growing almost indefinitely. As they mature, they take on a rigid "muscular" appearance. Casting just the right shade, wisteria is the perfect cover for a sturdy arbor or trellis. It also looks great on fences. Requires annual pruning to look its best and to bloom prolifically. Plant in full sun. Hardy to Zone 5.

Chapter 10

Using Plants for Color and Texture

. . . .

In This Chapter

▶ Using annuals, perennials, and bulbs in your landscape

▶ Growing plants in containers for a more beautiful landscape

▶ Planning an ornamental-edible landscape

. . . .

*B*rightly colored flowers and interesting foliage textures give a landscape vitality and personality. When landscape professionals talk about flowers, they're usually talking about annuals, perennials, and bulbs. These words refer to different types of plants, but the distinctions between them are not as clear-cut as you may like. *Annual* plants usually grow for one season and then die. *Perennials* live on year-to-year if they're grown in the proper zones (see Chapter 12). *Bulbs* arise from some type of swollen below-ground, rootlike structure that allows them to live on year to year in many areas, so technically they can be considered perennials. However, some plants that are technically perennials, including some bulbs, are usually grown as annuals. And some annuals, perennials, and bulbs aren't grown for their flowers, but for their foliage texture or color. But don't worry about all this — we clear everything up in this chapter and even help you grow these flower in containers, if you want to.

Also in this chapter, we take a look at plants for the ornamental edible landscape — plants that look good in most landscapes and also provide food. If you like fresh fruit and vegetables but don't want a yard that looks like a farm, edible landscaping is for you.

Annuals for Flowers and Foliage

Annuals are the workhorses of the flowering landscape — they provide the quickest and showiest color. If you want flower color, if you want your landscape to be bright, and if you want your landscape to look good *right now,* annuals are your answer.

What's an annual?

Technically, an *annual* is a plant that lives for one season and dies. Annual-flowering plants grow quickly, put on a spectacular flower show for several months, and then expire. When the plants die, they are usually removed and replaced. Annual plants come in all shapes and sizes, from low-growing alyssum (which rarely gets more than 6 inches high) to the tallest sunflower (which can be more than 10 feet high).

Our definition of *annual,* however, is a bit misleading for two reasons. First, some plants that are actually *perennials* (that is, the plants live on from year to year) are often used as annuals in climates where they can't survive year-round because of extreme heat or cold. Some flowering plants, such as geraniums and primroses, are long-lived in some climates, but because their bloom is so spectacular in a particular season, they are planted for that seasonal bloom and are then removed from the landscape when their bloom is finished.

Our definition of annual plants is also a bit misleading because two kinds of annuals exist: cool-season and warm-season annuals. The distinction between these two types is important because it determines when you plant annuals and when they bloom. The two following sections list some of the most reliably colorful annuals, divided into cool-season and warm-season types, and arranged alphabetically according to botanical name, but listing the common name first. For a bigger selection, see *Annuals For Dummies* by Bill Marken and the Editors of the National Gardening Association (IDG Books Worldwide, Inc.).

Annuals can be planted by sowing seed directly in the garden, by starting seeds indoors and moving small transplants (seedlings) outside later, or by purchasing small transplants at the nursery.

Cool dudes

Cool-season annuals (such as pansies, violas, and primroses) thrive in spring and autumn. Planted in late summer or early spring, these plants grow quickly and bloom while the weather is still on the cool side. When the days get longer and hotter, most cool-season annuals stop blooming. At that time, we advise taking them out of the garden, although they may live a while longer if you choose to leave them in.

In mild-winter climates, many cool-season annuals that are planted in late summer bloom throughout winter. In general, cool-season annuals can withstand mild frosts.

✔ **Snapdragon.** *Antirrhinum majus.* Plants with wonderfully colorful spikes of white, yellow, orange, red, purple, and multihued flowers. The common name comes from the hinged blossom, which opens and shuts like jaws when squeezed on the sides. Varieties range from 12 to 36 inches high. Plant them in full sun from transplants (already growing plants).

- **Flowering cabbage or kale.** *Brassica* species. These vegetable relatives look very much alike. They are grown for their brightly colored, ruffled or frilly foliage arranged in a head like a cabbage. The foliage is usually green with purple, pink, or white markings. Plants grow 12 to 18 inches high. Plant in full sun from seed or use transplants.

- **Pot marigold.** *Calendula officinalis.* Easy-to-grow annuals with yellow or orange (or sometimes white) daisylike flowers. Pot marigold is a nice cut flower. The compact plants reach 12 to 30 inches high. Plant in full sun from seed or use transplants.

- **Dusty miller.** *Centaurea cineraria.* One of the most valuable gray-foliaged plants, which is useful for highlighting other colors. Dusty miller makes other plants look brighter. It is perennial in mild climates and produces yellow flowers in summer, starting when the plant is in its second season. The plants have finely cut leaves and a mounding habit, and they grow about 18 inches high. Plant in full sun from transplants. *Senecio cineraria* is another gray-foliaged plant that is often sold as dusty miller. *Senecio cineraria* grows slightly taller (to about $2^1/_2$ feet high) than *Centaurea cineraria.*

- **Annual chrysanthemum.** *Chrysanthemum paludosum.* A glorious miniature bloomer from seeds or transplants. Small white-and-yellow daisylike flowers cover the plant. Annual chrysanthemums grow best in full sun and reach 12 to 18 inches high.

- **Larkspur.** *Consolida ambigua.* Wonderfully delicate spikes of spurred flowers in pastel shades of white, blue, pink, and purple. Larkspurs grow 12 to 48 inches high, depending on variety. The plants are easy to grow from seed and do best in light or partial shade.

- **Chinese forget-me-not.** *Cynoglossum amabile.* Wispy clouds of tiny, deep blue, pink, or white flowers; a classic for shady landscapes. Chinese forget-me-nots grow 12 to 18 inches high. The plants are easy to grow from seed and *reseed* (grow the next year from seeds spread by their flowers) readily. *Myositis sylvatica,* the common forget-me-not, is similar and is equally good in shady landscapes.

- **California poppy.** *Eschscholzia californica.* The much-loved California wildflower is easily grown from seed and reseeds readily. California poppies bloom mostly in shades of yellow and orange (or sometimes white). The plants reach 10 to 24 inches high. Grow in full sun.

- **Sweet peas.** *Lathyrus odoratus.* Much-loved annual vining plant with intensely fragrant blooms. Sweet peas come in single colors and multicolors — almost every hue except true blue and green. Sweet peas make a wonderful cut flower. Most varieties need a fence or trellis for support (see Chapter 5 for more on fences and Chapter 7 for the scoop on trellises), but bushier, low-growing types, such as 'Little Sweetheart,' don't need supports. Plant in full sun from seed.

- **Sweet alyssum.** *Lobularia maritima.* Ground-hugging annual (usually under 6 inches high) that covers itself with tiny, bright white, purple, or pink blooms. Alyssum flowers best in cooler weather and is quite hardy, but it often blooms into summer, too. Alyssum is one of the finest edging and container plants. Easy to grow from seed and reseeds readily. Plant in full sun.

- **Stock.** *Matthiola incana.* One of the most deliciously-fragrant annuals, with intense, spicy scents. Flower spikes reach 12 to 30 inches high (depending on variety) in shades of white, pink, purple, and red. Stocks are best started from transplants. Grow in full sun.

- **Geranium.** *Pelargonium* species. Old-time favorites that are often used as perennials in mild-winter climates. Geraniums have huge clusters of white, pink, red, purple, orange, or bi-colored flowers in spring and summer. The plants grow from 8 to 36 inches high, and some have variegated leaves. Start from transplants and grow in full sun to light shade.

- **Primroses.** *Primula* species. Perennials in many mild climates, but usually grown as annuals. Primroses have brightly colored flower clusters atop straight stems that seldom reach more than 12 to 18 inches high. Many colors of primroses are available to choose from. Fairy primrose, *P. malacoides,* produces airy clusters of white, pink, and lavender blooms above hairy leaves. English primrose, *P. polyantha,* has brighter, often multicolored flowers above deep green, crinkled leaves. Plant in full to partial shade and start with transplants.

- **Nasturtium.** *Tropaeolum majus.* Sprawling annual with neat round leaves and bright orange, yellow, pink, cream, or red flowers. Nasturtiums grow about 15 inches high on the ground, but the plants can climb up to 10 feet when given support from a trellis or fence. Nasturtiums are easy to grow from seed; plant in full sun or light shade.

- **Pansies** and **violas.** *Viola* species. Flowers often resemble colorful little faces. Imagining prettier flowers than pansies and violas is difficult. These annuals bloom in almost every single color and multicolor except green. Pansies have slightly larger (but fewer) blooms than violas. Both feature neat, compact plants that seldom grow more than 8 inches tall. Pansies and violas can be grown from seed, but they are usually started from transplants. Plant in full sun or light shade.

When it's hot, they're hot

Warm-season annuals (such as zinnias, marigolds, and petunias) prefer the hot months of summer. Planted after the last frost in spring, these plants grow quickly and bloom when the weather is hot. Warm-season annuals usually continue to flower until the first frost in autumn, but because they bloom poorly in cool weather, we recommend pulling them out before a frost does them in.

Some overlap in bloom time between cool- and warm-season annuals exists, so if you orchestrate your planting just right, you may never be without blooms.

- ✔ **Bedding begonia.** *Begonia semperflorens.* Versatile annuals that are most useful in shady landscapes (although some types can take more sun). The flowers of bedding begonias come in shades of white, pink, and red. Red-flowering plants, which can take more sun, have bronzy-red leaves. Most varieties grow about 12 inches high. Bedding begonias are best started from transplants.

- ✔ **Madagascar periwinkle.** *Catharanthus roseus.* (Also known as annual vinca.) These cheery plants are workhorses in the summer landscape. Compact with deep green leaves, Madagascar periwinkles produce an abundance of white, pink, red, or lavender blooms that often have a pink or white spot in the center. They grow 12 to 20 inches high and are best in full sun (but can take some shade). These plants can be grown from seed, but are more easily grown from transplants.

- ✔ **Coleus.** *Coleus hybridus.* Grown for its intensely colored foliage, which comes in a variety of color combinations and different leaf shapes. Coleus grows best in the shade and is best planted from transplants. It can also be grown as a houseplant. Pinch off the flowers to keep the plant compact.

- ✔ **Cosmos.** *Cosmos bipinnatus.* Bright green, airy plants with a brilliant bloom of white, pink, lavender, purple, or bi-colored daisylike flowers. Most types grow tall (upwards of 5 feet high), but dwarf varieties stay more compact. Easy to grow from seed or transplants, and the plants reseed. Plant in full sun.

- ✔ **Sunflower.** *Helianthus annuus.* Few annuals make a statement the way that sunflowers do. Most sunflowers reach 8 to 10 feet high and are topped with huge, sunny, yellow blooms. But sunflowers also come in small-flowered forms in shades of red, orange, and white. Some dwarf varieties, such as 'Sunspot,' stay under 2 feet tall. All sunflowers have edible seeds. Plant from seed in full sun.

- ✔ **Impatiens.** *Impatiens wallerana.* The stars of the shady landscape and one of the most popular annual flowers. The 1- to 2-inch-wide blooms come in bright shades of white, red, pink, and lavender. Bi-colored varieties of impatiens are also available. Impatiens plants have dark green or bi-colored leaves and grow 12 to 30 inches high. Grow from transplants.

- ✔ **Lobelia.** *Lobelia erinus.* Low-growing (and often spreading) plants covered in deep to light blue blooms. Few blues are as bright as those of lobelia, but white- and pink-flowering forms are also available. All lobelias reach about 4 to 6 inches high. They can be grown from seed but are more easily started from transplants. Plant in full sun to light shade.

- **Flowering tobacco.** *Nicotiana alata.* Small, tubular, often-fragrant blooms in shades of white, pink, red, and purple. Flowering tobacco plants grow 12 to 48 inches high, depending on variety. Plant flowering tobacco in full sun or light shade. Can be grown from seed or from transplants.

- **Petunia.** *Petunia hybrida.* Much-loved annuals with single and double, usually trumpet-shaped flowers in a myriad of single and bi-colored shades. Petunias are compact plants that range from 10 to 24 inches high. Start from transplants and plant in full sun.

- **Sage.** *Salvia* species. Tall spikes of bright white, red, blue, or purple flowers atop compact, sun-loving plants. Some types of sage are perennials in mild-winter climates. Sages range in height from 10 to 36 inches. Plant in full sun and use transplants.

- **Marigold.** *Tagetes* species. Marigolds are one of the most popular summer annuals, with blooms in sunny shades of yellow, orange, and red. Many varieties are available. Blossoms can be big or small, as can the plants. Plant in full sun. Easy to grow from seed or transplants.

- **Verbena.** *Verbena hybrida.* Brightly colored clusters of white, pink, red, purple, or blue flowers on low-growing, spreading plants. Verbenas grow 6 to 12 inches high. Plant in full sun. Easiest to start from transplants.

- **Zinnia.** *Zinnia elegans.* A cut-flower lover's dream. Zinnias come in a huge range of flower colors (except blue), flower shapes and sizes, and plant heights. Small types, such as 'Thumbelina,' stay under 12 inches high. 'State Fair' grows up to 5 feet high and has long stems for cutting. Plant in full sun. Easy to grow from seed or transplants

Planting annuals for a riot of color

When planting annuals, you have three choices in what you start with:

- Some annuals can be planted from seed that is sown directly where the plants are to grow and bloom.

- Other annuals can be started from seed indoors and transplanted to the landscape later.

   For more information on starting annuals from seed, pick up a copy of *Annuals For Dummies* by Bill Marken and the editors of the National Gardening Association (IDG Books Worldwide, Inc.).

- *Transplants* of varying sizes (from small plants in six-packs to larger ones in gallon cans) can be purchased at nurseries and planted in your landscape.

   Transplanted annuals at the nursery can give you instant color because they are already in bloom. And if your landscape is full of young plants, some instant bloom really helps make things look better. You can wake up in the morning to a dull, immature green landscape and turn it into a riot of color before noon by simply visiting your nursery or garden center. Besides, with all the other things you may have to deal with when improving your landscape, you probably won't have time to spend six to eight weeks doting over germinating seeds.

Before planting, make sure that you prepare the soil properly (see Chapter 12), and make sure that you match the requirements of the plant — sun or shade — with the conditions at the planting site.

To transplant annual seedlings, do the following:

1. **Use a hoe, spade, or trowel to make a small hole for each transplant. (See Figure 10-1.)**

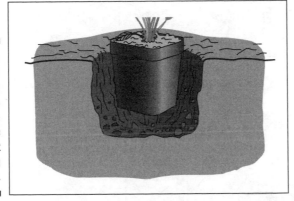

Figure 10-1: Dig a hole large enough to fit the plant's roots without crowding them.

2. **Unpot the seedling by turning the pot upside down, cupping the seedling with your hand, as shown in Figure 10-2.**

   If you're planting from six packs (small plastic trays that contain six seedlings), use your thumb to press on the bottom of individual cells to remove the seedling.

   Be sure to keep the roots and soil intact. If the seedling doesn't readily come out, gently rap the edge of the pot or gently press on the bottom of each cell with your hand — don't yank the plant out by its stem.

3. **Gently spread out matted roots (as shown in Figure 10-3) and check their condition.**

   For larger plants, you can gently cut the bottom of the rootball with a knife and *butterfly* (spread) the rootball apart.

   If the roots are wound around the outside of the pot, work them loose with your fingers so they can grow out into the soil. Unwind larger roots and break smaller ones until their ends are all pointing outwards.

Figure 10-2:
Gently turn
the pot
upside
down to
remove
seedling.

Figure 10-3:
Breaking a
few roots
won't hurt
the plant, as
long as the
mass of
roots
remains
intact.

4. **Fill each planting hole with water.**

   You may also want to add a diluted liquid fertilizer to help your plants get off to a fast start.

5. **Put each prepared seedling in the hole that you made.**

   Set the seedling in the hole so the top of the rootball is at the same level it was in the pot. (See Figure 10-4.)

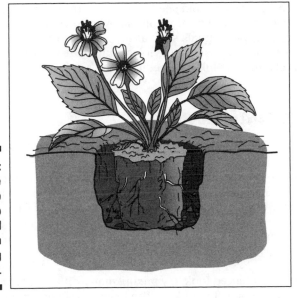

Figure 10-4:
Set the seedling so that the top of rootball is level with surrounding soil.

6. **With your hands, firm the soil around the roots, as shown in Figure 10-5.**

   Try to make a small basin sloping toward the plant to hold water.

Figure 10-5:
Firm the soil around the plant just enough so that it can remain upright.

After planting, water thoroughly. Keep the bed moist until the seedlings are established and begin to grow strongly. In extremely hot, dry weather, provide temporary shade for the transplants with paper tents (made like party hats) or wood shingles pushed into the ground on the south or west side of the plant.

Many plants that bloom easily from seed can reseed themselves and come back year after year on their own. Most annual wildflowers reproduce themselves this way. Leave annuals such as alyssum, calendula, cosmos, forget-me-nots, marigolds, pansies and violas, sunflowers, vinca, and zinnias to go to seed for a landscape full of "freebies" next season.

Getting annuals together

The diversity among flowering annuals makes them very useful in the landscape. For the brightest blast of color, we like to plant annuals in large groups. Low-growing types usually work best for this type of planting, and you can go with just one color or mix a number of colors. But the important thing is to plant many annuals and plant them close together (usually 6 to 12 inches apart). Space the transplants evenly in staggered rows (like the ground covers discussed in Chapter 11) — the plants will grow quickly and fill in the spaces to give you a solid bed of bright color.

If you prefer a less-regimented look, try mixing many different types of annuals together in one bed. Try to keep the lower-growing plants in front and the taller ones in back, but really, no hard rules about plant placement exist. We also like to keep to a particular color scheme, such as mixing only complementary colors, but you can go with whatever color scheme you like.

Low-growing annuals, such as alyssum and lobelia, are useful as edgings. You can plant these low-growers along walkways or in front of other annuals, in front of perennials, or even in front of flowering shrubs, such as roses.

Treating them with care

Some annuals have unique habits that call for special treatment, but these plants also present special opportunities. Most sweet peas are climbing vines that need some kind of a support, such as a trellis. (See Chapter 7 for information about trellises.) Place the trellis right by a window so that the sweet peas' sweet fragrance can waft through the house. Tall sunflowers are spectacular focal points for any spot where you have room for them, but they also make a beautiful tall "wall" around a vegetable garden or along a back fence.

Really, the best way to use annuals is to put them wherever you have room. Just one or two plants can turn a blank spot into a colorful focal point. Simply scattering some seed in open areas, where newly planted ground covers have yet to fill in, for example, can result in a colorful mulch that changes with the seasons. For the longest season of color, pick off faded blossoms to encourage new bloom.

Perennials for Permanent Impact

Perennial plants, grown for their flowers, their foliage, or both, are with us like the seasons — perennials return with their beauty, year after year. Compared with annuals (which have to be replanted every year), *perennials* are left in place to grow, get bigger, look better, and bloom more, season after season.

The plants known as perennials are a diverse group. Perennials include some of the best-loved flowering plants, such as daisies, mums, and carnations. Spectacular foliage plants, such as ornamental grasses, hostas, and lamb's ears, are also perennials.

Perennials can be planted in containers (see "The Containerized Landscape" section, later in this chapter) or worked in among trees and shrubs for seasonal color. Many perennials also make excellent ground covers (see Chapter 11).

Creating a perennial border

The classic use of perennials is to combine many of them in a large planting bed, known as a *perennial border*. A well-designed perennial border has something in bloom throughout the growing season. It not only has a well-thought-out color scheme, but also relies on plant texture for visual interest. Designing a spectacular planting can take years of experience, but even beginning landscapers can create a workable, pleasing border, adding to it over the years as their knowledge increases.

For most landscapers, a perennial border is constantly evolving, which is part of the fun of creating it. If certain plants don't work, you can replace them with something else. If the border has some downtime when nothing is in bloom, add some flowering annuals to fill in the gap, or plant some flowering shrubs, such as floribunda roses, which bloom over a long season.

Many landscaping books give specific plans for perennial borders and some nurseries even sell plants or seeds that fit predesigned borders. Although the use of these plans and designs may be a good way to start a perennial border, blooming times and growing conditions vary so much from place to place that you may end up making changes to the border. In any case, you want to make changes to such predesigned plans because designing your own, unique landscape is part of the fun.

Even though individual experience is the best teacher, here are some things that we find useful in designing a perennial border.

- ✔ **Start with a plan and keep records.** Draw your bed out on paper, making sure to give plants the room that they need to grow. Work with a simple color scheme, such as three of your favorite colors, and plant only things that bloom in those shades.

- ✔ **Plan for a succession of bloom.** Think seasonally, aiming for something always in bloom. Keep records of blooming times so that you know where there are gaps to be filled the next planting season. And don't forget winter. Even in cold climates, you can use shrubs that have colorful berries or attractive bark.

- ✔ **Prepare the soil carefully.** You won't be remaking this bed every year. Dig deep, add organic material, and, most important, eliminate weeds.

- ✔ **Plant in groups.** One plant, alone, gets lost in the masses. We find that grouping plants in odd numbers — 3s, 5s, and 7s — looks the most natural.

- ✔ **Don't forget the foliage.** Use plants with dramatic foliage to set off the flowers. Ornamental grasses or bold-textured shrubs make excellent focal points.

- ✔ **Use grays and whites.** Gray foliaged plants (such as lamb's ears) and plants with white flowers highlight other colors and can be used to tie everything together. These plants also reflect light and look great on those nights when the moon is bright.

- ✔ **Consider the background.** A dark green background enriches the color of most flowers. Consider planting a hedge (possibly of flowering shrubs or evergreens) at the back of the border.

Our favorite high-performance perennials

Here are our favorite perennials, arranged alphabetically according to botanical name, but listing the common name first. A few others, which are often grown as annuals, are described in the "Annuals for Flowers and Foliage" section, earlier in this chapter. Some perennials are technically *biennials,* meaning that they mostly grow foliage the first year, bloom the second year, and then die. For more information on these and other perennials, see *Perennials For Dummies* by Marcia Tatroe and the Editors of the National Gardening Association (IDG Books Worldwide, Inc.).

- ✔ **Yarrow.** *Achillea* species. A useful group of easy-care, summer-blooming perennials with ferny gray foliage and tight, upright clusters of yellow, red, or white blooms. Yarrows range in height from low-growing ground covers to tall plants (up to 5 feet high). One favorite is *A. filipendulina* 'Moonshine', with bright yellow flower clusters atop 2-foot stems. Plant in full sun. Where summer rain is common, some types can become invasive and weedy. Most are hardy to Zone 3.

- **Artemisia.** _Artemisia_ species. Very useful group of mounding, silver-foliaged plants that are great for highlighting other plants. One of the best is the hybrid 'Powis Castle' with lacy, silver foliage on a mounding plant about 3 feet high. Plant in full sun. Hardy to Zone 5.

- **Columbine.** _Aquilegia_ species. Widely adapted perennials with fernlike foliage and beautiful, spurred flowers. Columbine blooms in spring and early summer in many single colors and multicolors. Many natives are included in wildflower seed mixes. The plants range in height from about 18 inches to 3 feet. Columbine is easy to grow from seed and will reseed. Plant in full sun to light shade. Hardy to Zone 3.

- **Asters.** _Aster_ species. Colorful, late-blooming perennials with daisylike flowers, mostly in shades of blue, purple, red, pink, and white with yellow centers. Asters usually bloom in the late summer to autumn. Some begin flowering in early summer or late spring. _A. frikartii_ produces blue flowers almost year-round in mild-winter climates. Asters grow about 2 feet high. Plant in full sun and divide every two years. Hardy to Zone 4.

- **Basket-of-gold.** _Aurinia saxatilis._ Brilliant gold blooms cover the gray foliage in spring. Basket-of-gold grows about 12 to 15 inches high and spreads. The plant also withstands drought. Plant in full sun. Use in foreground. Hardy to Zone 3.

- **Bellflower.** _Campanula_ species. Much-loved family of mostly summer blooming perennials with bell-shaped flowers in shades of blue, purple, or white. There are many species, varying from low-growing spreading plants to taller types, some of which are 6 feet high. Flower size and shape also vary.

  Favorites include the Serbian bellflower, _C. poscharskyana_ (a low, mounding plant, 4 to 8 inches high, with blue flowers). Another favorite is the peach-leaf bellflower, _C. persicifolia,_ which is also spreading, can reach up to 3 feet high, and has blue or white blooms. Campanulas grow best in light shade but can take sun in cool-summer climates. Hardy to Zone 3.

- **Chrysanthemum.** _Chrysanthemum_ species. A very diverse, useful group of perennials. This group includes the familiar mums, so useful for autumn bloom, and types such as _C. coccineum_ (the painted daisy), _C. frutescens_ (the marguerites), and _C. superbum_ (the Shasta daisies), all of which are well known as daisies. All chrysanthemums are wonderful cut flowers. Although chrysanthemum plants vary in height, flower color, bloom season, and hardiness, one exists for almost every landscape and situation. Most grow best in full sun.

- **Coreopsis.** _Coreopsis_ species. Easy-to-grow plants known for their sunny yellow, daisylike flowers borne from spring through summer. _C. grandiflora_ is one of the most common. This variety grows about 3 feet high and has single or double flowers. Plant in full sun. Hardy to Zone 5.

✔ **Dianthus.** *Dianthus* species. Lovely family of usually fragrant, spring- and summer-flowering plants that includes carnations, *D. caryophyllus.* Many varieties of dianthus can be grown as annuals. Favorites include sweet William, *D. barbatus* (which grows 6 to 18 inches high and has tight clusters of white, pink, red, purple, and bi-colored flowers), and cottage pinks, hybrids that have very fragrant, frilly, rose, pink, white, or bi-colored flowers on stems reaching about 18 inches high above a tight mat of foliage. Plant in full sun or light shade (in hot-summer areas). Hardy to Zone 3.

✔ **Purple coneflower.** *Echinacea purpurea.* Tall, purple or white, daisylike flowers top this fine, long-lasting perennial. Purple coneflower reaches 3 to 5 feet high and blooms in summer. Plant in full sun. Hardy to Zone 3.

✔ **Blanketflower.** *Gaillardia grandiflora.* These sunny-colored, daisylike flowers are a combination of red and yellow or are straight red or yellow. Blooms heavily in summer and grows 2 to 3 feet high. Plant in full sun. Hardy to Zone 2.

✔ **Blood-red geranium.** *Geranium sanguineum.* One of the best of the species *geraniums,* which is a large group of fine perennials. Dainty-looking, purplish-pink, red, and white flowers appear in abundance above good-looking, deeply cut leaves that turn red in the autumn. Blood-red geranium blooms spring to summer and mounds to about 18 inches high. Many varieties are available. Plant in full sun to light shade. Hardy to Zone 4.

✔ **Daylilies.** *Hemerocallis* species. A dependable group of summer-flowering perennials with stalks of large, trumpet-shaped flowers in single and bi-colored shades of yellow, orange, pink, red, and violet. Some daylilies are fragrant. Lilies have grassy foliage that reaches 12 to 24 inches high. Plant in full sun. Hardy to Zone 3.

✔ **Coral bells.** *Heuchera sanguinea.* Wiry spikes of tiny, bell-shaped, white, pink, or red flowers are held 12 to 24 inches above lovely, lobed leaves. Coral bells bloom in the spring. Plant in light shade, although they can take sun in cool-summer climates. Hardy to Zone 3.

✔ **Plantain lily.** *Hosta* species. Useful foliage plants that make a nice contrast to other shade-loving flowers. Plantain lily leaves are usually heart-shaped and are often crinkled or variegated. Flower spikes appear in summer. Plants and leaves range from small to large. One favorite is the blue-leaf plantain lily, *H. sieboldiana,* which has large (10 to 15 inches), crinkled, blue-green foliage and pale purple flowers; it grows 3 feet high. Hardy to Zone 3.

✔ **Candytuft.** *Iberis sempervirens.* In early spring, snow-white flowers completely cover this dainty, compact plant. Candytuft grows from 4 to 12 inches high and makes a wonderful edging. Plant in full sun. Hardy to Zone 4.

- **Ornamental grasses**. The term *ornamental grasses* designates a large group of wonderful plants grown for their grassy foliage and feathery, plumelike flowers. Ornamental grasses make stunning focal points among other blooming plants. The dried flowers often look good well into winter. Some favorites include purple fountain grass, *Pennisetum setaceum* 'Rubrum', with purplish-red leaves and plumes that reach over 6 feet high; the huge (often more than 8 feet) variegated eulalia grass, *Miscanthus sinesis* 'Zebrinus', with yellow-striped leaves and broomlike plumes; and blue oat grass, *Helictotrichon sempervirens,* with gray-blue foliage 2 to 3 feet high. Growing conditions and hardiness vary.

  Beware! Some ornamental grasses get very large and can become invasive.

- **Garden penstemon.** *Penstemon gloxinioides.* Spring-blooming, mounding plants that grow 2 to 4 feet high. Garden penstemon features spikes of tubular flowers in many single and bi-colored shades of white, pink, red, and purple. Plant in full sun. Hardy to Zone 8. Check nursery catalogs for other species that are hardier.

- **Summer phlox.** *Phlox paniculata.* Large clusters of small white, pink, red, salmon, and purple flowers bloom in mid- to late summer. The plants grow 2 to 4 feet high. Plant in full sun. Hardy to Zone 3.

- **Gloriosa daisy; Black-eyed Susan.** *Rudbeckia hirta.* Free-blooming, easy-to-grow perennial or biennial. These plants have large yellow, orange, maroon, or mahogany daisylike flowers with dark, domelike centers. Some kinds are bi-colored. These plants bloom from summer to autumn. The plants grow 2 to 4 feet high, are easily grown from seed, and reseed themselves heavily. The plants can be invasive. Plant in full sun. Hardy to Zone 4.

- **Salvias.** *Salvia* species. So many excellent perennial salvias are available that we could write a book about them alone. Most are best adapted to dry-summer areas with mild winters. Many are shrublike; others are perennials that are usually grown as annuals.

  Still others are valuable herbs. Favorite flowering types include *S. superba,* with violet-blue summer flowers reaching 2 to 3 feet high, and *S. azurea grandiflora,* with 4- to 5-foot-high, rich gentian-blue flowers in late summer. Plant in full sun. Hardy to Zone 6.

- **Lamb's ears.** *Stachys byzantina.* A lovely, low-growing foliage plant with soft, fuzzy, silver-gray leaves. It grows 6 to 12 inches high and has purplish-white flowers in summer. Lamb's ears is a fabulous edging plant for flowering perennials. Plant in full sun. Hardy to Zone 4.

Planting perennials

Before planting, prepare the soil site as described in Chapter 12.

Perennial plants are usually sold in six-packs, 4-inch pots, or 1-gallon pots. Many mail-order suppliers ship a wide selection of plants bare-root. See Chapter 8 for information on planting from pots, the "Annuals for Flowers and Foliage" section in this chapter for directions on planting from six-packs, and Chapter 9 for how to plant bare-root.

Container-grown perennials can be planted any time that you can work the ground. However, the best time to plant such perennials is in the autumn or early spring because the plants have time to get established before hot weather begins.

Caring for perennials

Many perennials benefit from being cut back at various times during their growth cycles.

- ✔ To stimulate branching on lower stems and make the plant bushier, for example, pinch out new growth at the top of the plant.

- ✔ *Deadheading* is the process of pinching or cutting off faded flowers while the plant is in bloom. Deadheading forces the plant to spend its energy on developing more flowers instead of setting seed. The result of deadheading is usually a longer bloom cycle.

- ✔ Some perennials, such as coreopsis and gaillardia, rebloom if cut back by about one-third after the initial bloom cycle.

- ✔ Most perennials (some shrubbier types are an exception) should be cut back to a height of 6 to 8 inches at the end of the growing season. This cutting back rejuvenates the plant and results in a better bloom next season. Where the ground freezes in winter, mulch plants with at least 6 inches of organic matter.

- ✔ Taller perennials, such as delphiniums, and bushy types, such as peonies, may need to be staked to prevent the flowers from falling over.

If older plants become overcrowded or bloom poorly, they can be rejuvenated by *dividing*. In fact, division is a good way to increase plant numbers. (Check out *Perennials For Dummies* by Marcie Tatroe and the Editors of the National Gardening Association (IDG Books Worldwide, Inc.) for more on plant division.)

Boisterous Bulbs

For many people, especially people who have never had much luck growing plants, bulbs are a dream come true. Think of bulbs as flowering power-houses: plants that have packed most of what they need for a season's worth of growth into some type of below-ground storage device — the bulb. Plant a bulb at the right time of year and at the proper depth, and you're almost guaranteed a spectacular bloom. (See Figure 10-6.)

What are bulbs?

When you think of bulbs, you probably think of daffodil or tulip bulbs — brownish things that look something like an onion — which are indeed bulbs. But the term *bulb* as used in landscaping refers to a great number of different plant bulbs. Besides the true bulbs, such as tulip bulbs, there are corms, rhizomes, tubers, and tuberous roots and each one of these looks different — underground stems surrounded by modified fleshy leaves, swollen underground stem bases, thickened and branching storage stems, or swollen roots.

But enough of that. All you really need to know is which bulbs to plant, where and how deeply to plant them, and — most important of all — which end is up!

Figure 10-6: Colorful spring bulbs, like tulips, bloom year after year with little care.

You can separate bulbs into two groups. One group (including the daffodils, some tulips, and grape hyacinths) is called *naturalizers*. Bulbs that naturalize are left in the ground, year after year. Over time, the bulbs increase, and their bloom gets better and better. Some bulbs, such as tulips, need more cold than others to naturalize. In climates where the ground freezes, the bulbs bloom on forever. If the ground rarely freezes, which is the case in many mild-winter climates — Zones 9 to 11 (see Chapter 12 for information about zones) — the blooms get smaller each year and eventually stop coming altogether.

A second group of bulbs (which includes begonias and dahlias) has to be replanted every year. Bulbs may need to be replanted for many reasons: some bulbs may not be hardy enough to survive over winter in your climate, while other bulbs may rot in wet soils. Still other bulbs may not get enough chilling to rebloom year after year — in a sense, you can call these *annual bulbs*, because, like annuals flowers, they must be planted every year.

Although some bulbs have to be replanted every year, you don't have to buy new bulbs every year. After they finish blooming, you can dig up most bulbs, store them, and replant them at the appropriate time to bloom again next season.

Discovering some great bulbs

Here are a few of our favorite kinds of bulbs, arranged alphabetically according to botanical name, but listing the common name first. For more information, consult *Flowering Bulbs For Dummies* by Judy Glattstein and the Editors of the National Gardening Association (IDG Books Worldwide, Inc.). Perhaps even better, collect bulb catalogs — one of the easiest ways to do this is to subscribe to a landscaping magazine, such as *National Gardening,* which contains coupons for many landscaping catalogs, including some bulb specialists.

- **Lily-of-the-Nile.** *Agapanthus orientalis.* Very dependable, summer-blooming bulb with tall stalks of bright blue flowers reaching from 4 to 5 feet high. Lily-of-the-Nile's straplike foliage is evergreen in mild climates. Dig and store the bulbs over winter in cold-winter climates. Lily-of-the-Nile gets by on little water. 'Peter Pan' is a compact variety, reaching only 8 to 12 inches high, so it's excellent in containers. Varieties with white flowers are also available. Plant in full sun or light shade. Hardy to Zone 9.

- **Begonias.** *Begonia tuberhybrida.* One of the most beautiful of all flowering plants. Many varieties of begonias are available to choose from. Some varieties have large flowers (up to 8 inches across). Other flowers are smaller and are borne on "weeping" or drooping plants. Few begonias grow more than 12 to 18 inches high. Begonias bloom in summer, and their flowers come in almost all shades except blue and green. The foliage is good-looking and succulent. They make ideal container plants and grow best in light shade. Hardy to Zone 9. Dig up and store the bulbs over winter in all regions.

✔ **Fancy-leaved caladium.** *Caladium hortulanum.* Brightly colored foliage plant for shady situations. Caladiums feature large leaves, which are tropical looking and painted with shades of green, white, pink, and red. The plants grow from 12 to 24 inches high and are great in containers. Hardy only in Zone 10 but can be dug up and stored or grown as an annual in any zone.

✔ **Canna.** *Canna* species. Upright, summer-blooming plant with showy flowers in shades of yellow, orange, salmon, pink, and red. Some have bi-colored flowers. The plants have large, tropical-looking leaves. Some cannas grow more than 5 feet high, but many are lower growing. Plant in full sun. South of Zone 7, cannas can be naturalized with little care. Elsewhere, dig and store them over winter.

✔ **Lily-of-the-valley.** *Convallaria majalis.* Small, dainty clusters of very fragrant, bell-shaped flowers. Blooms in summer. The plants grow from 6 to 8 inches high. Plant in light shade and acid soil and keep the soil moist. Naturalizes in cold-winter climates and is hardy to Zone 4.

✔ **Dahlia.** *Dahlia* species. A huge, diverse family of hybrids with an incredible array of flower form and sizes. Some dahlia blossoms are tiny balls; other blossoms are huge, star-shaped blooms more than 8 inches wide. Summer-blooming in almost every color but blue, dahlia plants range in size from 6 inches high to more than 5 feet high. Plant in full sun and water regularly. Hardy to Zone 9, but they grow in any zone as long as tubers are dug and stored over winter. Smaller varieties are often grown as annuals.

✔ **Freesia.** *Freesia* species. Dependable spring-blooming bulb that naturalizes freely in mild climates. Freesia's arching clusters of trumpetlike flowers come in almost every color. Some freesias are fragrant. The plants grow to about 18 inches high. Plant in full sun or light shade. Hardy to Zone 9, but the bulbs must be dug or used as an annual elsewhere.

✔ **Snowdrops.** *Galanthus* species. Lovely, drooping, bell-shaped white flowers. Bloom in very early spring and naturalize nicely in cold-winter climates. Snowdrops grow from 8 to 12 inches high. Plant in full sun or partial shade (snowdrops are great under trees). Hardy to at least Zone 4. The giant snowdrop, *G. elwesii,* naturalizes farther south, into Zone 9.

✔ **Gladiolus.** *Gladiolus* species. Much-loved cut flower with tall spikes of trumpetlike flowers. Comes in almost all shades except blue. Most bloom in summer and grow to 4 to 5 feet high, but smaller types are available. Plant in full sun. Hardy to Zone 9, but dig the bulbs or use the plants as annuals elsewhere. Baby gladiolus, *G. colvillei,* is lower growing and hardier. Baby gladiolus bulbs can be left in the ground and can naturalize in most areas.

✔ **Common hyacinth.** *Hyacinthus orientalis.* Wonderfully fragrant spikes of white, red, pink, yellow, blue, or purple bell-shaped flowers in early spring. Common hyacinth grows to about 12 inches high. Hyacinths look best when planted in masses or containers. Plant in full sun or light shade. Hyacinths do best in cold-winter climates, but they need chilling elsewhere. Hardy to Zone 4.

✔ **Iris.** *Iris* species. A huge group of elegant, spring-to-summer–blooming plants. You can choose from many different types. Favorites include the bearded iris, which has huge blooms and gracefully arching petals. Irises come in many shades and reach from 2 to 4 feet high. The plants spread freely. Plant in full sun or light shade. Most need to have water regularly. Hardiness varies, but most survive into at least Zone 5, some to Zone 3.

✔ **Snowflake.** *Leucojum* species. Very similar to snowdrops (see "Snow-drops" earlier in this list) with white, drooping flowers in early spring. Snowflake plants naturalize in cold-winter climates. Plant in full sun or light shade. Hardy to Zone 5.

✔ **Lilies.** *Lilium* species. Large family of beautiful, mostly summer-blooming bulbs. Most have large, trumpet-shaped flowers, but a great diversity of lilies exists. Colors come in almost every shade but blue, and plant heights range from 2 to 6 feet. Plant lilies so that the roots are in the shade but the tops can reach for the sun. Water regularly during summer. Most are hardy to Zone 4.

✔ **Grape hyacinth.** *Muscari* species. Wonderful little bulbs that form carpets of fragrant, mostly blue, spring flowers and grassy foliage. Grape hyacinths grow from 6 to 12 inches high and naturalize freely. Plant in full sun or light shade. Hardy to Zone 3.

✔ **Daffodil and narcissus.** *Narcissus* species. Carefree bloomers that flower spring after spring, even in mild climates. If you plant only one type of bulb, this should be it. Narcissus plants generally bear clusters of small, often fragrant, flowers. Daffodils have larger blooms. You can choose from many daffodil and narcissus varieties (mostly in white and yellow shades). 'King Alfred' is one of the all-time favorite, large-flowered, yellow trumpet types. Plant daffodils and narcissus in full sun to light shade. Hardy to Zone 4.

✔ **Persian buttercup.** *Ranunculus asiaticus.* Bright-colored, spring-to-summer flowers in shades of white, yellow, orange, red, and purple. Some Persian buttercups are multicolored. The plants grow from 12 to 24 inches high and have deeply cut leaves. Plant in full sun or light shade. Hardy to Zone 8 but dig and store the bulbs in autumn.

✔ **Tulips.** *Tulipa* species. Much-loved, spring-blooming bulbs with the familiar cup-shaped flowers in almost all shades (including multicolors) except blue. Tulips usually grow from 10 to 24 inches high and are best planted in full sun. They rebloom only in cold-winter climates; they're hardy to Zone 3. Elsewhere, the bulbs must be dug and chilled before replanting. However, many species of tulips, such as *T. clusiana*, naturalize even in mild-winter areas. Most tulips thrive as far south as Zone 8.

✔ **Calla lily.** *Zantedeschia* species. Spectacular, tropical-looking plants with large, usually white, cup-shaped summer flowers and bright green, arrow-shaped leaves. Yellow, pink, and red shades are also available. Calla lily plants generally grow from 2 to 3 feet high, but dwarf forms are also available. Best grown in light shade, but can take sun in cool climates. They need regular watering and are hardy to Zone 8.

Buying bulbs

Bulbs are sold through the mail and at local nurseries. Hardy bulbs, such as daffodils and tulips, are best planted in autumn, while tender bulbs, such as begonias and dahlias, should be planted a few weeks before the last frost date in spring. Nurseries should have the best supplies at the appropriate planting time for your area.

Always purchase top-quality bulbs — they give you more bang for your buck. Never forget that, with bulbs, bigger is better. Larger bulbs, although more expensive, give you more bloom. Bargain bulbs are often poor performers. Avoid bulbs that are soft and mushy or have obvious signs of decay.

If you live in a warm-winter climate, you may have to refrigerate bulbs that require winter chilling (such as hyacinth and tulip) before planting. Check the bulb package for such a recommendation or ask at your nursery. To chill bulbs, place them in the refrigerator (not the freezer) for six to eight weeks prior to planting.

Planting bulbs

Plant bulbs wherever you want to see them bloom: in the smallest little spot by the front door, in pots, in large swaths under trees, or among other flowering plants. Some bulbs, such as the English bluebell, look particularly good in woodland settings, while others, such as tulips, do well in formal landscapes.

One of our favorite designs involves planting large beds of tulips or daffodils. We then plant low-growing annuals or perennials (such as sweet alyssum, pansies, violas, or iberis) right on top of these bulb beds. The bulbs come up through the other flowers and create wonderful combinations. And after the bulbs are through blooming, the other flowers cover up the leftover foliage of the bulbs.

Plan for a long season of color with bulbs. Even though some of the most familiar bulbs (such as daffodils and tulips) bloom in spring, other bulbs (such as dahlias) bloom in summer and autumn.

Bulbs work especially well in containers. With containers, you can really pack bulbs in tight for a spectacular bloom (but the tighter you pack the bulbs, the less likely they'll bloom the following year). Bulbs can even be *forced* to bloom out of season or indoors. Forcing tricks the bulbs into blooming whenever you want them to. It takes some time and work, but it results in great looking pots stuffed with glorious color. For more information on how to force bulbs, see *Flowering Bulbs For Dummies* by Judy Glattstein and the Editors of the National Gardening Association.

The two most important things that you should know about planting a bulb are to set the bulb at the right depth and to make sure that you put the bulb in the hole rightside up.

The chart in Figure 10-7 shows the recommended planting depths and proper positioning for common bulb types. As a general rule, most bulbs should be planted at a depth equal to three times their diameter. Remnants of roots on the bottom should tell you which side of the bulb should go down. If you have any doubts, ask at your local nursery.

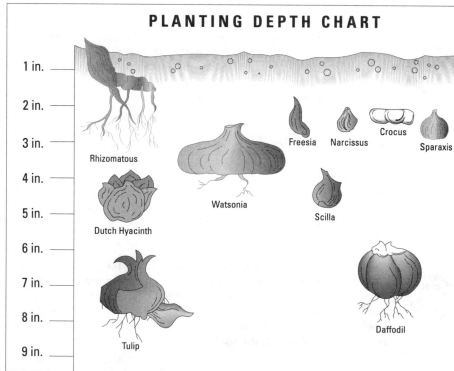

Figure 10-7: Use this bulb-planting depth chart as a guide when you plant your own bulbs.

PLANTING DEPTH CHART

1 in.
2 in.
3 in.
4 in.
5 in.
6 in.
7 in.
8 in.
9 in.

Rhizomatous

Freesia Narcissus Crocus Sparaxis

Watsonia

Scilla

Dutch Hyacinth

Tulip

Daffodil

Bringing all the flowers together

For the longest bloom, you'll probably want to mix different types of flowers together. The rules for doing so are pretty much the same as for planting a perennial border as described earlier — plan for a long season of bloom, have a color theme, blend plant textures, use grays — that kind of stuff.

You can plant bulbs individually by using a hand trowel or bulb planter, available at garden supply stores. If you're planting many bulbs, digging one big trench or hole and lining up the bulbs in the bottom is usually easier.

Most bulbs require well-drained soil because bulbs can rot in soggy, overly wet ground. Before planting your bulbs, mix a slow-release, complete fertilizer into the soil in the bottom of the hole. You can find appropriate fertilizers (labeled *bulb food*) in nurseries and garden centers. After planting the bulbs, water them thoroughly.

Caring for bulbs

With many bulbs (especially those bulbs that bloom in spring), you won't have much else to do. Plant the bulbs and forget them. The bulbs grow, bloom, die back, and come back again the following year. Summer-blooming bulbs, like dahlias and begonias, however, need to be watered and fertilized regularly during their growth cycle. Most bulbs, in fact, benefit from a once-a-year application of nitrogen fertilizer during their growing season.

Pinch off faded blooms just as you would for most flowers. But after the bloom is finished, don't cut down the bulbs' foliage. Let the foliage die down naturally so that it can continue to feed the bulb and build next year's bloom.

Digging and storing bulbs is necessary for begonias, dahlias, and tender bulbs that are grown in cold-winter climates. Wait until the foliage is almost dried out and gently dig the bulbs up. (A spading fork works well.) Brush the dirt off the bulbs and allow them to dry for a week in a cool, dark place. After drying the bulbs for a week, discard any damaged or rotting bulbs and dust the remaining bulbs with sulfur or another fungicide. Finally, pack the dusted bulbs in dry peat moss or perlite and store them in a cool, dark place until replanting time.

If digging and storing bulbs is too much work, just treat bulbs like annuals and plant new ones every year.

Dividing bulbs

Some bulbs, particularly smaller types of bulbs (such as crocuses and daffodils), can be left undisturbed for years. But other bulbs multiply so rapidly that they become too crowded and deplete the nutrients in the soil around them. Few blossoms, unusually small, are a sure sign that your bulbs need more room.

Dividing is done just after the foliage turns yellow and begins to die back. Dig up the clump by using a garden fork, being careful not to injure the bulbs. Then break off the individual bulbs, keeping the roots intact. Replant the bulbs immediately or store them in a dry place until autumn planting time. Water the area well and allow any foliage to mature and die before removing it. The newly planted bulbs should bloom the following spring.

- Larger bulbs (for example, lily) or corms (for example, gladiolus) develop small, immature offspring at the base of the bulb. Remove these offsets after the plant has bloomed and the leaves have died; then plant them in a container or in an inconspicuous area where they can grow for a year or two until they are big enough to bloom.

- Tuberous-rooted plants, such as dahlias, are propagated a little differently. After the plant blooms (as the leaves fade), dig the plant up. A clump of fat, tuberous roots is attached to the stalk. Cut the roots into several groupings, leaving part of the stalk intact on each of the clusters. Each cluster should include at least one growth bud at the base of the section of stalk. Then replant the clumps in various spots; plant the clumps at approximately the same depth that they were planted before they were dug. Or store them in peat or sawdust until you are ready to plant.

- True bulbs, such as lilies, are propagated by using yet another method. Most true lilies resemble artichokes, with many swollen, scalelike sections. These individual "scales" can be removed and grown to form new bulbs, for planting the following spring. This process is somewhat involved, however, and best left to the more advanced landscaper.

The Containerized Landscape

Why add potted plants to your landscape? Here are a number of reasons:

- **You can grow plants in places that don't have soil, as shown in Figure 10-8.** Container plants add character to patios, decks, porches, and windows. They make basically flat places interesting and soften the edginess of hard materials like wood, brick, and concrete. But even more important, if you live in an apartment or small home with very little outdoor space or anywhere with muddy gumbo or hard rock for soil, growing in containers may be your only chance to have plants.

Figure 10-8:
Containers filled with summer annuals including begonias, lobelia, geraniums, and marigolds.

✔ **You can move plants around.** Containers allow you to show off plants when they are looking their very best. For example, when your potted azalea is in bloom, it goes right on the front porch. When it's out of bloom, it moves out of the way for the next show-off. Plants growing in containers can also be moved to protected areas if bad weather threatens.

✔ **Containers can make plants look better**. Lance's wife says that a handsome plant growing in a good-looking container is like a handsome man in the finest uniform. It just can't help but look better. A nice pot can turn even an ordinary plant into a piece of art. We wonder what a uniform could do for Lance?

Think of it this way. If your yard is really an outdoor room, potted plants can be your decorations — the items that turn a simple room into a comfortable home. Container plants help give your landscape a lived-in look.

What to grow and how to grow it

Almost any plant can be grown in containers. Your local nursery is proof of that. But, of course, larger plants will eventually outgrow their pots, so plant size should be a consideration. If you really want to know the possibilities, get yourself a copy of *Container Gardening For Dummies* by Bill Marken and the editors of the National Gardening Association (IDG Books Worldwide, Inc.). But let me whet your appetite with just a smattering of plants you can grow in pots:

- **Small trees:** Japanese maples
- **Shrubs:** camellias, azaleas, and roses
- **Fruiting plants:** dwarf citrus, apples, peaches, and pears
- **Berries:** strawberries and blueberries
- **Annual flowers:** petunias, marigolds, and impatiens
- **Flowering perennials:** salvias, geraniums, and ornamental grasses
- **Bulbs:** tulips and daffodils

Heck, try whatever you want!

Setting the stage

That's how you should feel when planting containers and arranging them in the yard — set the stage, put on a show. Here are some tricks for getting the best display:

- **Use some big pots.** Splurge a little and buy a few really nice size clay or wooden pots. Particularly if you have a big deck or patio, a few nicely planted big pots will bring it into scale with the rest of the yard, as well as with patio or deck furniture.

  Match the size of a plant with the size of the container. Bigger plants are better off in bigger pots, but a small plant can look dwarfish in very large containers.

- **Match pot and plant.** You have a huge choice of container sizes, styles, and materials, so think carefully about how you match plants with pots. A glazed ceramic pot may beautifully accentuate the Oriental feel of a Japanese maple, but look a little funny filled with bright yellow marigolds. A dwarf fruit tree matches nicely with the rustic feel of a half whiskey barrel, but more refined plants may look a little campy.

- **Group different pot sizes and shapes.** Start with one big one and then surround it with smaller pots of varying shapes and sizes. It helps to stick to one style of pot, like clay or wood. Things get pretty busy looking if you mix too many different kinds of pots.

- **Plant flowers the way you arrange a bouquet.** Put taller, upright plants like salvia or zinnias in the center of pot, something a little smaller like Madagascar periwinkle around that. Then line the outside with a spreading plant, like alyssum or lobelia, which will cascade over the edge. And, of course, only mix plants that have the same sun requirements. And plant everything a little closer than you would in the ground.

- **Use foliage color and texture.** Flowers will eventually go out of bloom, but if you mix in some nice foliage plants, like gray-leafed dusty Millers, ornamental grasses, or ferns, the pots will still look good.

✔ **Move the best plants forward.** When a pot is really looking good, move it up front where people can see it.

Caring for potted plants

Growing plants in containers is a bit of a different deal than growing them in the ground. That's why, if you are serious about container landscaping, get a copy *of Container Gardening For Dummies* by Bill Marken and the editors of the National Gardening Association (IDG Books Worldwide, Inc.) to get the whole scoop. But in a nutshell, here are some things you need to know:

✔ **Start with good soil.** Buy potting soil at your local nursery or garden center. Don't fill pots with garden soil. It causes nothing but headaches.

✔ **Make sure pots have drainage holes.** Roots will drown otherwise. Most pots have them, but you may have to drill a few in wood pots or half barrels.

✔ **Water frequently.** Container plants dry out quickly and need to be watered often, especially big plants in small pots. In hot weather, pots may need to be watered daily, especially if the plants have been growing in the container for a while. When you water, make several passes with the hose, making sure the entire rootball is getting wet.

✔ **Fertilize frequently.** Frequent watering washes nutrients, especially nitrogen, from the soil. Use a water-soluble fertilizer about every two weeks. Follow label instructions.

✔ **Transplant when necessary.** Plants that have been in a pot too long get rootbound, meaning the pot is full of a mass of tightly-woven roots that are very hard to get wet. If that happens, move the plant into a larger container, loosening the roots around the outside of the rootball as you do so.

Figures 10-9 and 10-10 show how to plant in pots.

Eating Your Landscape

Many food plants — vegetables, fruits, berries, herbs and nuts — are good-looking plants in their own right, with handsome foliage, fragrant flowers, and/or colorful fruit. With that said, it's not surprising that many people are starting to work these kinds of plants into the landscape as ornamentals, in other words, just for the sheer beauty of the plant. So if you have been thinking how nice it would be to grow your own fresh produce, but don't like the idea of a farm-like fruit orchard or vegetable patch, you may consider an ornamental-edible landscape. It can be beautiful, nutritious, and delicious all at the same time.

Figure 10-9:
Fill the container with potting soil and scoop out holes for each plant.

Figure 10-10:
Place the plant in the hole so it sits at the same level as in the nursery pot. Firm the soil around the plant so it stands on its own, and water thoroughly.

But before we give you some ideas on how to create an ornamental edible landscape, we should tell you that food-producing plants can't really be considered low maintenance. To get a quality harvest, most require close attention to watering, fertilizing, pest control, and sometimes pruning. Fruit trees in particular, require a lot of care. And although you may like the thought of having a plum tree next to your patio, if you don't get around to picking the fruit, you're going to have one messy, smelly, fly-infested patio when the fruit falls to the ground.

If you really want to go the edible landscape route, pick up a book devoted to the subject so you understand all the problems as well as possibilities. There are several described in the Appendix, but one sure-fire book is *Vegetable Gardening For Dummies,* by the Editors of the National Gardening Association (IDG Books Worldwide, Inc.).

The beautifully-delicious possibilities

Here are some of the ways food plants can be incorporated into the landscape:

- ✔ **Fruit and nut trees:** Apples, pears, plums, peaches, and nectarines have fragrant flowers, attractive foliage, good tasting fruit and manageable habits. The same can be said of small nut trees, like almond trees. Fruit and nut trees can be used like any small flowering tree — along fences, as background, as small shade trees, or even planted by patios or walks if you make sure to harvest the fruit (see Chapter 8 for more on trees). You can also use dwarf varieties, which grow smaller than standard-size fruit trees, as background, container plants, or unpruned hedges.

  If you live in a mild winter area, don't forget citrus trees — one of the most handsome of the fruiting trees. The bright green foliage, fragrant flowers and colorful fruit make oranges, lemons, and limes exquisite ornamentals to use as screens, hedges, or patio trees. Persimmons, with shiny yellow green foliage, colorful fruit, and bright orange-red fall color, are also outstanding ornamentals.

  Some larger nut trees, particularly pecans and walnuts, can also be used as shade trees, but the size of the trees makes the nuts difficult to harvest.

- ✔ **Vegetables planted with flowers:** The foliage texture and color of many vegetables makes them ideal for planting with flowers (see Figure 10-11). Our favorite ornamental vegetables include red or green leaf lettuce, red or green chard (or the rainbow foliage colors of 'Bright Lights'), red flowering scarlet runner beans (plant them near sunflowers so they can climb up the stalks), red cabbage, purple leafed eggplant, colorful peppers, deep green spinach, crinkly kale, statuesque onions (especially when they bloom), bold foliaged, red ribbed rhubarb, and even

Figure 10-11:
Flowers and vegetables combine for a beautiful and productive planting area.

heavy producing cherry tomatoes, especially the yellow fruited varieties. But really, you can try anything: Let watermelons and cantaloupe sprawl through other ground covers; plant carrots, beets, and turnips with alyssum; or plant any compact variety in pots. Be creative.

✔ **Fruiting shrubs for borders, background, hedges and screens:** Blueberries, gooseberries, and currents have flowers, fall color, and fruit. Use them like most small shrubs.

✔ **Fruit vines for arbors and trellis:** Grape and kiwi vines are vigorous plants that you can train over a sturdy trellis or arbor. Grapes vines with their lobed leaves, bright fall color, and dangling clusters of fruit work particularly well.

✔ **Berries and vegetables as ground covers.** Plant both strawberries and low-growing types of blueberries as small-scale ground covers. You can even grow the sprawling sweet potato plant as a ground cover.

✔ **Herbs everywhere.** Parsley, chives, sage, creeping thyme, oregano, rosemary, and lavender are all great looking plants. Mix them with flowers or vegetables. Use low-growing, spreading ones like rosemary, creeping thyme, and catnip as ground covers. Or try tall growers, like dill and fennel, as feathery background plants.

Rules of the ornamental-edible road

When using fruit-bearing plants in the ornamental edible landscape, apply these tips. For more information about varieties, check with your local cooperative extension office or a trusted nursery person.

- **Plant varieties adapted to your area.** Not all fruit can be grown everywhere, so choose ones proven in your area. Whenever possible, plant varieties with resistance to diseases or pests common to your region.

- **Don't plant more than you can eat.** Remember, when fruit drops, it makes a sticky, smelly, fly-ridden mess. Harvest on time, even if you won't eat it all, and give the harvest to friends.

- **Prune for shape.** Most fruit trees will produce more fruit than you need. Where most farmers prune to keep trees as productive as possible, you should prune to keep the trees in bounds. Don't be afraid to prune hard to keep plants in line.

Here are few of the most important tips to successfully planting flowers with vegetables:

- **Match bloom seasons of flowers with growth cycles of the vegetables.** In other words mix flowers that grow in cool weather with vegetables that like similar conditions. Consider picking up copies of *Perennials For Dummies* by Marcia Tatroe, *Annuals For Dummies* by Bill Marken, and *Vegetable Gardening For Dummies* (all written in conjunction with the Editors of the National Gardening Association and published by IDG Books Worldwide, Inc.). That should make our stock go up.

- **Match cultural needs.** Most vegetables need regular water, so don't combine vegetables with flowers that like it on the dry side. Otherwise you may either have to do a lot of individual watering or some of your plants are going to be unhappy.

- **Give vegetables enough room.** Seed packets and books on vegetable gardening recommend the amount of space you should leave between individual vegetable plants. Try to leave at least that much room between flowers and vegetables, too. You may be able to push them a little closer but don't get carried away. If the flowers have a spreading habit, you can even plant things farther apart.

- **Put short plants in front, tall in back.** Make a smooth transition in sizes from the front of the bed to the back. That way you can see everything — smaller plants won't be blocked or shaded by taller ones.

- **Leave room to harvest.** Use stepping stones or paths to give access for harvesting vegetables without damaging flowers. See Figure 10-12 for an example.

✔ **Create a color theme.** Use colors that will blend well. For example, pink pansies planted at the base of ruby rhubarb, white alyssum with green chard, red leaf lettuce with purple Johnny-jump-ups, or red petunias at the base of pepper plants.

Figure 10-12: Neatly-designed vegetable garden is an attractive family gathering place in this small, but productive, backyard.

Chapter 11

Covering Lots of Ground

· ·

In This Chapter

▶ Choosing your lawn size

▶ Deciding which type of grass to grow

▶ Planting your lawn from seeds or sod

▶ Putting in native grasses and meadows

▶ Planting and maintaining ground covers

· ·

*F*or most people, a landscape isn't complete without at least *some* lawn. The lush color and smooth, uniform look are a practical and attractive way to complement the house and the trees, shrubs, and other plantings. And it's tough to beat having a grassy area as a place for family and pets to relax and play. Many grasses can handle heavy foot traffic and some even thrive in moderately shady areas. So lawns solve certain landscaping problems.

But lawn isn't a good choice of ground cover in many situations.

✔ Lawn grasses don't grow well in deep shade, and only a few kinds of lawn truly thrive in hot, dry regions.

✔ Lawns are hard to establish and to maintain on steep pieces of ground.

✔ If you have a lot of lawn, the mowing and maintenance can eat up your time.

✔ In parts of the world where water is scarce, traditional lawn grass isn't an environmentally sound choice.

If any of these situations apply to you, then you want to plant ground cover instead of a traditional lawn. The most appealing aspect of all the other ground-cover plants — meadow and prairie grasses, wildflowers, woodland perennials, and low-growing shrubs — is that they give your landscape a natural look and require very little maintenance. The selection of good ground-cover plants is so broad that you can find several to fit any landscaping style or regional climate.

But because most people start with a lawn, that's where we start.

More Lawn or Less Lawn?

The utility of a well-kept lawn is undeniable. That's why for decades, putting in a lawn was the first thing that people did when they bought a new home. But recently, many people have started to question the amount of time, money, and resources that lawns demand. You may be doing the same.

Putting in a lawn is a lot of work. Then, you must maintain it, year after year. A lawn also uses resources — water, fertilizer, and pesticides — that may be in short supply in some areas or can be sources of pollution if not used correctly.

With planning, however, you can satisfy your penchant for a lawn without putting too many demands on your leisure time or the environment.

- ✔ If you have a newly built home and you're starting from scratch with the landscaping, think seriously about how much weekend time you want to spend pushing the lawn mower (or sitting on the riding mower) and what's appropriate water use for your part of the country — then size your new lawn area accordingly. (See Chapters 8, 9, and 10 for help in deciding how else you can use the rest of your land and what to plant there.)

  If you already have a lawn, the sidebar "Don't like the lawn you have?" further on in this chapter tells you how to easily reseed with one of these improved varieties and keep it in top shape.

- ✔ Forget about the idea that your lawn must be square. Figure 11-1 shows a unique lawn shape.

- ✔ Choose for your lawn one of the many new low-maintenance grass varieties available today.

- ✔ Select a grass that's adapted to your climate to reduce the amount of work and resources required to keep your lawn looking good.

Putting In a New Lawn

You create lawns by planting *turfgrasses* — grasses especially bred for this particular use — and this can be done in several ways.

The most economical way to plant grass is by spreading seed. Proper soil preparation and follow-up care are the keys to success here. The first week or two after planting, pay constant attention to your newly seeded lawn, to make sure the seeds don't dry out. (Weed seeds are likely to germinate during this time, as well.) The fastest way to put in a new lawn, however, is

Figure 11-1:
A small
lawn adds
richness
to the
landscape.

by *laying sod* — setting large sections of fully grown turf in place on the soil.
The idea of an instant lawn certainly has its appeal, but sod is an expensive
option, and you still have to prepare the soil as thoroughly and maintain the
newly planted area until the sod gets its roots in the ground.

Some types of grass are available only as sod, or as *plugs* (chunks of turf) or
sprigs (single plants or stems) that are set into little holes in the soil. It can
take a couple of years before the grass completely fills the area and looks
like a real lawn. Keeping weeds out of the bare soil until the lawn fills in is
critical. Grasses that must be planted this way are noted in the "Which grass
is best?" section, which describes the common turfgrasses.

Which grass is best?

Growing the appropriate variety of grass for your area of the country is
critical. It'll make all the difference between a thriving lawn and one that
doesn't survive the winter or languishes in the heat of your climate.

Turfgrasses fall into two broad groups: cool season and warm season.
Cool-season grasses grow best between 60°F and 75°F and can withstand
cold winters. Warm-season grasses, which grow vigorously in temperatures
above 80°F, are planted in mild-winter regions. In general terms, cool-season
grasses are grown in Zones 6 and colder; warm-season grasses are grown in
Zones 7 and warmer.

Each type of grass has its named varieties, many of which have been bred for conditions like drought or shade tolerance or for sheer ruggedness. Your local extension office or garden center can recommend varieties for your area.

Try the following cool-season grasses:

- **Fine fescue.** A fine-textured turfgrass. Quick to germinate and get established; does well in less-than-ideal growing conditions. The most shade tolerant of the cool-season grasses. Drought tolerant and requires little feeding. Newer varieties offer insect resistance.

- **Kentucky bluegrass.** The most common lawn grass for cold-winter regions. Slow to get established, but with its spreading habit, it fills in nicely. Fine texture with a rich green color. A heavy feeder. Very hardy; many disease-resistant varieties are available.

- **Perennial ryegrass.** This finely-textured grass is one of the quickest types to get established and will grow in up to 60 percent shade, but it doesn't tolerate the temperature extremes of bluegrass or hold up under mowing as well. Newer varieties offer insect- and disease-resistance.

- **Turf-type tall fescue.** This coarse-textured grass makes a lush, rugged lawn under difficult conditions. New varieties are resistant to everything: heat, drought, diseases, and insects.

- **Crested wheat grass.** A native grass of the Rocky Mountains and High Plains; very drought tolerant.

For warmer climates, we like the following warm-season grasses:

- **Bahia grass.** This low-growing, coarse-textured grass is not as attractive as some of the other warm-season grasses, but it is low maintenance and grows in partial shade.

- **Bermuda grass.** The most common lawn grass in mild-winter climates. Texture ranges from coarse to fine, depending on the variety. This rugged, drought-resistant grass spreads quickly and can crowd out weeds. Needs frequent, close mowing. Some varieties offer disease and insect resistance. Common Bermuda grass can be grown from seed; the *improved hybrids* (recently developed varieties) can be planted only as plugs or sod and are not as weedy because they don't set seed.

- **Blue grama grass.** A fine-textured grass with flat, gray-green blades. Native to the Great Plains of the U.S.; very drought resistant and requires little or no fertilization.

- **Buffalo grass.** Fine texture and curled, gray-green blades. Another heat- and drought-resistant Great Plains native. Requires little mowing and little or no fertilization.

- **Carpet grass.** Coarse texture and low-growing, pointed blades. Spreads quickly and does well in sandy soil.

- **Centipede grass.** Coarse to medium texture and flat, blunt blades. A low-maintenance, shade-tolerant grass that does well on soils that are acidic or low in fertility. Some disease resistance.

- **St. Augustine grass.** This coarse-textured grass tolerates partial shade. In general, susceptible to insect and disease problems, although some improved varieties have been introduced in the past few years. Planted from sod or sprigs.

- **Zoysia grass.** A coarse- to fine-textured grass with stiff blades. Slow growing but very tough after it's established. Drought resistant and shade tolerant. Planted from sod or sprigs.

Before you plant

The first step in preparing the area to be sown is to test your soil to see whether it's fertile and has the proper pH to grow grass. Then you need to add the proper soil amendments, work them into the ground with a rototiller and level the whole area.

Seeding your lawn

The best time to seed a new lawn in cool climates is in the late summer or early autumn and in mild climates, in spring or early summer.

Your lawn is a landscape feature that you'll have for years to come, so skip the cheap stuff. How to recognize fine quality seed? Look for the following on the label:

- A variety name, such as 'Nugget' Kentucky bluegrass instead of generic Kentucky bluegrass

- Weed and other crop seed content of 0.5 percent or less; the highest-quality seed is free of weed and other undesirable crop seed

- *Germination percentage* (percentage of seeds in your bag that will sprout and begin to grow) of 85 percent or greater for Kentucky bluegrass and above 90 percent for all other grasses

Remember to measure the square footage of the area that you plan to seed; the label also indicates how large an area the package will cover.

When you're ready to plant, assemble all of the tools and equipment that you need: soil amendments, rotary tiller, grass seed, lawn spreader (a device, shown in Figure 11-2 that scatters seed evenly as you roll it over the soil — also called a drop spreader), board scraper (a board that you drag over the soil surface) or rake, lawn roller (a large, heavy drum, shown in Figure 11-2, with a handle that you roll over the scattered seed to press it into the soil; the drum can be filled with water to increase the weight), and mulching material such as straw. You can rent expensive tools for the day.

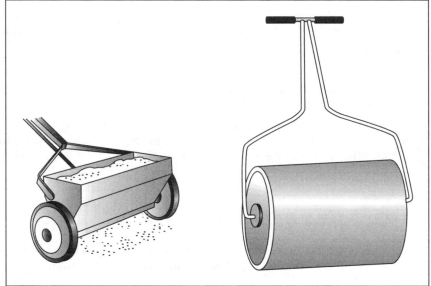

Figure 11-2: One of several types of lawn spreaders (left) and a lawn roller (right).

Then follow these instructions:

1. **If necessary, spread amendments over the soil to correct the pH and apply a complete fertilizer recommended for new lawns in the amount given on the bag.**

   Chapter 12 has more information about soil.

2. **Till the soil 6 to 8 inches deep to loosen it, as shown in Figure 11-3.**

   Don't overcultivate — leave small lumps and cracks to catch seed so that the grass sprouts quickly. Remove stones and debris.

3. **Level the soil with a board scraper or rake to eliminate high spots.**

   Without this step, shown in Figure 11-4, your mower would cut the grass too short as well as depressions where it might miss spots or where water can collect (see Chapter 4 for information on solving drainage problems).

Figure 11-3:
Tilling
works
amendments
into the soil.

Figure 11-4:
Leveling the
soil with a
rake.

4. **Roll the seedbed with a half-filled roller to firm the soil.**

   Make sure that the soil is dry before you roll; otherwise, it compacts, preventing seeds from sprouting.

5. **Sow the seed with a mechanical spreader or by hand, as shown in Figure 11-5.**

   Don't be tempted to oversow; if you do, the plants won't develop properly.

Figure 11-5:
Spreaders
are ideal for
sowing
grass seed.

6. **Rake the surface lightly, barely covering about half the seed and leaving the rest exposed.**

   The seed needs light to germinate.

7. **Roll once more with the half-filled roller to press seeds in contact with the soil. (See Figure 11-6.)**

8. **Lightly mulch the seedbed.**

   Mulch keeps the soil moist until the seeds germinate. A light mulch — less than ¼-inch deep — is all you need. If you are planting a large area, ask your nurseryman if you can borrow a cage roller — an easy-to-use device that lays down a thin layer of organic matter, shown in Figure 11-7. The mulch also keeps the seeds from washing away in a heavy rain.

9. **Give the newly seeded area a thorough initial soaking and then keep it well watered until the grass is established.**

   After the initial soaking, frequent light sprinklings will keep the seed moist. After the seed sprouts, each watering should penetrate the soil to a depth of several inches to promote good root growth.

Growing your lawn from sod

The best time to lay sod in cold-winter regions is in autumn; in mild-winter regions, the best time is early spring.

Figure 11-6:
Roll the surface to ensure good contact between seed and soil.

Figure 11-7:
A cage roller.

Sod is expensive, so buy from a quality supplier. Look for sections that are $\frac{1}{2}$-inch to 1 inch thick, with no brown patches or dried-out edges. Have the sod delivered on planting day so that it doesn't sit in a pile and heat up.

When you're ready to lay your new sod, assemble all the tools and equipment that you need: soil amendments, rotary tiller, sharp knife, board scraper or rake, and lawn roller. Prepare the planting area as you would for a lawn from seed (Steps 1 through 4 in the "Seeding your lawn" section of this chapter).

Then follow these instructions for laying sod:

1. **Roll out a piece of sod (green side up!) and press it into position.**

   Start along a straight edge, such as next to a walkway or driveway. If the lawn is irregularly shaped, stretch twine across the middle to establish a straight line. Fit the next section against it tightly but don't overlap.

2. **Continue laying sections, staggering them slightly, like bricks. (See Figure 11-8.)**

   Don't let the sod dry out. Lightly sprinkle finished sections as you go. Use a knife to cut sod to fit curved or irregular areas.

3. **Use a half-filled roller over the newly laid turf, going back over it a second time at right angles to the first pass.**

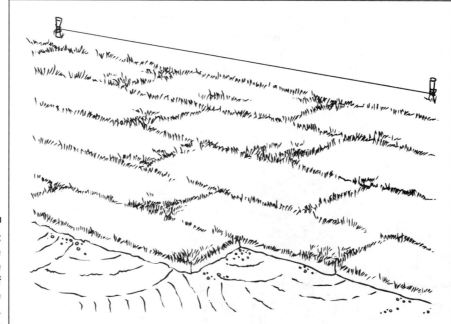

Figure 11-8: Stagger the ends of the sod as if you're laying brick.

4. **Water the lawn thoroughly and keep the sod moist until roots knit with the soil (try lifting an edge to check).**

   In hot weather, you may have to sprinkle the new sod several times a day to keep it moist.

Planting plugs and sprigs

To plant a lawn using grass plugs and sprigs, prepare the planting area as you would for a lawn from seed (Steps 1 through 4 under "Seeding your lawn"). Then follow these instructions for planting plugs and sprigs:

1. **Dig holes 2 to 3 inches deep and 6 inches apart for zoysia grass plugs; 12 inches apart for Bermuda grass plugs. Set the plugs in place. Water well.**

   See Figure 11-9. Sprigs can be set in shallow trenches, 10 to 18 inches apart, and then covered with soil, or you can broadcast small pieces over an area and then lightly cover as you would for seed. Ask your nursery person which method is best for you. After planting, water well and keep moist as you would for new sod.

2. **Keep the bare soil weed free until the lawn is established.**

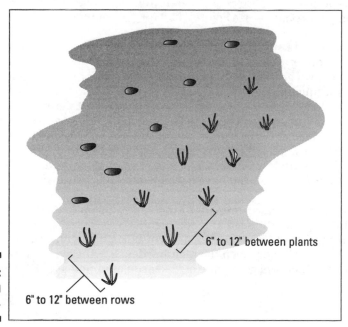

Figure 11-9:
Planting
plugs.

6" to 12" between plants

6" to 12" between rows

TIP

Don't like the lawn you have?

You can give your lawn a facelift by over-seeding with an improved grass variety. Here's how:

1. Mow your lawn closely and thoroughly rake out the thatch (that spongy layer of dead stems and junk between the leaves and the roots). If you have a large area, rent a dethatcher, a power driven machine that cuts out the thatch for you.

   Loosening compacted soil with a *coring machine,* a piece of power equipment that

cuts out small plugs of soil to improve air and water circulation around the grass roots, also gets rid of some of the thatch and allows the grass seed to come in contact with the soil.

2. Adjust the soil pH if necessary and fertilize. Sow seed at 1½ times the rate recommended on the package. Sprinkle a light layer of topsoil over the lawn (called *topdressing*) and water thoroughly.

Over in the Meadow

A trend in lawn alternatives is to use native grasses and other low-growing, prairie-type plants. These create meadowlike landscapes that can be beautiful year-round — see Figure 11-10 for an example.

ECO-SMART

Native grasses are superbly adapted to their native ranges and are often well adapted to other areas, too. Native grasses can survive on less water than traditional lawn grasses and can be left unmowed (or only need to be mowed infrequently) so are low maintenance. Common types of native grasses include crested wheat grass (a very drought-tolerant native grass of the Rocky Mountains) and blue grama grass and buffalo grass, both native to the Great Plains. Certain wildflower mixes (see the appendix for sources) composed of low-growing plants can also be used for meadowlike lawns. Meadow lawns are less formal-looking than most grass lawns but can be walked on or played on and have a wild beauty all their own.

To plant a meadow lawn, prepare the soil as you would for a regular grass lawn. Then, spread the seed at recommended rates on the package and make sure the seed bed stays moist. If you're using native grasses, occasional mowing will help keep the planting dense. Otherwise, allow the plants to set seed, which will germinate next season and increase the planting.

Figure 11-10:
A meadow lawn of native grasses is low maintenance and needs little water.

The Ground-Cover Alternative

Ground covers are usually low-growing, spreading plants that, when planted close together, form a uniform layer of foliage. Ground covers range from very low-growing plants that are just a few inches high to more shrubby types that are several feet high. Some of the lowest-growing ground covers, such as chamomile and creeping thyme, can handle a little foot traffic — you can plant these types between stepping-stones or in other areas where people occasionally walk.

Ground covers have an artistic side, too. You can create a nearly infinite variety of contrasts with ground covers, and you can mix in other shrubs, vines, annuals, and perennials for a variety of effects. Foliage textures can range from grassy to tropically bold, and colors can range from subtle shades of gray to vibrant seasonal colors. Ground covers provide a natural-istic appearance, so look to the local wild areas for ideas. Choose plants that mimic what you see in wooded areas, in unmown fields, in meadows, or on steep slopes.

Planting ground covers

Plants sold as ground covers usually come in small containers or in flats, depending on their growth habit. Those ground-cover plants that are grown in flats are cut into individual sections before planting.

For best results, ground covers should be planted in staggered rows (see Figure 11-11). Plant spacing is very important. If you space the ground-cover plants too far apart, they take a long time to fill in. Plant them too close together, and the plants may quickly become overcrowded. Recommended plant spacings are included in the plant descriptions given in the "Top ground-cover choices" section, further on in this chapter.

If you're planting your ground covers from containers, you can place the plants into individual holes. To plant small plants from pots or packs, dig a hole just deep enough for the rootball. For larger, container-grown plants, taper the hole outward at the base and create a mound for the rootball. For more information on planting container-grown plants, see Chapter 8.

If you're planting a ground-cover plant on a steep slope, set the plant on its own terrace or flattened spot (with the top of the rootball slightly above the soil level) and provide a watering basin behind the plant.

If starting from flats, prepare the whole planting area as if you were planting a lawn (see the "Planting day" section, earlier in this chapter). As with all plantings, you need to attend to soil needs (see Chapter 12) before introducing your plants to your landscape. Water plants adequately to help get them established; after the plants are growing well, many types need only minimum maintenance. Planting ground cover from flats is very much like planting annuals and perennials, described in Chapter 10.

Plan on controlling weeds between plants until the ground cover is established. We like to use an organic mulch or, for shrubby ground covers, *landscape fabric* (a porous material sold in rolls that permits water penetration but retards weeds) to control weeds. One advantage of organic mulches is that they also protect the plants in the winter.

Figure 11-11:
Plant ground covers in staggered rows.

Many spreading, nonwoody ground covers (such as English ivy, St. John's wort, and vinca) can be rejuvenated or kept looking fresh by occasional shearing. Cut the plants back to just several inches above the ground in spring and then fertilize them. Within a few weeks, the plants will regrow and look full, clean, and healthy.

Top ground-cover choices

Although the number of possible candidates is nearly infinite, the following common ground-cover plants have proved themselves in a multitude of situations and environments.

- **Woolly yarrow.** *Achillea tomentosa.* Evergreen. A tough, spreading ground cover that reaches 6 to 9 inches high. Its ferny, gray-green leaves are topped with small yellow flower clusters in summer. Woolly yarrow can take some foot traffic but can also be invasive. Plant 6 to 9 inches apart in full sun. Hardy to Zone 3.

- **African daisies.** A group of spreading, evergreen plants with daisylike flowers. Widely grown as ground covers in mild-winter climates. Generally hardy into Zone 9. Favorites include the trailing African daisy, *Osteospermum,* with white-to-purple spring flowers on 1- to 3-foot-high plants (depending on the species) and gazanias, *Gazania,* with sunny summer flowers in single and multicolored shades of white, red, pink, yellow, and orange borne on 6- to 12-inch-high clumping or trailing plants. Plant 1 to 2 feet apart in full sun.

- **Carpet bugle.** *Ajuga reptans.* Evergreen. Forms a low-growing, spreading ground cover with attractive dark green or purplish-green foliage reaching 2 to 6 inches high. Carpet bugle has blue flowers in summer. Plant in partial to full shade (some types with colored foliage can take more sun), 6 to 12 inches apart. Hardy to Zone 4.

- **Kinnikinnick.** *Arctostaphylus uva-ursi.* Evergreen. Several selections of this hardy, shrubby plant make excellent ground covers. Features shiny green foliage. The plants' small, urn-shaped, white spring flowers are followed by red berries. 'Point Reyes' and 'Radiant' are two fine choices and generally stay below 12 inches high. Plant in full sun about 3 feet apart. Hardy to Zone 2.

- **Barberries.** *Berberis.* Several types of barberries make excellent ground covers. One of the most popular is the deciduous *B. thunbergii* 'Crimson Pygmy'. This variety grows about 18 inches high, has purplish-red foliage (when grown in full sun), bright-red autumn color, and red berries. As a ground cover, plant 'Crimson Pygmy' 15 to 18 inches apart. Hardy to Zone 4.

- **Chamomile.** *Chamaemelum nobile.* Evergreen. Chamomile's fine-textured, aromatic foliage can take some foot traffic. Has small yellow flowers in summer. Chamomile stays low and compact in full sun, rarely getting over 6 inches high; plants grow taller in partial shade. You can mow chamomile or plant it between stepping-stones. Plant in full sun, spacing plants about 6 to 12 inches apart. Hardy to Zone 7.

- **Cotoneasters.** *Cotoneaster.* Deciduous or evergreen. Cotoneasters are a large family of shrubs that includes many dependable ground covers known for their bright-green foliage, small flowers, and red berries. Favorites include the evergreen bearberry cotoneaster, *C. dammeri* (which grows only 8 inches high and spreads up to 10 feet), the deciduous rock cotoneaster, *C. horizontalis* (which grows from 2 to 3 feet high and has orange-to-red autumn color), and the evergreen rockspray cotoneaster, *C. microphyllus* (which rarely exceeds 2 to 3 feet in height). Hardiness varies, but most cotoneasters can be grown into Zone 5 or 6. Plant at least 3 feet apart in full sun. (Some of the widest-spreading types should be spaced 5 feet apart.)

- **Winter creeper.** *Euonymus fortunei.* Very hardy, evergreen plant that comes in many fine ground-cover varieties. 'Colorata', the purpleleaf winter creeper, has bright green foliage that turns purple in autumn and winter. 'Colorata' grows about 2 feet high. 'Ivory Jade' has green leaves edged with white and also grows about 2 feet high. 'Kewensis' grows only 2 inches high and makes a very dense ground cover. Plant winter creeper in full sun, spacing the plants from 1 to 3 feet apart. Most are hardy into Zone 4 or 5.

- **Blue fescue.** *Festuca ovina glauca.* A mounding, grassy ground cover with silver-blue foliage. Grows 4 to 10 inches high and gets by on little water. Plant in full sun, spacing the plants 6 to 12 inches apart. Hardy to Zone 5.

- **English ivy.** *Hedera helix.* Evergreen. With its dark green, lobed leaves, English ivy is one of the most popular ground covers. Grows well under many conditions, including sun or shade. Many varieties (differing in leaf size, texture, and color) are available. English ivy can be invasive, climbing into trees and over structures if not kept under control. Space plants 12 to 18 inches apart. Hardy to Zone 5, although some small-leafed types are less hardy.

- **Aaron's-beard; creeping St. John's wort.** *Hypericum calycinum.* Evergreen. These adaptable ground covers thrive under a variety of conditions. They grow 12 inches high and have bright-yellow flowers in summer. The plants spread rapidly and can be invasive. Prefer full sun but will take partial shade. Space the plants 12 to 18 inches apart. Hardy to Zone 5.

✔ **Ice plants.** Evergreen. Many different, trailing, succulent ice plants are useful ground covers in mild-winter climates, especially arid areas. Two popular blooming types are rosea ice plant, *Drosanthemum floribundum,* which grows about 6 inches high and has pink flowers in spring and summer; and trailing ice plant, *Lampranthus spectabilis,* which grows 12 to 15 inches high, covering itself with pink, red, or purple flowers in spring. Plant in full sun, spacing them 12 to 18 inches apart. Hardy to Zone 9.

✔ **Junipers.** *Juniperus.* Evergreen. Many low, spreading junipers (differing in height and foliage color) are available. Junipers are tough plants that get by with little care but must have well-drained soil. *J. chinensis* 'San Jose' has grayish-green leaves and grows 2 feet high. *J. horizontalis* 'Bar Harbor' grows about a foot high and spreads up to 10 feet; the gray-green leaves turn bluish in winter. *J. h.* 'Wiltonii' is only 6 inches high and has silver-blue foliage. Plant junipers in full sun. Most should be spaced 2 to 5 feet apart, depending on the variety. Most are hardy into Zone 3.

✔ **Mondo grass or lily turf.** *Liriope* or *Ophiopogon.* Evergreen. Mondo grass and lily turf are two similar, grasslike plants that make attractive ground covers in shady situations. *Liriope spicata,* creeping lily turf, is one of the most adaptable, growing 6 to 10 inches high. *L. muscari* grows up to 24 inches high and has blue summer flowers that are partially hidden by the foliage. Some varieties have variegated leaves. *Ophiopogon japonicus* is a common mondo grass with dark green leaves; the plants grow 8 to 10 inches high. Space these plants 6 to 18 inches apart, depending on height. The hardiness of both species varies, but most can be grown into Zone 5.

✔ **Japanese spurge.** *Pachysandra terminalis.* Evergreen. Japanese spurge is an attractive spreading, foliage plant for shady, moist conditions. Features rich green leaves on upright 10-inch stems, with fragrant white flowers in summer. Plant in partial to full shade and space them 6 to 12 inches apart. Hardy to Zone 4.

✔ **Spring cinquefoil.** *Potentilla tabernaemontanii (P. verna).* Evergreen. This plant's dark green, divided leaves form a soft-textured cover 3 to 6 inches high. Has small clusters of yellow flowers in spring and summer and can take some foot traffic. Plant in full sun to partial shade and space the plants 10 to 12 inches apart. Hardy to Zone 4.

✔ **Creeping thyme.** *Thymus praecox arcticus.* Evergreen. A low-growing, creeping herb that is especially useful between stepping-stones. Can take foot traffic and can even be grown as a lawn alternative. Creeping thyme grows 3 to 6 inches high and has white-to-pink flowers in summer. Plant in full sun and space the plants 6 to 10 inches apart. Hardy to Zone 3.

- ✔ **Star jasmine.** *Trachelospermum jasminoides.* Evergreen. This spreading, vining plant has shiny green foliage and fragrant white flowers in spring. Grows about 18 inches high when left to sprawl. Confederate vine, *T. asiaticum,* is similar but grows slightly lower, has dull green leaves, and bears yellowish-white flowers. Plant in full sun and space the plants 2 to 3 feet apart. Hardy to Zone 8.

- ✔ **Dwarf periwinkle.** *Vinca minor.* Evergreen. This spreading, deep green ground cover is good for shady conditions. Grows from 6 to 12 inches high and has violet-blue flowers in spring and summer. Can be invasive. Space the plants 6 to 8 inches apart. Hardy to Zone 5.

Chapter 12

Solutions for Your Landscape Problems

· ·

In This Chapter

▶ Improving your soil

▶ Landscaping a shady area

▶ Understanding different climate zone maps

▶ Preventing winter injury of plants

· ·

You can design the most beautiful landscape on paper, with wonderful plant combinations and eye-catching color, but if the plants don't thrive where they are planted, they won't look good and neither will your yard. In this chapter, we discuss soil preparation, growing plants in shady areas and talk about winter hardiness.

Improving Your Soil

You can design the most beautiful landscape filled with perfect plants, but it's all for naught if you haven't spent some time to prepare the soil. Soil preparation ensures that plant roots have a balance of all of the things they need for healthy growth — air, water, and nutrients. Without any one of these, your plants languish. And with many permanent plants like flowering perennials, ground covers, and lawns, you only get one crack at soil preparation — prior to planting.

The best time to improve the soil is after any major drainage problems have been fixed (see Chapter 4), paths and patios are in (see Chapters 5 and 6), and any leftover junk and debris are out of the way. After that, it's time to take a close look at the soil you have, give it a good squeeze, have it tested, amend it, and then work it into shape.

LANDSCAPE LINGO

Turning up topsoil

Topsoil is that good native soil that was on your property before your house was built. Many times it is scraped away during construction of a new home, leaving some hard crude that most plants won't like. If the soil around your new home looks and feels more like pavement than dirt, you'd best consult with a landscape contractor about fixing it. It will probably take some work and heavier equipment to get things in order. And its definitely worth the extra effort. It is possible to buy and truck in new topsoil, but you have to be careful that it's similar to the original topsoil, not full of weed seeds and other junk, and that it is properly spread and worked in. The best advice if you are considering this alternative — get help from a professional.

Soils come in three main types with a lot of variations in between:

- **Sandy soils** are composed of mostly large mineral particles. Water moves through these soils quickly and, as it does, takes nutrients with it. Sandy soils are well aerated, quick to dry out, and often lack the nutrients that vegetable plants need.

- **Clay soils** consist of mostly small particles that cling tightly together and hang on to water. Clay soils are slow to dry out and have poor drainage.

- **Loam soils** are a happy mixture of large and small particles, and they usually contain an abundance of organic matter. Loamy soil is well aerated and drains properly, while being able to hold water and nutrients.

TIP

You get a pretty good idea of what type of soil you have by grabbing a moist handful and squeezing. When you let go, sandy soil falls apart and doesn't hold together in a ball. Clay soil oozes through your fingers as you squeeze and stays in a slippery wad when you let go. Loamy soils usually stays together after squeezing but fall apart easily when you poke it with your finger.

Adding dead stuff

LANDSCAPE LINGO

Your garden probably doesn't have perfect loam soil. To fix that mucky clay or loose sand, you need to add *organic matter* — once living stuff like compost, sawdust, shredded bark, or leaf mold (composted tree leaves). Organic matter helps loosen and aerate clay soils. Organic matter also improves the water- and nutrient-holding capacity of sandy soils. In other words, organic matter makes soil more loamy and perfect for plants.

Organic matter also provides the once-living material that attracts microorganisms, beneficial fungi, worms, and other soil borne critters that enhance the health of your plants. The very best organic material is compost, which is really the humus that remains after the composting process ends. Composting turns yard waste, agricultural waste, wood scraps, and even sludge into crumbly soil-like material.

Compost is usually clean, easy-to-use, and readily-available. You can buy it in bags or have it delivered by the truckload. Most waste disposal sites make compost and sell it relatively cheap. However, before you buy, ask if the compost contains any heavy metals, such as lead, and if it is all right to use in edible gardens. You may even be able to get a precise nutrient content from tests they have performed.

We recommend that you lay down a 1 to 2 inch layer of organic matter on the area where you're planting — go for the higher end in a new garden or if the soil is heavy clay or very sandy, less if you've been growing there for years or if the soil is pretty good. And then work it in to a depth of at least 6 inches. You need 3 cubic yards of compost to spread a 1-inch-thick layer over 1,000 square feet.

The best way to spread the compost is with a wheelbarrow and shovel, but if you're landscaping a large area, you may want to rent a small tractor with a front end scoop to simplify things.

Organic materials other than compost are okay, but they have a few problems. If you add sawdust to your soil, it robs the soil of nitrogen when it decomposes, so you have to add more fertilizer to compensate. Livestock manure is wonderful because it adds nitrogen to the soil. However, livestock often eat a lots of hay that's full of weed seeds, which end up germinating in your landscape. If you use manure, make sure it's fully composted — in other words, it's been sitting around for a year or two, very little of the original material is visible, and the salts have been leached out.

Putting your soil to the test

As if knowing whether you have a sandy, clay, or loam soil wasn't puzzling enough, you also need to know some things about your soil's chemistry. Don't worry, though, you don't need a lab coat.

Most plants are kind of picky about soil chemistry. Too much of this or too little of that, and you have problems. Anyway, the only way to see if your soil will be to your plants' liking is to have it tested.

Soils tests can be performed in either of two ways:

↙ **A do-it-yourself kit:** These tests measure the soils acidity and alkalinity, and sometimes major nutrient content. This basic *pH* (a number that represents the acidity and alkalinity of your soil) test is really easy to do. Buy the kit at a nursery, follow the instructions, and voilà! — you know what your soil pH is. However, these tests aren't always reliable, and besides, you want to know more than just the soil's pH. These tests are cheap and easy, though.

↙ **A soil lab test:** Your local cooperative extension office or a private soil lab can conduct a more complete and reliable soil test. (To locate a private lab, look in the Yellow Pages under *soil testing* or ask your cooperative extension office.) This test gives you your soil pH and its nutrient content. When you know the nutrient content, you can tell how much and what kind of fertilizer to use. (Many soil tests tell you exactly what to add.) A lab charges quite a bit more to conduct a test.

Besides providing pH and nutrient content, a soil lab test can also help identify local problems. For example, in dry summer areas, you may have salty soil. The remedy is to add gypsum, a readily available mineral soil additive.

Changes in pH and most nutrients are gradual. If you're testing a soil imbalance, you may want to test the soil every year, in which case, a home testing kit may be best. For maintaining soil that's already in good balance, test every three to five years. Autumn is a good time to have a soil test done, and it's a good time to add many amendments because they work slowly in the soil.

Adjusting soil pH

Soil gets scored on a pH scale with a pH of 1 being most acid and a pH of 14 being most alkaline. Most plants enjoy growing in a slightly acid soil with a pH between 6 and 7.5, but certain plants have specific requirements. Azaleas and rhododendrons, for example, must have an acid soil.

If the pH is not within a suitable range, plants can't take up nutrients like phosphorous and potassium even if they are present in the soil in high amounts. On the other hand, the *solubility* (ability to take up nutrients) of certain minerals such as manganese may increase to toxic levels if the pH is too low.

Generally, soils in areas with high rainfall tend to be acidic. In these areas, you likely have a pH of below 6, and need to add ground limestone to the soil. Where less rainfall occurs, soils are more alkaline, and you likely have a pH of above 7.5, and need to add soil sulfur.

All cooperative extension offices, any soil lab, and many lawn and garden centers have charts showing how much lime or sulfur to add to correct your pH balance. The scale is based on pounds of material to add per 1,000 square feet, so you have to get a tape measure and determine the square footage of your garden first. Then, if you don't feel like going out, you can use Tables 12-1 and 12-2 to figure out how much lime or sulfur you need.

Table 12-1 Pounds of Limestone to Raise pH, Per 1,000 Square Feet

PH Change Needed	Sandy Soil	Loam Soil	Clay Soil
4.0 to 6.5	60	161	230
4.5 to 6.5	51	133	193
5.0 to 6.5	41	106	152
5.5 to 6.5	28	78	106
6.0 to 6.5	14	41	55

Table 12-2 Pounds of Sulfur to Lower pH, Per 1,000 Square Feet

PH Change Needed	Sandy Soil	Loam Soil	Clay Soil
8.5 to 6.5	46	57	69
8.0 to 6.5	20	34	46
7.5 to 6.5	11	18	23
7.0 to 6.5	2	4	7

The best way to apply these materials is through a drop spreader (see Chapter 11). These simple machines don't cost very much and they help you spread the material more evenly. Some nurseries may loan you a spreader, or rent it to you at a cheap price. If you're careful and wear gloves, you can spread these materials by hand, just make sure that you work the soil well after spreading.

✔ Pulverized limestone is the most common and inexpensive acid neutralizer.

✔ Dolomitic limestone contains magnesium, as well as calcium, and is used if your test shows that your soil is low in magnesium.

✔ Pelletized pulverized limestone is a little more expensive than ordinary powdered limestone, but it's cleaner and easier to use. Because its particles aren't as fine as ground limestone, pulverized limestone isn't as dusty.

Spread a preplant fertilizer

One last thing to add to your soil is a *preplant fertilizer* to help correct phosphate and potash deficiencies that your soil test may have uncovered. If your soil fertility is low, you may have to add more fertilizer initially than you would if the soil were built up and high in organic matter. Although a soil test is always the most accurate way to decide how much fertilizer to add, a general rule is to apply 3 to 4 pounds of 5-10-10 fertilizer or its equivalent spread evenly over 100 square feet during the initial soil preparation.

Turning the soil

With various amendments and starter fertilizer spread over the area, you have to work everything into the soil. If the soil is dry, water well, and then let it set for a few days before digging. Don't work soil that's too wet. Soil that's in good condition to work crumbles easily in your hand with a flick of your finger.

The easiest way to turn the soil, especially on large plots, is with a rototiller. You can rent or borrow a tiller, or if you're serious about landscaping, buy one. We prefer types with rear tines and power driven wheels — they let you lean into the machine and use your weight to till deeper.

If you use a rototiller, adjust the tines so that the initial pass over the soil is fairly shallow. As the soil loosens, set the tines deeper with successive passes (criss-crossing at 90 degree angles) until the top 8 to 12 inches of soil is loosened. (To loosen the soil in smaller areas by hand use a straight spade and a digging fork.)

After turning the soil, level the area with a steel rake, breaking up clods and discarding any rocks. Make sure that you maintain any nature contours that promote drainage (see Chapter 4).

Handling Shady Areas

We've probably never been anywhere near your home or yard, but I can say one thing about it for sure — it has some shady spots. If nowhere else, it's shady along the north side of your house. It should also be shady in the morning on the west side of your house and shady in the afternoon on the east side. And that doesn't even include the shady areas under big trees that you may have on your lot.

How do we know this? Well, plants have different sun requirements — some like a lot, some like a little. Plant them in the wrong place and you have problems — shade lovers turn yellow, fry and die in the sun, sun lovers get leggy, won't bloom, and often become diseased in the shade. We can give you an easy tip on where to put plants that like a lot of sun — you plant them in a sunny spot. But things are a little trickier with plants that grow in shade. That's because not all shade is the same. Here are the three types:

- **Partial shade:** This is the sunny in the morning, shady in the afternoon, and vice versa scenario. Many plants thrive in cool morning sun and afternoon shade. In fact in very hot climates, partial shade is often the ideal situation. Shade in the morning and sun in the afternoon is a different story all together. In the afternoon, the sun is hotter, further stressing plants that would rather have shade. In such situations, you're better off planting sun-loving plants.

- **Dappled or filtered shade:** This is the kind of shade you get from tall trees. As long as the canopy isn't too dense, dappled or filtered shade is a great situation for shade lovers (including you on a hot summer day!). There is, however, one caveat. Large trees often have very greedy roots. If you're planting under existing trees, be ready to watch the plants carefully and water more often than usual. Tree roots suck up water and nutrients quickly, making it difficult for new planting to get established. You should also know that, depending on how plants are positioned or how big the trees are, dappled shade can be more like partial shade if plants get direct sun early in the morning or late in the afternoon.

- **Full shade:** This is where it's shady all day. It could be in a woodsy area under a large canopy of trees or the shade on the north side of your house. Or it could be on the woodsy north side of your house — now that's very shady. In fact, it may be too shady for all but cave dwellers.

If you plant small trees in your landscape, they won't cast much shade until they get bigger. So what do you plant underneath? Plants that thrive in the sunny conditions before the trees get big and shade-loving plants later on? You're probably better off planting sun lovers (or ones that can grow in partial shade) that will grow well initially. The truth is that as a landscape matures, you often have to make changes. But if a plant is described as growing well in sun or partial shade, it's probably a good choice for such a situation.

Let the sun shine in, shade the sunshine out

You may be confronted with a location that is too shady. If this location is under trees, you have a few choices to let in more light:

✔ **Prune trees.** Hire an arborist to thin out branches and open up the canopies. You get more light and probably better looking, healthier trees.

✔ **Remove trees.** Maybe not all of them, but just a few. Just remember, trees that shade your house are valuable for the cooling they provide. Taking out the wrong tree can turn your yard from woodsy to deserty in a hurry. You may also consider replacing trees that cast dense shade with smaller trees or ones with more open canopies.

On the other hand, you can find many wonderful plants, like azaleas, rhododendrons, begonias, camellias, and ferns that are worth creating shade for just so you can grow them. Obviously, you can plant trees, but don't forget that you can also build arbors and gazebos to create shade. You can find out more about landscape structures in Part II of this book.

Shade-loving plants

"It's about time," you may be saying. "I'm finally going get specific plants for specific types of shade." Sorry, but there are too many types of shade. How well certain plants will grow in those various shades also depends on how hot a climate you live in.

What we give you, instead, are lists of different kinds of plants that grow in some type of shade. You can go read their descriptions in Chapters 8 through 11. Chances are that if a plant is described as growing in full sun or part shade, it's better for areas with brighter light. If it says plant in shade, it will do okay in full shade and possibly in very heavy shade. In either case, you can't really find any hard and fast rules.

Check out your neighborhood and see which plants are growing well in shady conditions similar to yours. That's often the best guide. But even with that information, you may have a failure or two before you find a group of plants that all thrive.

From a design standpoint, plants with big leaves, white flowers, or variegated white foliage put on the best show in shady landscapes. In fact, planting any light colored flowers is a good way to light up a shady area.

Trees for shady landscapes

The following are mostly small trees that grow especially well under the canopy of taller trees. For more information, see Chapter 8.

✔ Japanese maple

✔ Flowering dogwood

✔ Serviceberry

✔ Katsura tree

✔ Silverbell

Shrubs for shade

For complete descriptions of shrubs, see Chapter 9.

✔ Glossy abelia

✔ Barberries

✔ Boxwood

✔ Camellias

✔ Euonymus

✔ Gardenias

✔ Hydrangeas

✔ Heavenly bamboo

✔ Tobira

✔ Azaleas and rhododendrons

✔ Viburnums

✔ Mahonia

Vines for shade

These are good choices to train on a shady wall or trellis. For more information, see Chapter 9.

✔ Creeping fig

✔ English ivy

✔ Chinese jasmine

✔ Virginia creeper and Boston ivy

✔ Star jasmine

Annual flowers for shade

These are broken down according to cool season and warm season plants, depending on whether they grow best in the cool months of spring and fall, or the hot months of summer. For additional information, see Chapter 10.

Try the following cool-season annuals:

- Larkspur
- Chinese forget-me-not
- Sweet alyssum
- Geraniums
- Primroses
- Nasturtium
- Pansies and violas

Check out the following warm-season annuals:

- Bedding begonias
- Madagascar periwinkle
- Coleus
- Impatiens
- Lobelia
- Flowering tobacco

Flowering perennials for shade

Many other perennials can grow in partial shade, but they will produce fewer flowers.

For more information, see Chapter 10.

- Columbines
- Bellflowers
- Dianthus
- Blood-red geranium
- Coral bells
- Plantain lily (hosta)

Flowering bulbs for shade

Many early spring blooming bulbs, including daffodils, can be grown in the shade of deciduous trees. Such bulbs will grow and bloom before the tree's canopy becomes too dense with foliage. For more details on bulbs, see Chapter 10.

- ✔ Lily of the Valley
- ✔ Begonias
- ✔ Fancy caladium
- ✔ Freesias
- ✔ Snowdrops
- ✔ Common hyacinth
- ✔ Iris
- ✔ Snowflake
- ✔ Grape hyacinth
- ✔ Calla lily

Lawns and ground covers for shade

Most lawn grasses don't grow well in shade. The most shade tolerant are fine fescues and St. Augustine grass, but you may be better off planting a ground cover. The following are shade tolerant ground covers. For more information on lawns and ground covers, see Chapter 11.

- ✔ Carpet bugle
- ✔ English ivy
- ✔ Aaron's beard
- ✔ Mondo grass
- ✔ Japanese spurge
- ✔ Spring cinquefoil
- ✔ Star jasmine
- ✔ Dwarf periwinkle

What's Winter Hardy?

Terms such as *cold hardy, frost hardy,* and *winter hardy* are used to describe woody plants that can survive freezing temperatures without injury during the winter. So, this section is for those of you who live where it gets cold in winter. Of course, "cold" is a relative term. For plants, it's *cold* in Venice, California (where coauthor Philip Giroux lives), on those rare occasions when the thermometer dips to 30°F. In Burlington, Vermont (home of the National Gardening Association), cold is a lot colder: –20°F is not unusual.

And don't forget ferns

No discussion on shade landscapes is complete without mentioning ferns. Their arching, feathery leaf (fern leaves are actually called *fronds*) patterns are as at home in the shade as are hammocks.

You can find many ferns to choose from. Tree ferns, such as *Dicksonia antarctica*, the tasmanian tree fern, and *Cyathea cooperi*, the Australian tree fern, have long arching fronds and tall stalks that can reach over 15 feet under ideal, moist conditions. They're not very hardy though, and can't be grown in areas colder than Zone 9.

Some hardier native ferns include the Autumn fern, *Dryopteris erythrosora*, which can be grown into Zone 5. This fern is interesting because its 2-foot long leaves are pinkish when they unfold and turn rust brown in autumn. The Alaskan or soft shield fern, *Polystichum setiferum*, is also hardy into Zone 5; has lacy, flattened fronds that can grow up to 4 feet high; and is easy to grow. A close relative, the sword fern, *P. munitum*, produces upright fronds on a spreading plant. In its native western United States, it's a tough plant that can get weedy if given too much water. It is hardy into Zone 7.

That's only a taste of the ferns. If you're really into them, your local nursery probably carries an even wider selection.

Even though landscapers are natural born experimenters, imagine investing a few thousand dollars and your free time in summer planting a new landscape only to watch the plants curl their toes and die their first winter. To avoid that is exactly why climate zones were invented.

Climate zones are most critical for permanent landscape plants — the type of plants you find in this book. If you want a tree, shrub, vine, or perennial to survive and grow year after year, the plant must tolerate year-round conditions in your area — most often, this means the lowest and highest temperatures. Other factors are important too, namely the amount and distribution of rainfall (or availability of irrigation water) and soil conditions.

Perhaps the safest course to ensure plant adaptability is to grow only plants that are native to your particular region — they are most likely to have the constitution to survive in your landscape. However, plants don't stay in their regions of origin any more than landscapers do. Plants native to China, Siberia, or Mexico thrive alongside each other in many American landscapes. Furthermore, a landscaper in California may want to grow a plant native to the Great Plains. In these cases, he or she needs some way to compare the landscape's climate with the climate where the plant is known to grow well. This is when zone maps play a critical role.

Peeking at the USDA Zone Map

All the plants in this book (explored in Chapters 8 through 11) are coded with a hardiness zone that corresponds with the zone system devised by the United States Department of Agriculture in 1960, and most recently revised in 1990. Figure 12-1 shows the Canadian USDA zones, Figure 12-2 shows the European zones, and Figure 12-3 gives you the zones in the United States. The zone numbers given for plants refer to these maps. If you live in one of the plant's recommended zones, you have some assurance the plant is hardy enough to survive winter.

The latest version of the USDA Zone map divides North America and Europe into 20 separate zones. Zones are numbered 1 through 11, but Zones 2 through 10 are subdivided into "a" and "b" regions — but only in North America, not in Europe. Each zone number is 10°F warmer (or colder) in an average winter than the adjacent zone. The greatest virtues of the USDA map are its widespread use and the fact that many plants have been categorized according to its zones.

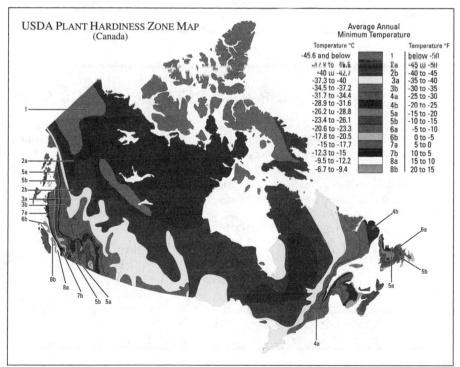

Figure 12-1:
Plant
hardiness
zones for
Canada.

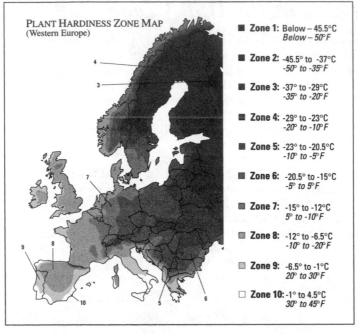

PLANT HARDINESS ZONE MAP
(Western Europe)

■ **Zone 1:** Below – 45.5°C
Below – 50°F

■ **Zone 2:** -45.5° to -37°C
-50° to -35°F

■ **Zone 3:** -37° to -29°C
-35° to -20°F

■ **Zone 4:** -29° to -23°C
-20° to -10°F

■ **Zone 5:** -23° to -20.5°C
-10° to -5°F

■ **Zone 6:** -20.5° to -15°C
-5° to 5°F

■ **Zone 7:** -15° to -12°C
5° to -10°F

■ **Zone 8:** -12° to -6.5°C
-10° to -20°F

■ **Zone 9:** -6.5° to -1°C
20° to 30°F

□ **Zone 10:** -1° to 4.5°C
30° to 45°F

Figure 12-2:
Plant
hardiness
zones for
Europe.

Exploring the AHS plant heat-zone map

The significance of winter's lowest temperatures decreases as you shift from places where winter freezes may kill many plants to areas where freezes merely mean frost on lawns and windshields. But on the other hand, areas with mild winter temperatures often have soaring summer temperatures. Landscapers have discovered that summer high temperatures can limit plant survival just as surely as winter low temperatures.

In 1997 the American Horticultural Society (AHS) published a zone map that accounts for plant's adaptability to heat. Called The Heat Map, this 12-zone map of the United States indicates the average number of days each year when given regions experience temperatures of 86°F or higher. According to the AHS, that's the temperature at which many common plants begin to suffer physiological damage. The zones range from 1 (one day or less at 86°F or warmer) through 12 (210 days or more per year).

The AHS Heat Zone Map is still new and not widely published. You can buy your own color poster of it for $15. To order, call the AHS at (800) 777-7931, ext. 45.

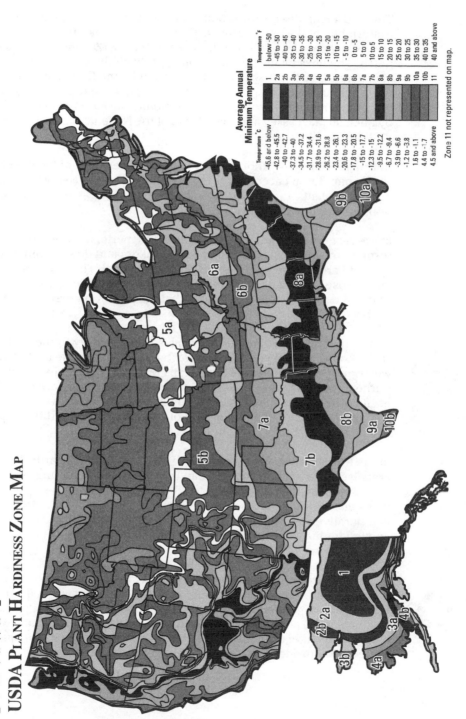

Figure 12-3:
Plant
hardiness
zones for
the United
States.

USDA PLANT HARDINESS ZONE MAP

The USDA map does a fine job of delineating the landscape climates of the eastern half of the United States. That area is comparatively flat, so zones are mostly parallel, east-west lines separated by 120 miles or so as you move north. The lines tilt northeast as they approach the Eastern seaboard. They also demarcate the special climates formed by the Great Lakes and by the Appalachian mountain ranges. For color versions of the USDA zone maps of North America and Europe, check out *Gardening For Dummies,* 2nd Edition, by Michael MacCaskey and the Editors of the National Gardening Association (IDG Books Worldwide, Inc.).

But these maps have shortcomings. In the eastern half of the country, the USDA map doesn't account for the beneficial effect of a snow cover over perennial plants, the regularity or absence of freeze — thaw cycles, or soil drainage during cold periods.

In the rest of the country (west of the 100th meridian, which runs roughly through the middle of North and South Dakota and down through Texas west of Laredo), the USDA map is even less useful. The key problem is the map's absolute reliance on average winter minimum temperature, a system that can equate regions of climates that differ in every way but temperature, such as San Diego and Florida.

Due to the influence of mountain ranges and proximity to the ocean, the USDA Zones are less useful in the western U.S. than in the East. If you live in western North America, the zone maps featured in the Sunset Western Garden Book (Sunset Publishing Corporation, 1997; $35), are probably more useful. The criteria that define the different western zones are winter cold, summer heat, amount and duration of precipitation, humidity, seasonal winds, and number of sunlight hours.

In the low-elevation West, winters are mild. Vancouver, Seattle, Portland, San Francisco, Fresno, Los Angeles, San Diego, Phoenix, and Tucson all experience average winter lows of 27° to 48°F (with all-time lows mostly in the high teens and low 20s). And between 27° and 32°F, plant damage from freezing is comparatively unimportant. In most places, freeze damage is not significant enough to qualify as the single defining climatic factor — but it's the primary criterion for USDA zones.

At the same time, the West gets from a fraction of an inch to maybe 10 to 11 inches of rain each year. That's not enough to grow a lawn, a flower garden, or a vegetable garden without regular irrigation, but it is enough to grow western native plants. That's why, in the late 20th century, many western landscapers have turned to native plants and highly efficient irrigation systems to provide foliage and flowers in the dry season.

Maximizing winter hardiness for plants

Landscapers can, to some degree, help plants adapt to winter.

- ✔ Reduce the amount of nitrogen fertilizer that you apply after mid-July and stop by late summer.

  Commercial growers decrease the rate of nitrogen fertilizer by approximately one half and double the rate of potassium application in late summer.

  Plants should enter the autumn season as healthy as possible, but not rapidly growing, or their acclimation may be affected.

- ✔ Because plants — especially evergreens — often dry out or "dessicate" during winter, the soil in which evergreens are being grown should be well irrigated in mid-to-late autumn, before the soil freezes. If the landscape where evergreens are located is in a dry site, sandy soil, or under the overhang of a roof, irrigate the soil in midwinter when the temperature is above freezing.

  This practice is especially beneficial for plants, such as rhododendron, which continue growth late into the season and are susceptible to early freeze damage. Because woody plants appear to have a built-in mechanism to reduce water levels when they acclimate, reducing soil water may not benefit the development of maximum midwinter cold hardiness.

Uncovering how winter damages plants

Winter injury describes several types of plant damage caused by environmental conditions during late fall, winter, or spring. Damage ranges from a marginal scorching of leaves to complete killing of plants. You may have difficulty differentiating winter injury from disease, insect, or chemical injury. Winter-injured plants often leaf out normally in the spring only to collapse after stored food reserves have been totally used up by the plant. Occasionally, damage does not become apparent until one or two years after the injury occurred.

Frost injury

Late spring and early autumn frosts injure plants that are not yet sufficiently dormant and able to withstand cold temperatures. This type of injury can occur on native plants, but more exotic plants are usually more vulnerable. A result of late spring frosts can be the death of expanding flower buds on species such as magnolia or lilac, or the death of young, succulent, actively growing shoots.

Clip and destroy dead tissues in the spring. The plant won't suffer any long-term effects.

Low temperature injury

Cold temperatures damage plants in several ways. Damage is most common in early fall or late spring, when there is little or no snow cover. Plants are also likely to be damaged during winters of little snow cover, and during periods of prolonged low temperatures. Rapid fluctuations in temperature are dangerous for plants no matter what time of year they occur.

✔ Plants injured or killed directly by low winter temperatures are those planted in areas colder than their minimum hardiness zone. For instance, if a plant is rated as hardy in USDA Zones 5 through 9 and is planted in Zone 4, it will likely suffer in an average Zone 4 winter. Such species can't *harden off* (become accustomed and more resistant to cold) at an appropriate rate or to an extent sufficient to withstand prevailing winter temperatures. However, even hardy plants can be injured during unusually cold periods or when temperatures drop rapidly or change frequently.

✔ Both too much nitrogen fertilizer in late summer or fall, and late summer pruning can promote new growth that doesn't mature and may be damaged by freezing. Flower buds, vegetative buds, branches, stems, crowns, bark, roots, or even whole plants may be injured.

✔ Plants in containers are particularly vulnerable to low winter temperatures because their roots aren't protected by being below ground. Roots are much less hardy to cold than trunks and branches. Roots of even the hardiest shrubs and trees are killed at temperatures between 0 and 10°F. Place container plants in protected areas, sunk into the ground, grouped together, and heavily mulched to avoid low temperature injury to roots.

To prevent winter damage to your plants, avoid plants that aren't hardy where you live. To allow proper hardening of plant tissues, don't fertilize plants in late summer. Mulch around the bases of root-tender plants to help protect their crowns and roots from freezing temperatures. Even with good management, though, injury to young growth or insufficiently hardened tissues may still occur as a result of unusual weather patterns. Unfortunately, you can't do much to prevent injury in these instances.

In spring, after growth resumes, prune out injured and dead stems or branches or damaged plants, or replace damaged plants with kinds adapted to your zone.

Winter drought

This problem usually appears in late winter or very early spring on ever-green plants. The injury occurs during sunny and/or windy winter weather when plants lose water from their leaves faster than it can be replaced by roots that are frozen in soil. Broadleaf evergreens, such as rhododendron, exhibit browning or even total death of their leaf margins (leaf scorch) depending on the extent of injury. Narrowleaf evergreens, such as white pine, exhibit browning of needle tips when injury is slight. Extensive injury may result in browning and premature drop of entire needles.

Plants that are properly watered during dry periods in late autumn are better equipped to withstand this type of injury. Mulching around the root zones of susceptible evergreens will also help to minimize the damage. Placing a protective barrier of burlap over or around plants to protect them from winter winds and sun will help to reduce the incidence of this injury. Antidesiccant sprays applied once in late autumn and again in midwinter may also prove helpful.

Sunscald

This type of injury occurs when the sun heats tree bark during the day and then the bark rapidly cools after sunset. These abrupt fluctuations are most common on south or southwest sides of trunks and branches, and they may kill the inner bark in those areas. Young and/or thin-barked trees are most susceptible to winter sunscald.

Wrapping trunks of susceptible trees with protective "tree wrap" is the most effective way to minimize this type of winter injury.

Frost cracks

Frost cracks are splits in bark and wood of a tree that occur when winter sun causes a differential expansion of wood beneath the bark. The initial crack is often accompanied by a loud snap. In winter, the crack may become wider and narrower during colder or warmer periods. Such frost cracks often close and callus over during the summer, only to open again in subsequent winters. This callusing and recracking may lead to the formation of large *frost ribs* on the side of affected trees.

In midautumn, wrap the trunks of young trees with commercial tree wrap paper or burlap to protect against frost cracks. Brace large frost ribs to prevent reopening during the winter and enhance callusing and healing. Frost cracks in trees are ideal sites for the entrance of wood decay organisms. Check affected trees regularly to ensure that they are free from serious decay and, therefore, not a hazard to surrounding buildings and living things.

Snow and ice

Heavy snow or ice on weak limbs or on limbs with foliage (as in the case of evergreens) can result in breakage.

Prune trees and shrubs to reduce the amount of snow or ice they will collect and/or eliminate those branches which will be inherently weak. Branches with a wide angle to the main stem are generally stronger and can support more snow and ice than can those with a narrow or acute angle. Plant trees and shrubs away from places where snowmelt from roofs will drip on them. Build wooden barriers over small shrubs to allow snow and ice to slide off rather than accumulate.

Protecting landscape plants in winter

Take the following steps to decrease the likelihood of winter injury to your plants:

- **Plant on the north side.** Choose a location for marginally hardy plants with a northern or eastern exposure rather than south or southwest. Plants facing the south are more exposed to the sun on warm winter days and thus experience greater daily temperature variation.

- **Mulch.** Apply a layer of mulch, 2 to 2$\frac{1}{2}$ inches deep, after the soil freezes to keep the soil cold rather than protect the soil from becoming cold. This practice reduces injury from plant roots *heaving* (coming out of the soil) because of alternate freezing and thawing. Plants that benefit from this practice include perennials, *alpine plants* (plants adapted to very cold, usually high elevation areas), rock landscape plants, strawberries, and other shallow-rooted species. A mulch helps maintain even soil temperature and retains soil moisture.

  Apply bark products, composts, peat moss, pine needles, straw, hay, or any one of a number of materials that your local garden center carries. You can prop pine boughs or remains from a Christmas tree against and over evergreens to help protect against damage by wind and sun.

- **Tie your plants.** *Multiple leader* (that means branched) plants such as arborvitae, juniper, and yew may be damaged by the weight of snow or ice. Prevent plant breakage by fastening heavy twine at the base of the plant and winding it spirally around and upward to the top and back down in a reverse spiral. Use this technique as your plants become larger and begin to open at the top.

- **Use a burlap screen.** Stretch a section of burlap around four stakes to protect young plants from the south, west, and windward exposures. See Figure 12-4.

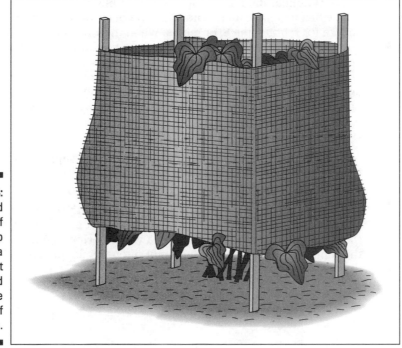

Figure 12-4:
A wind screen of burlap protects a young plant from wind and the rays of winter sun.

A wrap of burlap with the stakes can offer protection to plants against drying from sun and wind, and drift from de-icing salts applied to drives and streets. Wrap the "body" of the evergreens, but don't cover the top of the plant because some light is necessary, even during winter.

✔ **Use antitranspirants (antidesiccants).** Narrow and broadleaf evergreens lose moisture through leaves in winter. Because the soil moisture may be frozen, plant roots can't absorb what's lost and the foliage desiccates, turns brown, and may drop. This can be serious with evergreen azalea, holly, boxwood, and rhododendron.

First, make sure that evergreens are properly watered throughout the growing season and into the fall. Decrease watering slightly in autumn to encourage hardening off, then water thoroughly in October and continue until soil freezes.

Applying an antitranspirant, also called antidesiccant, reduces *transpiration* (loss of water from the leaves) and damage to the foliage from winter drought. At least two applications per season, one in December and another in February, are usually necessary to provide protection all winter. A number of products are available in most garden centers.

✔ **Prevent animal damage.** Some landscape plants, especially during a time when you have an extended period of snow cover, become a food source for rabbits, mice, or moles. When their normal food supply is covered with ice or snow, rodents turn to the bark and young stems of apple, flowering crabapple, mountain ash, hawthorn, euonymus, and viburnum, among others. Complete *girdling* (removal of the outer bark and transport cells of the plant) of stems by rodents kills the plants and partial girdling weakens the plant and creates wounds for borers and disease organisms to enter.

Protect stems and trunks of these plants in late autumn with plastic collars cut in a spiral fashion so that they can be slipped around tree trunks. You can also use *hardware cloth* (small mesh wire screen) as a stem wrap along with aluminum foil.

Spray or paint trunks, stems, and lower limbs with rodent repellents. A number of these materials are available in most garden centers. Repeat the application at least once during a warm period in midwinter. Mixing the repellents with an antitranspirant often results in extended effectiveness of these products.

Part IV
Putting It All Together

In this part . . .

The landscape plans in this part are intended to get you started. Because of so many factors that make each garden different — climate, terrain, your needs and desires, neighborhood traditions, and so on — any plan, except one designed exactly for you, can't be followed too literally. But they can help you with fresh ideas and can offer some interesting options for your landscape.

These garden plans, like all good designs, balance the pragmatic and the pretty. For a garden to work for you, it should make sense in practical ways — not too demanding of time and money, good for the land, and good for your family's lifestyle. It should also look great, and that's where the designer's bag of tricks comes into play: proportion, repetition, variety, harmony, surprise, color, and so on (flip to Chapter 2).

We begin with the major landscape elements in Chapter 13 and then subdivide the garden in Chapters 14 and 15. Consult Part III of this book to help select specific plants for your own situation.

Chapter 13

Plans for Your Whole Lot

*W*e realize that there may be no such thing as the typical lot waiting to be landscaped, but the situation that most of us picture is something like this: A front yard that's open to the street, a front door and walk that's used by guests and occupants, narrow side yards, and a decent-sized back yard. Does that sound like your lot? If so, you can use the four plans in this chapter.

Most home owners want a front yard that looks presentable at all times of the year and that provides some privacy from neighbors within shouting (or even whispering) distance. Another goal is an entry that clearly announces that *this* is the way to the front door — and makes the arrival interesting. Side yards are too often overlooked and under-used — here, we try to correct that. Our backyard plan addresses the familiar urge to create a multipurpose family place — for entertaining, relaxing, playing, plus growing flowers and vegetables.

A Park-like Front Yard

What do you want from your front yard? You may want shade trees and a big lawn that merges with the neighbors'. Or maybe a courtyard — an approach that has worked in Spain for hundreds of years — that provides privacy from a busy street. Or consider the overall effect of the front yard in Figure 13-1: spacious and simple, with a big lawn, shade trees, and evergreens creating a green, park-like effect. Guests have a pleasant walk to the front door any time of the year. Mixed perennials add bursts of seasonal color.

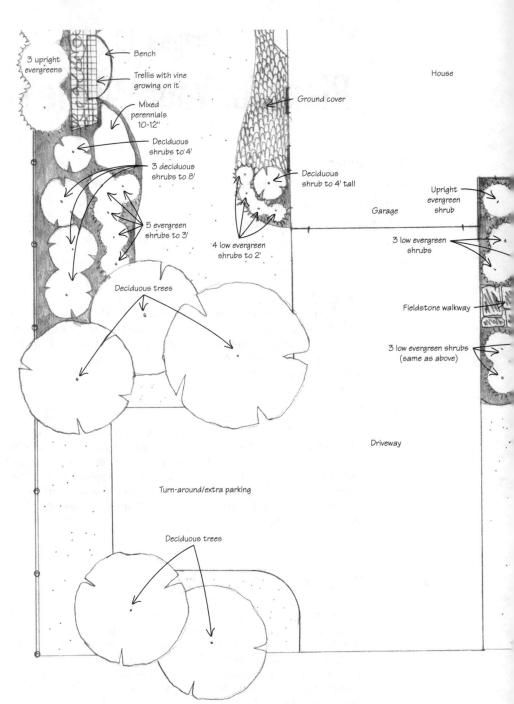

Figure 13-1:
A gracious
front yard.

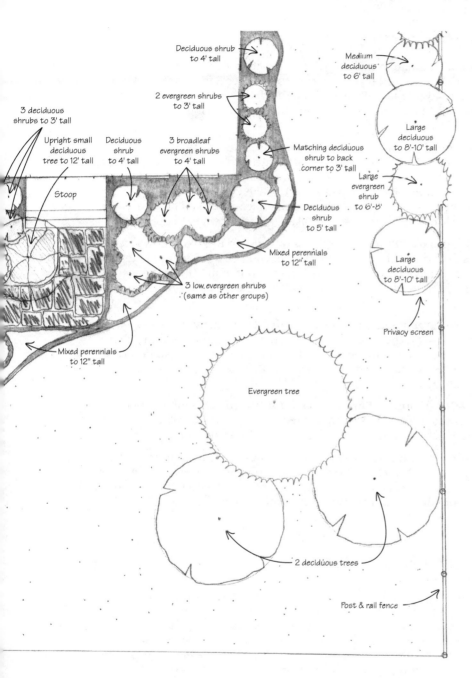

Deciduous shrub
to 4' tall

Medium
deciduous
to 6' tall

2 evergreen shrubs
to 3' tall

Large
deciduous
to 8'-10' tall

3 deciduous
shrubs to 3' tall

Upright small
deciduous
tree to 12' tall

Deciduous
shrub
to 4' tall

3 broadleaf
evergreen shrubs
to 4' tall

Matching deciduous
shrub to back
corner to 3' tall

Large
evergreen
shrub
to 6'-8'

Stoop

Deciduous
shrub
to 5' tall

Large
deciduous
to 8'-10' tall

Mixed perennials
to 12" tall

3 low evergreen shrubs
(same as other groups)

Privacy screen

Mixed perennials
to 12" tall

Evergreen tree

2 deciduous trees

Post & rail fence

This front-yard plan provides interesting features:

✔ **A gracious fieldstone walkway:** You can vary your walkway in size, shape, and the material you use (flip to Chapter 5 for more on building your walkway). This walk leads from the driveway to a spacious front stoop (which is covered in more detail in the following section, "A Friendly Front Entry").

✔ **A turnaround allows for extra parking:** Deciduous trees help define the turnaround area, as well as create a little mystery and screening for the side yard planting (covered in more detail in the "Side Yard Getaway Garden" section, later in this chapter). While your front yard may not be large enough to accommodate a turnaround, you may still be able to carve out a small, private, screened area, like the one shown in Chapter 14.

✔ **A deciduous tree that adds vertical interest to the front entry:** A tree that's so close to the house shouldn't exceed 12 to 15 feet in height. It should also have an upright growth habit so it won't block the view from the front door or jut into the walkway. See Chapter 8 for more on trees.

✔ **Mixed evergreen and deciduous shrubs:** These provide privacy where it's needed — on the property lines. Remember that deciduous plants won't provide much privacy during their leafless season, so don't use them where all-year screening is critical. Chapter 9 has more information on shrubs.

✔ **Foundation plants that are compact, for low maintenance:** Choose varieties that grow no taller than 4 feet (except for the plants at the corner, which can reach 6 feet, unless roof eaves don't allow room).

✔ **Repetition in plantings:** To provide continuity, the front entry planting has three groups of the same three low-growing masses of evergreens. And note that the same deciduous shrubs are used on both sides of the front door. Chapter 2 discusses repetition in more detail.

A Friendly Front Entry

Think of a front entry garden as a handshake, a hug, or a big, slurpy kiss — your personal way of greeting friends and family. This part of your yard is a personal statement, and it can reflect *you* — your favorite plants, touches of outdoor decoration, a wreath on the door at the holidays. Of course you also have to think of the mailman and others who use the entry for practical purposes — they should at least be able to find the front door. And speaking of the practical, you want something that's not unreasonable to maintain and keep tidy. Remember, this is the one part of your yard that you use every day of the year.

The front entry plan in Figure 13-2 falls in the category of a warm, but dignified greeting — sort of a friendly hug. It has an orderly, straight-ahead approach by way of the rectangular walk and the broad concrete stoop and steps. Skimping on the size of the front porch always seems like an un-friendly gesture — no place to stand comfortably while you're waiting. Fieldstone set into the walk lends a nice informal touch, but you can always substitute concrete, bricks, or gravel (see Chapter 5).

Keep the following in mind when considering this plan for your front entry:

- **Curved planting beds alongside the walk soften the geometry of the front porch, house, and walk.** Notice their asymmetry, which complements the offset door and adds interest to the design.

- **Plants are layered.** Tall plants in back against the house, medium-sized ones are in the middle, and low plants are in the front border. Chapter 2 explains layering in more detail.

- **Plantings are low-maintenance.** All except the capitata yew are dwarf or compact varieties, which will call for less maintenance. (The yew needs annual pruning, though.)

- **Flowers bloom throughout several seasons.** Red-leafed plants such as 'Crimson Pygmy' barberry repeat to provide color for a long season and to draw the eye across the whole planting. 'Miss Kim' lilac is repeated across the planting for the impact of its spring bloom.

  For additional color, use low perennials (up to a foot tall) throughout the season or add annuals for different color schemes every year. If you plant close to the house where shade is deep, make sure that you choose shade-loving flowers.

- **Use the front porch to display a small tree in a container, such as red-leafed Japanese maple (to repeat the red of the barberries): For even more color, fill in around the base of the tree with blooming annuals or perennials.**

Side Yard Getaway Garden

Space in the side yard is often neglected, mainly because it's a tight space that tends to be out of sight. Side yards also often suffer from too much shade from your house or the neighbor's — plus frequent problems with privacy.

At the same time, side yards offer great potential. Their restricted space can offer an intimacy that the rest of a yard doesn't. Shade, of course, can be turned into a blessing.

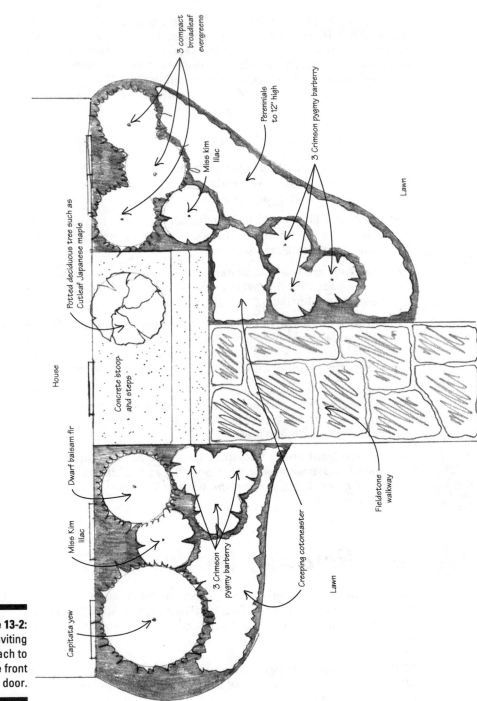

3 compact broadleaf evergreens

Perennials to 12" high

3 Crimson pygmy barberry

Miss Kim lilac

Lawn

Potted deciduous tree such as Cutleaf Japanese maple

House

Concrete stoop and steps

Fieldstone walkway

Dwarf balsam fir

Miss Kim lilac

3 Crimson pygmy barberry

Creeping cotoneaster

Lawn

Capitata yew

Figure 13-2:
An inviting approach to the front door.

This side yard plan (Figure 13-3) makes the most of a typical long narrow side yard shape. It's designed to be admired from outside and inside. Looking out the bay window at the bench, which serves as a focal point, the view is designed to be appreciated any day of the year.

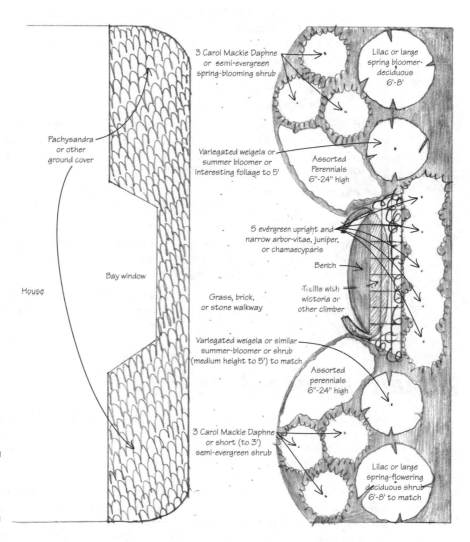

Figure 13-3: A peaceful side yard.

3 Carol Mackie Daphne or semi-evergreen spring-blooming shrub

Lilac or large spring bloomer- deciduous 6'-8'

Pachysandra or other ground cover

Variegated weigela or summer bloomer or interesting foliage to 5'

Assorted Perennials 6"-24" high

5 evergreen upright and narrow arbor-vitae, juniper, or chamaecyparis

Bench

Bay window

House

Grass, brick, or stone walkway

Trellis with wistoria or other climber

Variegated weigela or similar summer-bloomer or shrub (medium height to 5') to match

Assorted perennials 6"-24" high

3 Carol Mackie Daphne or short (to 3') semi-evergreen shrub

Lilac or large spring-flowering deciduous shrub 6'-8' to match

A few things to keep in mind about this side yard plan include:

- ✔ **A trellis over a bench makes a shady getaway.** Note the centered location of the bench, which creates a focal point. Chapter 7 has more information on benches and trellises.

- ✔ **The foundation of the house is covered.** At the base of the house, pachysandra or other evergreen ground cover that grows tall enough (to 12 inches) covers the exposed foundation — the plants enjoy the partial shade usually found at the base of a house. The ground cover that you select should form a solid mass and be subdued enough in leaf color and texture not to detract from the rest of the plantings. Chapter 11 can help with ground-cover selection.

  If the side of the house includes some bare wall panels, without windows, you may want to add shrubs along the house's foundation. The plants provide a cooling effect and reduce reflected heat, plus they offer a better view from the bench.

- ✔ **Plants provide privacy.** Plantings on the property line form a backdrop and privacy screen from the neighbors. See Chapter 14 for a plan for privacy planting.

- ✔ **Carol Mackie Daphne serves as bookends to planting.** It has white- or gold-edged leaves, and is attractive year-round; it is semi-evergreen and doesn't drop all its leaves in the fall.

- ✔ **The area has close-up color.** Colorful flowering plants are intended to be appreciated at close range. Consider wisteria, lilac, weigela, and assorted perennials.

A Multipurpose Back Yard

Out of sight of neighbors and passersby, the back yard would seem to be where you ease up a bit and let things go. But it's also the place where every family member wants their own pet projects — flowers, vegetables, a swing set, croquet, horseshoes, horses — whatever.

This backyard plan, shown in Figure 13-4, is for lucky homeowners with a big back yard, but you can choose to duplicate only a portion of this yard, if yours is smaller. Different activities are allotted their own, defined space, but without high dividing fences. The big, green lawn provides plenty of play space as well as visual relief for the more complex surroundings.

Note the following about this back yard plan:

- ✔ **Divided patio:** The patio is two levels — you step up to the dining area. Dividing the patio in this way makes the spaces seem more intimate. See Chapter 6 for more on planning and building a patio.

- ✔ **Safe play area:** The children's play area doesn't need fencing (except for the backdrop of side yard fencing). You want to be able to see playing children from the house and patio. See Chapter 15 for more details on this kids' area.

- ✔ **Shade trees:** A big tree near the patio provides shade where it's needed most — where you want to spend your summer days. Chapter 8 has more on selecting trees.

  More shade trees, strategically located, make the children's play area comfortable in hot weather.

- ✔ **Privacy shrubs:** Big evergreen and deciduous shrubs form privacy screens along the property lines. Chapter 14 has a special plan for privacy and Chapter 9 has more information on shrubbery.

- ✔ **Well-located vegetable garden:** The vegetable garden basks in the yard's sunniest spot — away from trees. It can be fenced (if you have visiting varmints or curious small children) or not. The fence and raised beds add an element of structure that makes the garden more presentable during its off-seasons. See Chapter 15 for an up-close and personal view of this vegetable garden.

- ✔ **Seasonal color:** A border of perennials and shrubs provides seasonal color right where you can see it most — at the edge of the patio. Select plants that are low enough not to cut off the view. Chapters 9 and 10 have the lowdown on shrubs and flowers.

- ✔ **Container flowers:** Annuals and perennials grow in containers to brighten corners of the patio. Choose pots that are 12 inches in diameter or larger, and cluster them in groups of at least three. See Chapter 10 for more on container gardens.

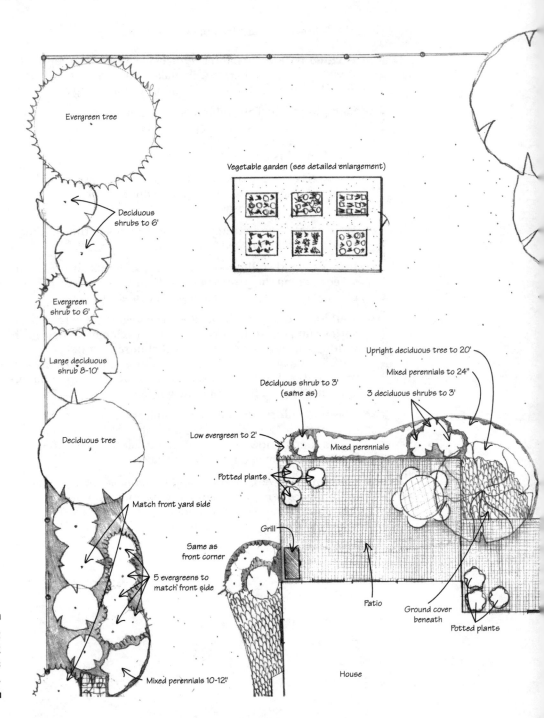

Evergreen tree

Deciduous shrubs to 6'

Evergreen shrub to 6'

Large deciduous shrub 8-10'

Deciduous tree

Match front yard side

Same as front corner

5 evergreens to match front side

Mixed perennials 10-12"

Vegetable garden (see detailed enlargement)

Upright deciduous tree to 20'

Mixed perennials to 24"

3 deciduous shrubs to 3'

Deciduous shrub to 3' (same as)

Mixed perennials

Low evergreen to 2'

Potted plants

Grill

Patio

Ground cover beneath

Potted plants

House

Figure 13-4:
This back yard has it all.

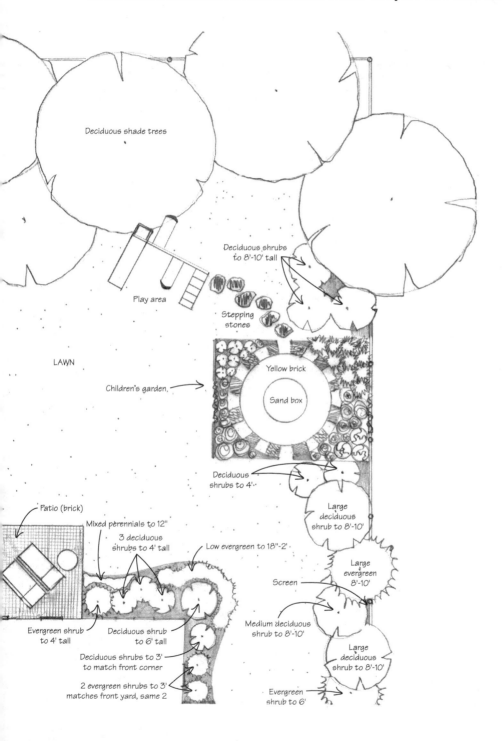

Deciduous shade trees

Deciduous shrubs
to 8'-10' tall

Play area

Stepping
stones

LAWN

Yellow brick

Sand box

Children's garden,

Deciduous
shrubs to 4'

Large
deciduous
shrub to 8'-10'

Patio (brick)

Mixed perennials to 12"

3 deciduous
shrubs to 4' tall

Low evergreen to 18"-2'

Large
evergreen
8'-10'

Screen

Evergreen shrub
to 4' tall

Deciduous shrub
to 6' tall

Medium deciduous
shrub to 8'-10'

Deciduous shrubs to 3'
to match front corner

Large
deciduous
shrub to 8'-10'

2 evergreen shrubs to 3'
matches front yard, same 2

Evergreen
shrub to 6'

Chapter 14
Plans for Special Situations

- -

In This Chapter

▶ Planting for privacy

▶ Creating a stunning low-water landscape

▶ Developing a woodland garden

▶ Landscaping around a pool

▶ Building a rock garden on a slope

▶ Carving a garden out of a small balcony

- -

*1*n this chapter, we try to help you plan the parts of your landscape that demand special treatment — is part of your yard wide open to the view from your neighbor's or the street? Do you have an area that slopes up from a lawn or the sidewalk? Have you recently installed a new swimming pool that's bare-naked on your lot?

In addressing sections of a landscape by themselves, we don't intend to contradict other chapters in this book that encourage you to integrate your whole property into a grand garden scheme. We just know that some situations require special attention. Or, that you may be doing your landscaping one section at a time — nothing wrong with that. But try to keep in mind how each section will fit into your overall scheme.

The idea here is to get you started. You probably have to adapt them for your own garden conditions and availability of landscaping material. The plans in this chapter suggest specific plants, which may or may not work in your garden and climate. For alternatives, check the plant lists that we give with each plan, and consult other chapters in this book: Chapter 8 for trees; Chapter 9 for shrubs and vines; Chapter 10 for annuals, perennials, and bulbs; and Chapter 11 for ground covers.

Planting for Privacy

The challenge in landscaping is to provide privacy while creating an enjoyable and useable space. For this plan, shown in Figure 14-1, we use both plants and fencing for privacy. When carefully selected and placed, plants can help screen neighbors, muffle noise, and create interest and beauty of their own. Remember, too, that plants eventually can grow much taller than a fence — if height is what you want.

When reviewing this privacy planting, consider the following:

- **Use fencing for privacy.** If you want a high degree of privacy, use solid stockade fencing. Otherwise, use a more open type of fencing with vines. See Chapter 5 for more fencing ideas.

- **Create a private patio.** A free-form patio gives an informal look. You can surface it with fieldstone, brick, concrete pavers, pea gravel, or even mulch. Chapter 6 can help you build a patio.

- **Use a mix of plants for privacy.** Evergreens are mixed with deciduous plants for screening (more on trees in Chapter 8). Evergreens provide year-round privacy, but deciduous plants may work fine for you, because their foliage blocks views during spring and summer when you're most apt to use the space.

  Keep in mind the eventual heights of the plants you choose. The taller plants in this plan generally reach 5 to 8 feet in height. For higher screening, consider plants in the section "Deciduous plants for screening," later in this chapter.

- **Pay attention to the shape of plants.** The rounded, enveloping shape of the planting creates a feeling of being wrapped in plants — like you're getting extra privacy.

Deciduous plants for screening

Consider using the following plants for tall screens or hedges.

- European beech *(Fagus sylvatica)*
- Osage orange *(Maclura pomifera)*
- Privet *(Ligustrum)*
- Russian olive *(Elaeagnus augustifolia)*
- Tallhedge buckthorn *(Rhamnus frangula* 'Columnaris')
- Weigela

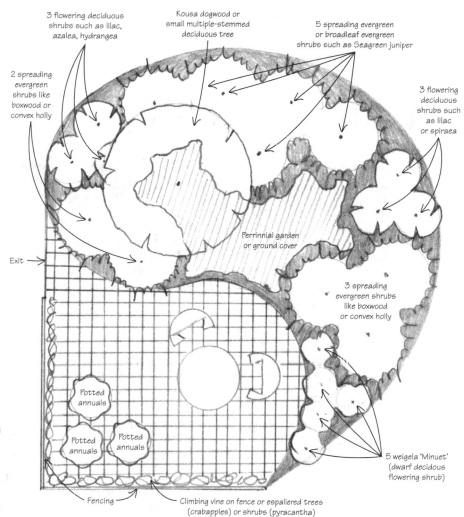

3 flowering deciduous shrubs such as lilac, azalea, hydrangea

Kousa dogwood or small multiple-stemmed deciduous tree

5 spreading evergreen or broadleaf evergreen shrubs such as Seagreen juniper

2 spreading evergreen shrubs like boxwood or convex holly

3 flowering deciduous shrubs such as lilac or spiraea

Perrinnial garden or ground cover

Exit

3 spreading evergreen shrubs like boxwood or convex holly

Potted annuals

Potted annuals

Potted annuals

5 weigela 'Minuet' (dwarf decidous flowering shrub)

Figure 14-1: Privacy for a sitting area.

Fencing

Climbing vine on fence or espaliered trees (crabapples) or shrubs (pyracantha)

Evergreen plants for screening

Try the following for extra privacy:

- Chamaecyparis
- Euonymus
- Incense cedar *(Calocedrus decurrens)*
- Juniper
- Photinia

  ✔ Privet *(Ligustrum)*

  ✔ Viburnum

  ✔ Yew *(Taxus)*

A Low-Water Garden

If you live in an area where water conservation is a priority — like much of the western United States — you may want at least part of your landscape to thrive without irrigation, after it's established. (Keep in mind that almost anything you plant needs watering to get it started and for the first year.)

This low-water plan, shown in Figure 14-2, works in most climates, with the plants that are hardy in Zones 3 to 8 or 9 (see Chapter 12 for more on plant zones). In Western climates that are milder, you can choose from additional palette of plants. Just because the planting has low-water requirements doesn't mean that it has to be boring — note the impact of color described in the following list.

Special features of this low-water plan include:

  ✔ **Layered plants:** The design is a fairly typical border with the low plants up front, tall ones at the back. Low plants grow underneath the window so not to obstruct the view. Russian olives are the big guys. (Chapter 2 discusses layering in more detail.)

  ✔ **Plenty of colors:** You can see a lot of silver — from the artemisa and the Russian olive. This goes nicely with the blue tones — the foliage of the junipers, along with the spring flowers of the ceanothus.

  Seasonal flowers add their colorful punctuation — spiraea in early summer and bright yellow potentilla for a long season. Croton, usually grown as an annual, also provides colorful leaves over a long season — if this isn't a low-water plant in your climate, better find a substitute.

Trees that require little water

You can find many low-water trees to choose from, depending on your climate. Check the adaptability of the following in Chapter 8.

  ✔ Chinese pistache *(Pistacia chinensis)*

  ✔ Crape myrtle *(Lagerstroemia indica)*

  ✔ Locust *(Robinia)*

  ✔ Olive *(Olea europe)*

  ✔ Russian olive *(Elaeagnus angustifolia)*

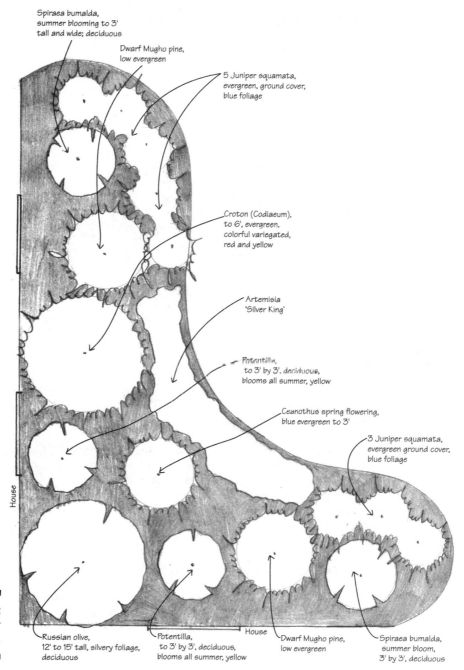

Spiraea bumalda,
summer blooming to 3'
tall and wide; deciduous

Dwarf Mugho pine,
low evergreen

5 Juniper squamata,
evergreen, ground cover,
blue foliage

Croton (Codiaeum),
to 6', evergreen,
colorful variegated,
red and yellow

Artemisia
'Silver King'

Potentilla,
to 3' by 3', deciduous,
blooms all summer, yellow

Ceanothus spring flowering,
blue evergreen to 3'

3 Juniper squamata,
evergreen ground cover,
blue foliage

House

House

Figure 14-2:
A low-water
garden.

Russian olive,
12' to 15' tall, silvery foliage,
deciduous

Potentilla,
to 3' by 3', deciduous,
blooms all summer, yellow

Dwarf Mugho pine,
low evergreen

Spiraea bumalda,
summer bloom,
3' by 3', deciduous

Shrubs that require little water

Chapter 9 offers more advice on shrubs.

- ✔ Artemisa
- ✔ Butterfly bush *(Buddleia)*
- ✔ Euryops
- ✔ Firethorn *(Pyracantha)*
- ✔ Heavenly bamboo *(Nandina domestica)*
- ✔ Lantana
- ✔ Lavender *(Lavandula)*
- ✔ Lemon bottlebrush *(Callistemon citrinus)*
- ✔ Oleander *(Nerium oleander)*
- ✔ Rosemary *(Rosmarinus officinalis)*
- ✔ Sage *(Salvia)*

A Woodland Garden

Maybe you have a garden at the edge of the woods and want to add to it, or perhaps you'd just like to create a woodsy feeling from scratch. Either way, you probably want landscaping that looks like nature created it.

The plan in Figure 14-3 is designed around several existing big shade trees, and features a number of touches that give a natural look. A meandering path seems to take you on a walk through the woods. The plants are all shade-lovers, which means mostly green, but you can brighten things up by including a few colorful bloomers. If the space that you have to work with isn't this large, consider winding a shorter path through an area of about half the size.

To capture this woodsy feel, try the following:

- ✔ **Create a natural path.** Use natural materials such as mulch, stepping stones, or pea gravel. The color section of this book has full-color examples of natural pathways.

- ✔ **Create a focal point.** In this plan, it's a bench at the end of the path. (See the color section of this book for more ideas on benches.) Your focal point can be a piece of outdoor art or an old log.

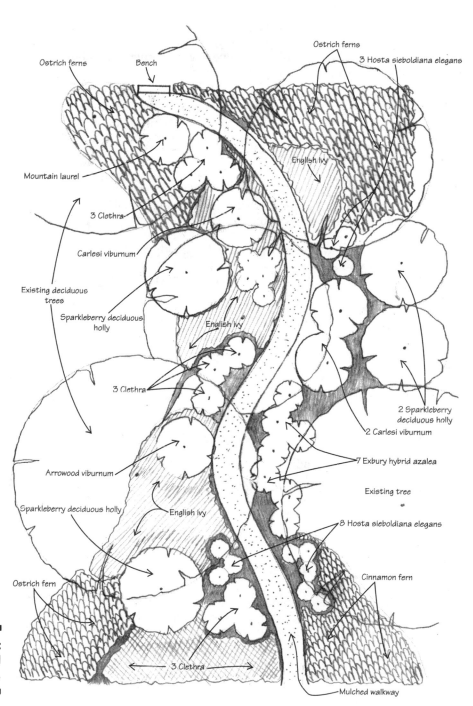

Ostrich ferns

Bench

Ostrich ferns

3 Hosta sieboldiana elegans

English Ivy

Mountain laurel

3 Clethra

Carlesi viburnum

Existing deciduous trees

Sparkleberry deciduous holly

English ivy

3 Clethra

2 Sparkleberry deciduous holly

2 Carlesi viburnum

7 Exbury hybrid azalea

Existing tree

Arrowood viburnum

Sparkleberry deciduous holly

English ivy

8 Hosta sieboldiana elegans

Cinnamon fern

Ostrich fern

3 Clethra

Mulched walkway

Figure 14-3:
A woodland garden.

- ✔ **Plant in groups.** Massed plantings of ground covers and ferns mimic nature's way. Ivy is a fast-growing ground cover choice, but it can invade other plantings like a weed. Other good choices include ajuga, asarum, pachysandra, and viola.

- ✔ **Choose low-maintenance plants.** Plants are selected so that they can grow naturally, without a lot of pruning or other care. Prune annually to keep plants healthy (shade conditions create more than the usual dieback of slender stems and twigs), so cut out dead wood as you notice it or at least once each spring.

- ✔ **Color naturally.** Color over a long season comes from a combination of blossoms and berries. Azaleas, viburnum, and mountain laurel bloom in the spring, and clethra and viburnum in summer. Fall foliage color and winter berries come from winterberry and viburnum.

A woodland garden, by nature, is a shady garden. The following are a few versatile shrubs that are well adapted to shade. All except heavenly bamboo, holly, and yew reward you with berries.

- ✔ Camellia
- ✔ Daphne
- ✔ Flowering maple *(Abutilon)*
- ✔ Fothergilla
- ✔ Heavenly bamboo *(Nandina domestica)*
- ✔ Holly *(Ilex)*
- ✔ Pieris
- ✔ Rhododendron
- ✔ Witch hazel *(Hamamelis)*
- ✔ Yew *(Taxus)*

Around a Pool

Landscaping around a pool first involves choosing the kind of look you want — tropical, natural, sleek, and so on. Keep the following practical considerations in mind when making your plans and selecting your plants:

- ✔ **Don't create shade.** Plants shouldn't cast shade where you don't want it. Choose low-growing or dwarf-type plants. Palms are different — even big ones may not cast too much shade.

✔ **Stay away from mess-makers.** Avoid leaf, blossom, and berry shedders that drop debris into your pool.

✔ **Avoid bee-attracting blossoms, like many summer annuals.**

✔ **Choose low-maintenance plantings.** If you're like most people, you want to use your poolside areas for relaxing and not for heavy-duty gardening.

The plan in Figure 14-4 concentrates planting for privacy and seasonal color in one corner. On the opposite side is a sunning deck — a great private area for viewing the garden.

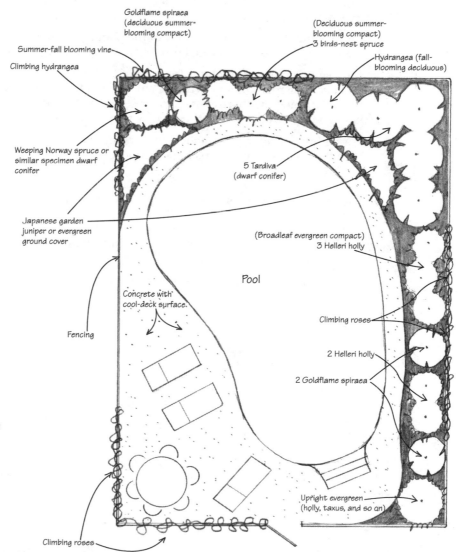

Goldflame spiraea (deciduous summer-blooming compact)

(Deciduous summer-blooming compact) 3 birds-nest spruce

Summer-fall blooming vine

Climbing hydrangea

Hydrangea (fall-blooming deciduous)

Weeping Norway spruce or similar specimen dwarf conifer

5 Tardiva (dwarf conifer)

Japanese garden juniper or evergreen ground cover

(Broadleaf evergreen compact) 3 Helleri holly

Pool

Concrete with cool-deck surface.

Climbing roses

Fencing

2 Helleri holly

2 Goldflame spiraea

Upright evergreen (holly, taxus, and so on)

Climbing roses

Figure 14-4: This poolside planting is designed to be low on maintenance.

Notice the following features of this plan:

- ✔ **Stick with low-maintenance materials.** The surface around the pool is easy-care and economical, with a material known as *cool-deck*.

- ✔ **Use fencing around the pool.** Consider using an informal post and rail fence or more formal aluminum with the look of wrought iron. If you need a solid fence, break up the monotony by growing vines on it. See Chapter 5 for the lowdown on fences.

- ✔ **Use plants for privacy.** Evergreens such as holly and conifers provide a privacy screen, plus interesting changes in texture.

- ✔ **Keep grass to a minimum.** There's no lawn inside the fenced area. The idea is to keep maintenance requirements low.

- ✔ **Reduce plant maintenance.** Many of the plants are compact, low-maintenance types (no special pruning or other care is needed).

- ✔ **Choose a few stunning plants for color.** Climbing hydrangea, spiraea, and climbing roses bloom in the summer, when the pool is used the most. (If you grow thorny roses, make sure that they don't grow close enough to pathways where thorns may scratch skin or clothing.)

    For additional color, plant annual flowers and bulbs as a front border. (See the color section of this book for more ideas on incorporating color into your landscape.)

Here are few suggestions for other plants to use around a pool (Chapter 9 has more on shrubs):

- ✔ **Low shrubs and ground covers:** agapanthus, juniper, moraea, rosemary.

- ✔ **Medium-sized to large shrubs:** holly, Japanese black pine, pittosporum, pyracantha.

Hillside Rock Garden

Instead of viewing a slope as a landscape liability, consider it a great opportunity — a place to display a rock garden. Rock garden plants are quite beautiful, and growing them on a slope near a walkway gives you the opportunity to view them up close.

This rock garden plan (Figure 14-5) can work in the back yard at the edge of a lawn or in front, right off of a side walk. It combines plants, steps, and boulders.

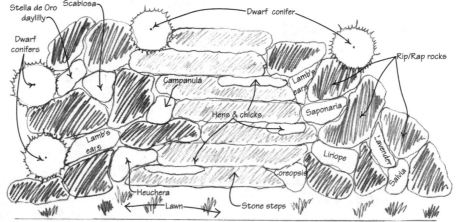

Figure 14-5:
Rocks and
rock garden
plants
stabilize and
beautify a
slope.

Keep the following in mind for creating a rock garden like this plan:

- ✔ **The steps are stones.** Use stones of different lengths for a more natural look. Choose stones with a smooth, flat surface, and put them in place firmly. Create planting pockets on the steps. Chapter 5 can help you build walkways and steps.

- ✔ **Rip-rap rocks help the soil.** Rocks of varying size stacked randomly are an economical way to retain soil on the slope — the steeper the hillside, the closer together the rocks should be to stabilize the soil effectively. Make planting pockets between the rocks to soften the harshness of the rocks.

- ✔ **Boulders add a natural touch.** Keep them in scale, not too big or too small for the site.

- ✔ **Color and texture come alive.** Typical rock garden plants are small and slow growing, offering a variety of textures that are best viewed close up. For color, include blooming perennials like lavender, coreopsis, and salvia. See the color section of this book for more ideas about using color in your landscape.

Small trees for a rock garden

You can find many potential rock garden trees for your own landscape (see Chapter 8 for more on trees):

- ✔ Dwarf arborvitae *(Thuja occidentalis)*
- ✔ Dwarf hemlock *(Tsuga canadensis)*
- ✔ Dwarf hinoki cypress *(Chamaecyparis obtusa)*

- ✔ Japanese maple *(Acer palmatum)*
- ✔ Mugho pine *(Pinus mugo mugo)*

Dwarf shrubs for a rock garden

Try these shrubs for your rock garden (Chapter 9 has more on shrubbery):

- ✔ Bog rosemary *(Andromeda polifolia* 'Nana')
- ✔ Dwarf heath *(Erica)*
- ✔ Dwarf Japanese holly *(Ilex crenata)*
- ✔ Dwarf junipers
- ✔ Dwarf Scotch heather *(Calluna vulgaris)*

Small perennials for a rock garden

The following perennials brings bursts of color to a simple rock garden:

- ✔ Bellflower *(Campanula)*
- ✔ Cranesbill *(Geranium)*
- ✔ Moonbeam coreopsis *(Coreopsis verticillata* 'Moonbeam')
- ✔ Primroses *(Primula)*
- ✔ Thrift *(Armeria)*
- ✔ Thyme *(Thymus)*
- ✔ Yarrow *(Achillea)*

Garden for a Small Balcony

A balcony offers a host of gardening challenges — no soil, perhaps a lot of shade or too much sun, and difficulty in bringing water to the garden. But with planning, a small balcony can offer some of the same amenities as a garden in the ground: lush green foliage, colorful flowers — even vegetables. And you have the garden right up close where you can appreciate it.

This plan for a balcony garden, shown in Figure 14-6, makes the most of small space. Plants provide seasonal interest and a bit of privacy, and you still have room for outdoor dining and relaxing.

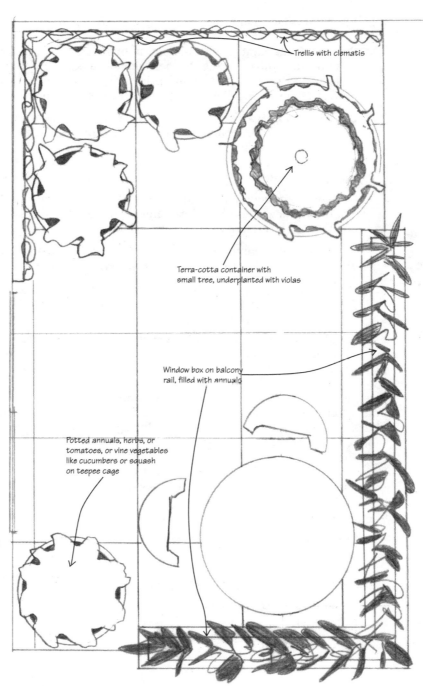

Trellis with clematis

Terra-cotta container with
small tree, underplanted with violas

Window box on balcony
rail, filled with annuals

Potted annuals, herbs, or
tomatoes, or vine vegetables
like cucumbers or squash
on teepee cage

Figure 14-6:
Add
flowers,
a tree,
or even
vegetables
to a small
balcony.

Keep the following in mind when planning a balcony garden:

- ✔ **Create a focal point.** The focal point in this plan is a small tree or *standard* (a shrub trained as a small, single-trunk tree). For extra color, underplant the tree with trailing spring or summer-blooming annual flowers (pansies, lobelias, marigolds, petunias, and so on).

- ✔ **Use window boxes.** Fasten window boxes to your balcony's railing, so that they're viewable from indoors or from outside. Use them to create more privacy or to frame a view. Change plantings in the window boxes seasonally by growing annuals in the summer and stuffing the boxes with greens and dried-berry plants for winter and the holidays.

- ✔ **Grow container plants.** Colorful pots of annuals provide surprising amounts of flower color at close range. Chapter 10 discusses container plants in greater detail.

  Water draining from the containers can stain the balcony surface or drip on your neighbor below — keep saucers under the pots.

- ✔ **Don't forget veggies.** Squeeze herbs and vegetables into your balcony garden. To save space, train climbers such as cucumbers and tomatoes on teepees or in cages.

- ✔ **Install an outdoor faucet.** Watering with a watering pot can be tedious, so consider installing an outdoor faucet. See Chapter 4 for more on irrigation systems.

Size (not too tall or spreading) and maintenance (not too demanding) are your main considerations when making plans for a balcony garden. Also check on your sun and shade exposure throughout the day. (Chapter 12 has more on shady conditions.)

The following are small trees and shrubs that need sun most of the day, and could serve as a focal point on a balcony garden.

- ✔ Camellia (needs shade in hot climates)
- ✔ Crape myrtle *(Lagerstroemia indica)*
- ✔ Hibiscus (standard)
- ✔ Japanese black pine *(Pinus thunbergi)*
- ✔ Japanese maple *(Acer palmatum)*
- ✔ Palms (indoor/outdoor)
- ✔ Tree rose *(Rosa)*

Chapter 15

Plans for "Theme" Landscapes

· ·

In This Chapter

▶ Designing a landscape for wildlife

▶ Creating a landscape for kids

▶ Discovering a highly-organized vegetable garden

▶ Putting in a pretty formal herb garden

▶ Establishing a meadow garden

▶ Setting up a water garden

· ·

*T*his chapter contains "theme" gardens — admittedly, somewhat of a catch-all category. These are gardens with specific purposes, and you don't usually create them out necessity, as you may a landscape that provides privacy or to prevent erosion on a slope. Mostly, you create theme gardens for fun — they make your yard more interesting and useful to you.

The theme gardens in this chapter range widely in complexity, from a rather simple wildlife garden to a fairly intricate water garden. Get professional help and advice, as needed.

For many of the plants, pay attention to your climate zones when selecting plants. Consult the plant lists and descriptions provided in Chapters 8 through 11. Of course, dealing with climate zones (covered in Chapter 12) isn't that vital when the plans call for annual flowers and vegetables — these are the one-season-only plants used in the vegetable garden and the kids' garden. The most important factor for these types of plants is when your planting season begins (last killing frost) and ends (first killing frost). Plant selection also depends on other climate variables, such as summer heat or autumn coolness.

A Landscape to Attract Wild Creatures

Nothing brings a garden to life more than living things — *desirable* living things, that is — not such bad eggs as gophers, voles, and deer. The sight and sound of birds is particularly appealing and easy to arrange. But you can also invite butterflies, chipmunks, and beneficial insects to your landscape. What brings creatures into a garden are plants — and certain plants bring certain creatures.

Following are a few general points to keep in mind when you want your garden to attract different types of life, like the plan in Figure 15-1:

- ✔ **Strive for diversity in your plant selection.** While this concept may conflict with a designer's approach to unity discussed in Chapter 2 (generally fewer plants), but for this plan, the more different types of plants you have, the greater the chances of attracting a variety of wild creatures.

- ✔ **Provide a year-round supply of water.** This can be a pond or a bird bath.

- ✔ **Grow plants that are native to your region.** These should be most familiar and attractive to your local creatures.

This plan for attracting wildlife includes a mix of plants designed to attract birds (including hummingbirds), butterflies, chipmunks, and insects. It also includes enough attractive plants to appeal to humans too.

- ✔ The post-and-rail fencing (see Chapter 5) has a rustic look that fits in nicely and supports a berry-producing pyracantha.

- ✔ Crabapple, cranberry bush *(Viburnum),* cotoneaster, blueberry, winterberry, and pyracantha all have berries that draw a variety of birds and animals.

  Try to use upright or vase-shaped trees (like the crabapple) so that other plants can grow underneath.

- ✔ Buddleia and butterfly weed *(Asclepias tuberosa)* are traditional butterfly lures.

- ✔ Tubular-shaped red or pink flowers generally attract hummingbirds. Weigela and monarda do the job here.

- ✔ You can find many other bird-attracting plants, and exactly which to choose depends on your climate and garden conditions. Here are a few: serviceberry *(Amelianchier)*, cedar, hawthorns, mulberry, holly, and junipers. For more specific recommendations, contact your local branch of the Audubon Society.

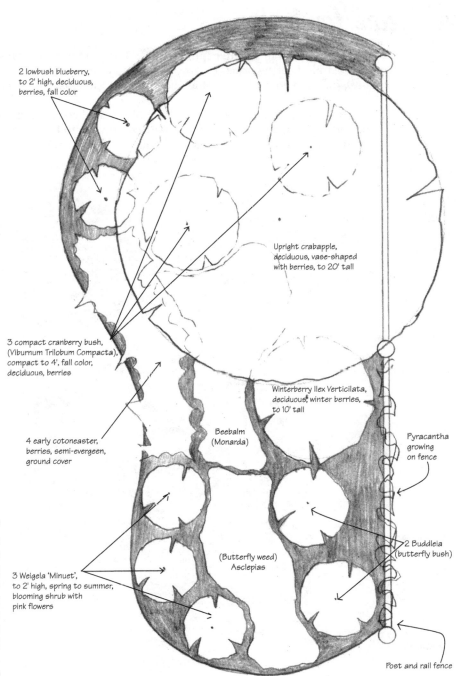

2 lowbush blueberry, to 2' high, deciduous, berries, fall color

3 compact cranberry bush, (Viburnum Trilobum Compacta), compact to 4', fall color, deciduous, berries

4 early cotoneaster, berries, semi-evergeen, ground cover

3 Weigela 'Minuet', to 2' high, spring to summer, blooming shrub with pink flowers

Upright crabapple, deciduous, vase-shaped with berries, to 20' tall

Winterberry Ilex Verticilata, deciduous, winter berries, to 10' tall

Beebalm (Monarda)

(Butterfly weed) Asclepias

Pyracantha growing on fence

2 Buddleia (butterfly bush)

Post and rail fence

Figure 15-1:
Grow flowering and berry-producing plants to attract birds and butterflies.

A Space for Kids

What do kids want in a landscape? Better not ask them, or they'll say a mudhole full of earthworms. As grown-ups, we want to turn kids on to the beauty, fun, and educational value of gardening. Kids just focus on the fun!

This kids' play area plan (see Figure 15-2) pleases all concerned parties. Designed in the shape of a clock, this garden appeals to the sense of fun, adventure, and taste buds of nearly all children.

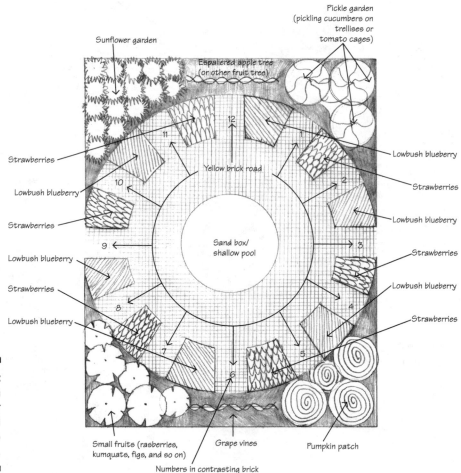

Figure 15-2:
This garden is fun for kids and striking to adult eyes.

Be extremely careful when selecting plants for your child's garden. If you have any questions, check lists of poisonous plants (which may be available from your county extension office) or consult your local nursery.

This plan is meant mainly as inspiration. Feel free to change its scale (the minimum space is 10 by 10 feet) or, instead of a clock, make it into a sun, a daisy — whatever suits your needs. This plan contains the following fantastic features:

- ✔ **At the center of it all is a little pond or sandbox.** Remember that the sandbox won't be fun for kids (or for you) if neighborhood or family cats have access to it. To block out sun, you can cover the sandbox with plywood or an outdoor awning cloth.

- ✔ **The brick clock garden is a real eye-catcher.** Strawberry and blueberry plants alternate in cutouts between numbers or spaces left blank. You can make numbers in the brick work (although this won't be easy) by cutting bricks and leaving space for cut bricks of contrasting color or sand or gravel.

- ✔ **The plants don't just sit there.** Various training devices get them off the ground and make them more interesting — trellises for cucumbers, cages for tomatoes, and so on. A section of fence can be used to train the apple tree into a flat *espalier* (plant that grows flat along a fence).

- ✔ **The plants are fun.** In addition to the berries, other edibles include pumpkins, figs, grapes. Sunflowers are big and striking — and irresistible to kids.

Fun plants

You can make a kids' play area more fun by including plants that have extra appeal for youngsters.

- ✔ **Gourds** are as easy to grow as squash. Harvest and dry the gourds for crafts projects or decorations.

- ✔ **Popcorn** can be grown just like sweet corn. But don't plant it near sweet corn unless you want to demonstrate the bizarre effects of cross-pollination.

- ✔ **Pumpkins** need a lot of room and water, but are an obvious draw. They also require patience — a good three or four months to reach harvest stage.

- ✔ **Mickey Mouse plant** is a little shrub with just one trick. Kids see a strong resemblance to Mickey Mouse in one stage of the black and red flowers. The plant's botanical name is *Ochna multiflora*.

Super-Neat Vegetable Garden

Who needs a plan for a vegetable garden? You may find it difficult enough just to find a sunny level spot, stick a few tomato plants in the ground, line up corn in rows, and let the squash sprawl. That's okay. But a well-designed vegetable garden can look downright handsome in its own right, and can be an important part of your landscape if it's situated in a prominent area. It also can be a lot more productive, by making maximum use of your space.

The tightly organized plan for a vegetable garden, shown in Figure 15-3, is handsome in its orderliness and highly efficient in its use of space.

Keep the following in mind when designing your vegetable garden:

- ✔ **Divide the garden.** Dividing the area into square or rectangular beds allows for easy access to each planting section. It also makes the garden ornamental as well as functional.

- ✔ **Build in walkways.** Pathways between the beds allow you to get around without muddying your feet. Paths can be surfaced with a variety of different materials including mulch, pea gravel, brick, stepping stones, or sawdust. See Chapter 5 for more on walkways and the color section of this book for full-color examples.

- ✔ **Interplant.** *Interplanting* (planting one kind of plant between another) is key for space efficiency. For example, radishes can be interplanted with peppers. By the time the peppers have spread out, the fast-growing radishes have finished their season and are out of the way.

- ✔ **Go organic.** Pungent plants, such as garlic, basil, and marigolds, are interplanted with tomatoes to ward off insects, naturally. Even if they didn't help with your pest control, they'd still be a nice addition to any vegetable garden.

- ✔ **Create shade.** Corn is a tall crop that's used to shade the ground for cool-season crops like lettuce.

- ✔ **Grow up.** By using teepees, trellises, and fences you can train vining crops (such as peas, beans, and cucumbers) up the structures to save ground space and make picking easier. Vertical structures also add visual interest to a vegetable garden — most plants otherwise stay low to the ground.

  Tomato cages are another good way to introduce verticality into a vegetable garden. Near the base of vine teepees, underground crops like potatoes and onions work well because they take so little space.

Figure 15-3:
This vegetable garden is attractive as well as productive.

Growing vegetables is fun, and discovering more about the subject can be absorbing. For information on essential topics such as selecting varieties, in-season maintenance, rotating crops, composting, and much more, consult *Vegetable Gardening For Dummies* by the Editors of the National Gardening Association (IDG Books Worldwide, Inc.). The book also has other vegetable garden plans for your consideration.

A Pretty, Formal Herb Garden

You can find all sorts of reasons to grow herbs somewhere in your garden — use them fresh or dried in cooking, breathe in their aromatic fragrances as you brush past them, or rely on their color and beauty to add life to your garden.

You can also mix herbs in with other plants — rosemary and lavender are basic landscape plants, but are also herbs. Grow them in containers, so that you can snip parsley right out your back door. Grow a traditional formal herb garden. Or, combine them with perennials for looks and because many herbs and perennial flowers thrive under similar conditions.

The herb garden shown in the traditional circular plan (Figure 15-4) is definitely on the formal side. It takes careful planning and installation, along with a good deal of maintenance, but it could easily turn out to be the high point of your garden.

Use the following tips when creating your own herb garden:

- **Establish a focal point.** Consider something man-made such as a sundial, bird bath, gazing ball, or outdoor sculpture. Don't be afraid to improvise.

- **Establish pathways.** Use brick for traditional, formal pathways. More informal alternatives include stepping stones, bluestone, mulch, or pea gravel (small stones with smaller aggregate mixed in so it can be packed down).

- **Keep herbs separate.** Define and separate the herb plantings with buried edging, which could be brick, metal, or wood. This is especially important to control the spreading tendencies of mint and spearmint. If you'd rather not worry about mints getting out of bounds, better substitute a more docile herb.

- **Create herb hedges.** Lavender and rosemary around the outside can be pruned into hedges for a formal look.

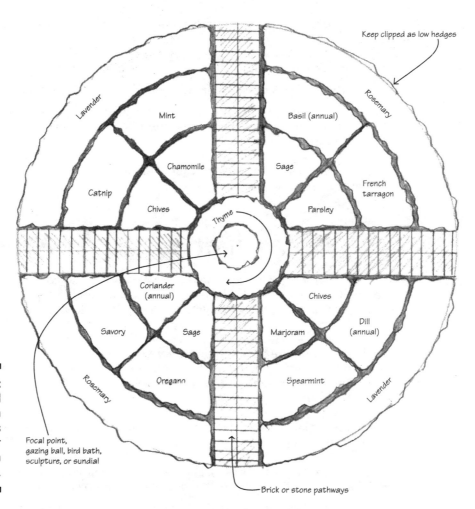

Keep clipped as low hedges

Rosemary

Lavender

Mint

Basil (annual)

Chamomile

Sage

Catnip

French tarragon

Chives

Parsley

Thyme

Coriander (annual)

Chives

Savory

Sage

Marjoram

Dill (annual)

Rosemary

Oregano

Spearmint

Lavender

Focal point, gazing ball, bird bath, sculpture, or sundial

Brick or stone pathways

Figure 15-4:
This formal herb garden supplies all your kitchen needs.

> ✔ **Maintain, maintain, maintain.** Any formal herb garden needs regular maintenance — mostly pruning and trimming to keep plants confined to their spaces. For bushy growth, pinch and trim plants while they're small and tender-stemmed — don't wait until they get too tall and woody.

The plants specified in this plan are selected on the basis of size and complementary appearances (leaf texture, flower color, and such). Before making substitutions, check into the growth habits of the plants that you're considering.

As a rule, most herbs, particularly those shown in this plan, need similar care:

✔ Provide a spot in full sun.

✔ Herbs don't need soil that's rich or high in organic matter.

✔ Keep the soil well drained and keep plants on the dry side. A few herbs, such as parsley and chives, need more water than others, so keep an eye on them.

Winter performance depends on your climate. In mild climates, many herbs stay evergreen all year.

Meadow Garden That Passes for Real

This plan is for a garden that looks like a meadow installed by Mother Nature. Of course, this plan takes a lot of planning and forethought — do you think that Cindy Crawford gets her "natural" look without makeup?

Another myth about creating a meadow garden is that you just throw out seeds and let nature take over. In reality, you have to prepare the soil just as you would for almost any other kind of garden. This said, there's nothing more glorious than a meadow or wildflower garden in bloom — it's well worth the work.

Note the special features of this plan for a meadow garden, shown in Figure 15-5:

✔ **The plants behave wildly.** Some are actual wildflowers, but all of them have the ability to reseed themselves as wildflowers do.

The wild form of loosestrife (*Lythrum*) is considered a noxious weed, but the cultivar 'Robert' specified here will behave itself.

✔ **The space can be enlarged.** Simply repeat the pattern for greater length and width.

✔ **You can adapt the plan for constant blooms.** Take into account the blooming dates of various plants in your region and spread them around in the design so that you always have something blooming.

✔ **The look is natural.** If you need a fence, a natural-looking style like post-and-rail is most appropriate (see Chapter 5).

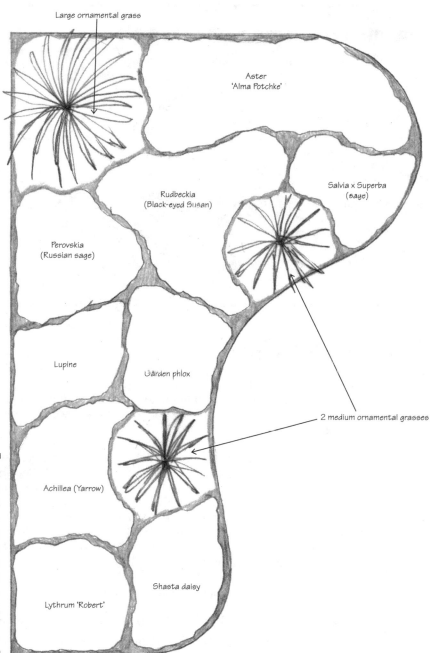

Large ornamental grass

Aster
'Alma Potchke'

Salvia x Superba
(sage)

Rudbeckia
(Black-eyed Susan)

Perovskia
(Russian sage)

Lupine

Garden phlox

2 medium ornamental grasses

Achillea (Yarrow)

Shasta daisy

Lythrum 'Robert'

Figure 15-5:
Ornamental
grasses
and long-
blooming
perennials
combine to
create a
natural-
looking
meadow
garden.

Wildflower gardens that come back from seed

For another kind of natural garden, consider sowing seeds of annual wildflowers — the kind that come back from seed year after year. The flowers that you can use vary widely from region to region, and so do planting times. In cold climates, spring is the main planting season, while in mild, winter-rain climates such as California, autumn is the chief planting season.

Here are some annuals that you can grow like wildflowers (that is, you sow seeds once and then let them reseed themselves):

- African daisy
- Baby blue eyes
- California poppy
- Clarkia
- Cornflower
- Cosmos
- Flax
- Forget-me-not
- Linaria
- Shirley poppy
- Wallflower

A Lush Water Garden

The most ambitious — but potentially most rewarding — of our theme gardens is a water garden — with pond and water-loving plants, plus moisture-loving plants that thrive at water's edge. It's lush, cooling, and always fascinating.

As daunting as a water garden may sound, take heart in the fact that many products and kits are now available. To create a pond, most people use a flexible liner made of PVC or butyl-rubber. Pumps are sold in a wide range of sizes and power, and are reassuringly reliable. Start with a trip to your garden center or hardware store, track down a knowledgeable salesperson, and pick up literature if you can. There are also many mail-order suppliers willing to send you water garden material; you find addresses in the back of gardening magazines. Chapter 7 can also help you design a pond.

Before you start planning, keep some important factors in mind.

- For pond health, a water garden should receive at least a half day of sun.
- Locate the pond in a wind-sheltered spot to avoid falling leaves.
- More than half of the water surface should be covered with plants.
- Safety is critical; you may need a fence to keep out curious children.

The toughest design challenges include the following:

- ✔ How do you gracefully fit a pond into the rest of the garden?
- ✔ What do you do at its edges?
- ✔ You don't want the pond just sitting there like an abandoned bath tub.

The water garden plan in Figure 15-6 is designed to look good and to blend naturally into the surrounding garden. It's based on a good-sized space, including several existing trees, but can be scaled up or down in size, depending on your available space.

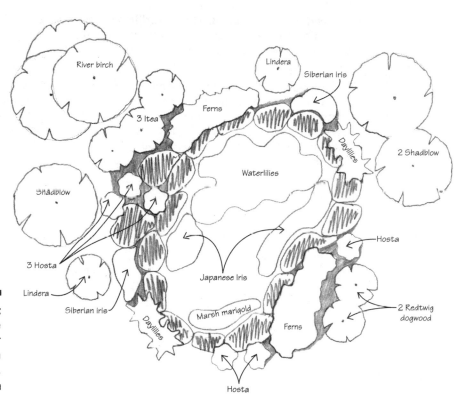

Figure 15-6: A complete water garden plan.

When reviewing your water garden plan, consider the following:

- ✔ **Use rocks.** The pond is made with a liner and rocks help hold it down, look natural, and soften the transition from the pond to the planting and beyond.

- ✔ **Use small plants.** The small plants at the edge of the pool — ferns, hosta, daylilies — all have hanging foliage to hide and soften the pond's edge.

- ✔ **Use large plants.** The larger plants — birch, shad, lindera, dogwoods — are all moisture-lovers that provide a transition to the rest of the garden.

- ✔ **Keep waterlilies in check.** The waterlilies in the pond should be grown in containers to keep them from running rampant, especially in small pools. Waterlilies require quiet water and shouldn't be grown near a fountain.

- ✔ **Use containers.** Marsh marigolds and Japanese iris are best grown in containers to keep them from spreading, and so that they can be moved around for best placement. Use underwater shelves to keep them at the correct heights under water. You can also use stacked bricks — remove bricks one at a time as plants grow taller.

Part V
The Part of Tens

The 5th Wave   By Rich Tennant

©RICHTENNANT

"Here's to your gorgeous new patio, which, incidentally, we
just discovered was built on our property instead of yours.
Cheers, everyone!"

In this part . . .

Good landscaping does so much more than just make your house look good. So much, in fact, that we can't fit them into the other parts of this book. So, here are some other ways to use landscaping to get the most out of your home and yard — simple ways to cut you energy bills, make your home look unique, and help you sell your house.

Chapter 16

Ten Ways to Make Your Surroundings Unique

. . . .

In This Chapter

▶ Making your landscape match your home and surroundings

▶ Fitting your landscape to your lifestyle

. . . .

Suppose that last night you came home from work feeling pretty tired. You pulled into your neighborhood filled with pretty much identical houses and you couldn't remember which one was yours. Thank goodness for numbered addresses!

But you can't help feeling that you have to do something about this — after all, character and uniqueness are what make a house a home. You need to make some changes, so that at least you can find your way home at night.

This chapter has some ideas — besides painting your house purple.

Work on Your Front Yard

An easy way to improve your front yard is as follows:

- ✔ Add a brick or stone walkway from the street (see Chapter 5).

- ✔ Add unique lawn edging, using concrete or brick.

- ✔ Add a single, beautiful, accent tree (like a Japanese maple) or a cluster of matching trees (like weeping birch) near the entrance. Or, group flowering trees along your entry walkway. Flip to Chapter 8 for more on trees.

- ✔ Add garden lighting (covered in Chapter 7) — path lights, uplights on trees, or lights around major shrub plantings.

> ✔ Add a water feature or sculpture as part of your entry walkway.
>
> ✔ Make part of the front yard a semienclosed courtyard, furnished with attractive garden furniture and accented with containers. If the area faces east, it can be a shady retreat in the summer months.

Reflect the Architecture of Your Home

Take a look at the architecture of your house. What style is it? Colonial, Tudor, or Spanish mission? After you determine the style, do some research at your local library to find out what kind of plants, landscape materials, and features are traditionally used with that style. Look for photographs of homes in the area where the style originated.

Perhaps you'll decide that a Tudor home isn't complete without neat little boxwood hedges. Or that your Spanish style home looks better with native Mediterranean plants. And if you can't get a statue of Paul Revere for the front of your colonial home, try adding a new brick walkway up to the front door.

Go Native

Take cues from the plants that grow naturally in your area. After all, these are plants that are superbly adapted to your climate and are probably the easiest to care for. Join your local native plant society (your nursery or local botanic garden should be able to put you in touch with one) and explore some of the most beautiful plants around.

Plant a Theme Garden

Plant the kinds of plants that you've always loved. Who says you can't live in a citrus orchard? Or landscape your home with nothing but roses and then go into the cut flower business (I know someone who did). Why not put in a pond with wild looking water plants? Chapter 15 shows you all sorts of plans for theme gardens.

Many people plan their landscapes around food production. Build raised beds of vegetables and fruits (see Chapter 10 for more on edible landscapes). The neighbors may not like it at first, but after they benefit from all the food you can't eat, you're in.

Design for Exercise

Work your exercise habits into your landscape. That way, you can't help but get in shape. Plan for a par course, a place to lift weights, or just a soft, grassy spot to do sit-ups.

Design for Sports

This is kind of like the previous section on exercise. What's your favorite family sport? Consider installing a tennis or handball court, swimming pool, basketball hoop, batting cage, putting green — whatever.

Designing for sports doesn't have to be very expensive. Check out Figure 16-1 for the dimensions for badminton and lawn croquet — your lawn may be the perfect size.

Remember what they say about the family that plays together.

Design a Kid's Garden

Consider building a safe playground area with slides and swings, like the one shown in Figure 16-2. And how about a bike path around the perimeter of the property, a fort or tree house, a sandbox (see Figure 16-3 for ideas), or a vegetable garden just for kids with beans, sunflowers, and fragrant plants. (Turn to Chapter 15 for a kid's vegetable garden plan.)

Whatever you do, just get those kids out of the house, for Pete's sake!

Put In a Wildlife Refuge

Hey, we're serious. Design a garden that attracts wildlife — everything from birds to squirrels and butterflies. Flip to Chapter 15 for a sample plan.

Look for information from The National Wildlife Federation — they'll tell you all you need to know to bring in the flocks at www.nwf.org or 1-800-822-9919.

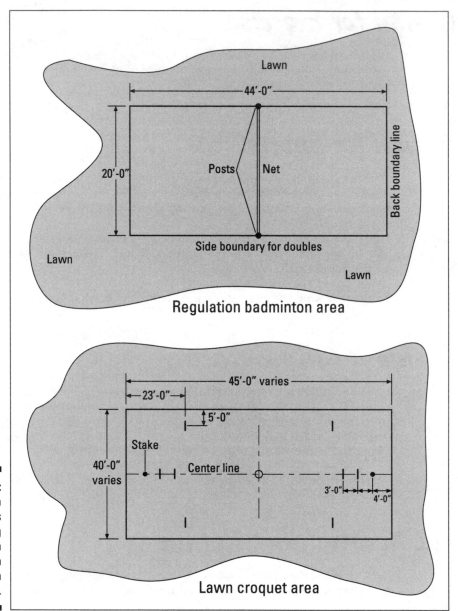

Figure 16-1: Lawn dimensions for playing regulation badminton or lawn croquet.

Figure 16-2:
A kids' play
area.

Accessorize

Put in stuff — birdbaths, sundials, statues, antique garden tools and farm
equipment, garden art, wall ornaments, big rocks (our favorite), fountains,
whirligigs — you name it. Watch out, though — you may get addicted to
collecting this stuff.

Containerize

Buy some nice containers (made of wood, ceramic, or clay), put some
attractive or colorful plants in them, and set the stage on the porch, patio,
deck, in window boxes, or wherever you find room. Using containers in your
landscape gives the yard immediate character, whether you have any open
soil or not. If Chapter 10 doesn't give you enough ideas, pick up a copy of
Container Gardening For Dummies by Bill Marken and the Editors of the
National Gardening Association (IDG Books Worldwide, Inc.).

Figure 16-3:
In-deck
sandbox
includes a
cover to
keep out
pets.

Colorize

Put in some flowers — a lot of flowers. Start by choosing a color theme, flip to Chapter 10 on information on all sorts of flowers, and plant in every open space that you can find.

Take a look at the color photo section (near the center of this book) for ideas on using color.

Chapter 17
Tens Ways to Conserve Energy

· ·

· ·

ou've probably taken refuge in the shade on a hot, sunny day — who hasn't? Well, public utility companies also want you to know that the shade (and other good landscaping techniques) can cut your energy consumption by as much as 30 percent.

But conserving energy is a little more complicated than putting in a few shade trees (which Chapter 8 gives advice on). This chapter looks at ten ways to conserve energy through creative landscaping.

Plant Trees on the West Side of Your House

Shading the west-facing side of your home and thereby blocking out the hottest sun of the day has the greatest impact on air conditioning needs during the summer.

Plant Trees on the East Side of Your House

Shade trees on the east side of your home block morning sun, which warms the house early in the day. This is the second most important place to plant trees.

Plant Solar-Friendly Trees

Solar-friendly trees are leafless (called *deciduous*) in winter and have fairly open *canopies* (the leafy portion of the tree). They allow winter sun to reach solar collectors and also to warm the house. In very hot climates, such as the desert southwest, *evergreen trees* (they stay leafy all year) may provide valuable shade in the warm winter months. In Palm Springs, California, it's pretty hot even in the winter.

Plant Trees on the South Side of Your House

In areas of the world with long, hot summers, planting trees on the south side of the house can provide shade in the warm months of early fall and late spring. Use deciduous trees, which are leafless in winter, or shorter trees so that the winter sun can warm the house in the winter. If you have solar collectors, use short trees that won't block them.

Plant Trees Outside of Windows

Summer sun shining through windows can quickly warm up your house. To block the sun without blocking the view, plant deciduous trees just to the south or west of the window. Keep the trees at least 10 feet from the house to avoid damage to the foundation.

Don't Block Cool Summer Breezes

If you cool your house by opening windows so that a nice cool evening breeze can blow through, don't plant trees or shrubs where they block windows or buffer the breeze. If necessary, prune the plants so that they shade windows from above, but still let the wind through.

Shade Air Conditioners

An air conditioner has to work harder (using more energy) if the hot sun is beating down on it. Plant small trees nearby or protect it with a fence and open arbor. Don't plant too close, though — an air conditioner needs circulation.

Shade Paving

Sunny driveways, patios, and walks can store a lot of heat during the day. When the heat is released at night, it keeps the house warmer longer, increasing the time the air conditioner must run. Plant trees on both sides of large expanses of concrete to keep them cooler during the day and night. Using light-colored materials for your walkways, like concrete, decreases the amount of heat absorbed during the day.

Plant Windbreaks

A properly-positioned windbreak can reduce cold winter winds by up to 50 percent (depending on the density and height of the windbreak), thus reducing the need for winter heating by as much as 20 percent. Tall, fast-growing, evergreen trees planted closely together — perpendicular to prevailing winds — are the most effective windbreaks. For maximum protection, the windbreak should be planted within a distance four times the height of the tallest tree. So, your house should be within 200 feet of a 50-foot windbreak.

Take Advantage of Trellises, Arbors, and Shrubs

If you don't have room to plant trees, build arbors to shade windows, patios, driveways, or parts of the house. Use vine-covered trellises to shade windows. (You can find out more about both arbors and trellises in Chapter 7.) A short windbreak or screen of smaller shrubs can provide some protection from cold winds. (Check out Chapter 9 for more on shrubs.)

Chapter 18

Ten Ways to Increase Your Home's Resale Value

In This Chapter

▶ Finding quick, inexpensive improvements

▶ Attracting potential home buyers

Suppose you just got a big promotion and have to move to company headquarters. Now you have to sell your house — fast. This chapter gives you quick, sure-fire ways to work wonders with your landscape — and most can be done in a single weekend.

Prune

Pruning makes a world of difference in the way your landscape looks:

✔ A good (emphasis on *good* — there is a right and wrong way) pruning job gives your house a well-kept look and enhances the beauty of the plants.

✔ Pruning opens up desirable views (from both inside and out) and gives your house better visibility from the street.

✔ Pruning trees can increase the sunlight into the home, making the interior brighter and more inviting.

Hire an arborist or tree service to prune trees and shrubs. Or, for smaller plants, do it yourself. (See Chapter 9 for more on pruning shrubs. For information on pruning trees, check out free tree care consumer information on the Web site of the International Society of Arboriculture — www.ag.uiuc.edu/~isa/consumer/consumer.html.)

Plant Flowers

Planting flowers is one of the easiest ways to improve the curb appeal of your house. Visit your local nursery or garden center and buy plants that are already in bloom — especially annuals. Plant them close together, wherever you have an open space.

And make sure you put some flowers in pots on your patio or deck. For more information on blooming plants, flip to Chapter 10.

Plant Big Plants

Nurseries and garden centers carry what are called *specimen plants* — large ones often require a truck to get them home and a landscape contractor to plant them. Although expensive, strategically placing a few specimen plants near entryways or around patios and decks gives a landscape a more mature look. And maturity translates to value.

You can also use a large tree or several large shrubs to screen out unsightly views, such as telephone poles or the neighbor's RV.

Weed and Mulch

Spray, hoe, or pull weeds so that your house looks cared-for and lived-in. Make sure you get the ones growing in pavement cracks. Moisten the soil prior to weeding (or wait until after a rain), and the weeds come out much easier. Your nursery also carries various tools that can make weeding less of a chore.

After weeding, apply a thick layer of organic mulch, such as ground bark or wood chips, to dirt paths, unplanted areas and any open ground around plants. Spreading a thick mulch really spruces a place up. If you need a lot of mulch, purchase it by the truckload from a local nursery or garden center (if you don't have a truck, they can usually deliver it for you). Buying a lot at one time saves you money.

Replace Your Old Lawn with New Sod

Nothing makes a house look better than a bright green new lawn — and with sod, it's almost instant. But make sure you do it right — by killing the old lawn and preparing the soil before resodding. It may take longer to sell your house than you think, and you don't want the new lawn to start dying out in a couple of weeks. Chapter 11 tells you all about planting a new lawn from sod.

Rebuild or Replace Your Old, Leaning, Wooden Fence

Rejuvenating a fence makes your whole lot look better. Sometimes all you need to do is replace a few posts or boards. Other times, you're better off ripping out the old fence altogether. Just remember, building a whole new fence may take some time, so plan ahead. See Chapter 5 for instructions on how to build a fence.

Clean, Repair, Refinish, or Stain the Deck

Spend some time working on your deck. Renail boards, tighten railings, and secure steps. Rent a power water jet at a local rental yard to wash off dirt and mold — use it carefully though, because it can damage a deck if used improperly. If your deck's really in bad shape, you may want to use sandpaper to refinish parts of it. Otherwise, visit your local hardware or home improvement store and ask the salesperson about products that you can use to clean an old deck. Some are pretty easy to use.

If you really want the deck to look good, apply some kind of stain or preservative. For the scoop on decks, flip to Chapter 6 or pick up a copy of *Decks and Patios For Dummies* by Robert Beckstrom and the Editors of the National Gardening Association (IDG Books Worldwide, Inc.).

Clean and Repair Patios and Pathways

Secure loose stones or bricks and give everything a good cleaning with a stiff broom and a strong jet of water. (You can rent a power scrubber at local rental yards — just make sure that you use it properly and don't tear your deck surface.) If you have algae or a difficult stain, ask a salesperson at your local hardware store or home improvement center for appropriate cleaning materials.

Correct Drainage Problems

Drainage problems are deal killers. Correct drainage problems that have caused water to build up against the outside wall, collect under the house, or drain into a neighbor's yard. Install underground drains to take the water to the street or *recontour* (rearrange gullies and mounds) the soil so that water drains away from the house. See Chapter 4 for more information on correcting drainage problems. Or, if necessary, hire a professional.

Appendix
Landscaping Resources

· ·

*W*hether you're creating your own landscape or making a career out of landscaping for others, you can find a deep and rich vein of information to mine. Books and magazines are a starting point, as are how-to videos, software, and the catalogs of suppliers. And now, with access to the Web, informational brochures from universities are easier to obtain from around the world.

In this appendix, we've assembled some of our favorite resources. We think you'll find them to be an eclectic mix — but useful, to be sure.

Yellow Pages

Don't forget to use your good-old Yellow Pages for finding local landscape resources, including construction material, landscape architects, or landscape contractors.

- ✔ For basic landscape material, look under "Building Materials." You can probably find a list of companies that sell and deliver the raw material that you need to install everything from asphalt driveways to fish ponds. Their inventories are comprehensive, and most companies also take special orders. You want to give them adequate lead time because special orders take time to put together and deliver to your home.

- ✔ For landscape architects, designers, and contractors, look under the specific profession.

Books

Thumbing through a book on garden design is a visual pleasure that helps you imagine one of the finished landscapes as your own. Books that have photographs — and more importantly, good ideas — stimulate creativity like no other medium. Some of our favorite books that address the fundamental theories of design along with the elements of great designs are as follows:

- *Dirr's Hardy Trees and Shrubs: An Illustrated Encyclopedia,* Michael A. Dirr, Timber Press, 1997. One of the best guides to landscape plants for gardeners who live east of the Rocky Mountains.

- *Gardens Are for People,* Thomas D. Church, Grace Hall, and Michael Laurie, University of California Press, 1995. This book is an updated revision of the 1960s classic by Church, the landscape architect often credited with inventing California's "outdoor living" lifestyle.

- *Garden Tools (Everyday Things),* Suzanne Slesin, Guillaume Pellerin, Stafford Cliff, and Daniel Rozensztroch, Abbeville Press, 1996. The second in a series of books about the history of gardening and landscaping collectibles. Documents the evolution of tools as you know them today. Fascinating photographs.

- *Landscape Plants for Western Regions,* Bob Perry, Land Design Publications, 1992. Comprehensive guide to plants for water conservation, especially for the Western regions of the United States. This book includes design checklists and plant compatibility.

- *Los Angeles Times Planning and Planting the Garden,* Robert Smaus, Harry N. Abrams, 1990. Practical suggestions for a design notebook for your garden. Reviews and discusses parts of the garden as they relate to the overall design.

- Sunset's *Western Garden Book,* the editors of Sunset Books and Sunset Magazine, Sunset Publishing Corp., 1995. It's a good and reliable reference wherever you live, but it's essential if you live in western North America. Likewise, its companion, *The SouthernLiving Garden Book* (Oxmoor House, 1998) is required if you live in the southeast.

- *Understanding Ordinary Landscapes,* Paul Groth and Todd W. Bressi, Yale University Press, 1997. Enough basic information to launch anyone into the landscape design process.

Favorite books that, like this one, cover landscaping basics include:

- *Decks & Patios For Dummies,* Robert Beckstrom and the Editors of the National Gardening Association (IDG Books Worldwide, Inc.). Practical and easy-to-access guide to building these essential features.

- *Gardening by Mail: A Source Book,* Barbara J. Barton, 5th Edition, 1997, Houghton Mifflin Co. Everything for the garden — it's just that simple. A complete mail-order catalog.

- *Western Landscaping Book,* Fiona Gilsenan and Kathleen Norris Brenzel, Sunset Publishing Corp. A masterful job of using photos and drawings to introduce readers to the western style of outdoor living that was popularized by *Sunset Magazine* years ago.

Magazines

Periodicals are a good way to invigorate your interest in landscaping and increase your knowledge of some of the challenges of landscaping. Magazines keep you current on design trends and new plant introductions that can make your yard unique.

- *Landscape Architecture* is a trade magazine that addresses issues ranging from residential design and urban planning to hotly-contested environmental issues on a grand scale. Each issue contains a buyers' guide on a variety of products. Even if you're only planning your own landscape, not a career, this magazine helps you think like a professional. Call 202-686-2752 to subscribe.

- *Garden Design* successfully blends great design with gardening. Subscribe by calling 800-234-5118.

- *The Garden* is a publication of the United Kingdom's Royal Horticultural Society (RHS). It beautifully depicts the fascinating world of landscaping and provides glimpses of England's grand estates. A treasure chest of information and inspiration. To join the RHS, call 0171 821 3000, fax 0171 828 2304, or visit the RHS Web site at www.rhs.org.uk.

Videos and Software

These guides provide an audio/visual experience that helps you translate your design ideas into a workable, successful landscape design. Many of the hosts of these programs stroll through the virtual design, giving you a feeling for space and design relationships.

Videos

- *Plant Usage In Landscape Design* (36 minutes). Focuses on site analysis and the appropriate plants to select for the site. You explore space development, privacy issues, creating vistas, erosion control, and more.

- *Landscaping With Container Plants* (27 minutes). Explores the use of containers in the landscape and the contribution they have added to patios, decks, gazebos, and more.

- *Xeriscape: Appropriate Landscaping to Conserve Water* (26 minutes). This video looks at various soils; tips for site analysis; and the use of texture, form, and adaptability of drought-tolerant plants in the landscape.

✔ *Fertilizing Landscape Plants* (26 minutes). The video discusses the basic elements that you need to make your landscape healthy and vigorous. Shows you how to develop a fertilizing program through the year.

All of the videos listed ($95 each) are available from American Nurseryman, Book Department, 77 West Washington St. Suite 2100, Chicago, IL 60602-2904, 800-621-5727. Or, send an e-mail to books@amerinursery.com.

Software

These computer-based design programs are mostly used by professionals, but that doesn't mean you can't become a pro as well.

✔ *LandDesignerPro for Windows*. This program for professionals provides a host of drafting tools to give you the foundation for a successful design project. This program offers elevations, provides you with "show and grow" that enables you to see the landscape you've chosen in its maturity, and gives you cost estimates. $640 with the plant database, $495 without.

✔ *Time-Saver Standards for Landscape Construction Details CD:* Provides professionals with over 350 landscape design and construction details. This interactive CD library calls up generic details and appropriate methods of installation notes along with current cost data. $295.

These two software packages are available from American Nurseryman, Book Department, 77 West Washington St. Suite 2100, Chicago, IL 60602-2904, 800-621-5727. You can also send an e-mail to books@amerinursery.com.

✔ *Complete LandDesigner* (Win 95) from Sierra Online (800-757-7707 or www.sierra.com). This is a full-featured program that includes an extensive plant database provided by White Flower Farm. $50.

Mail-Order Sources for Trees, Shrubs, and Vines

Every landscaper gets stuck, from time to time, looking for a particular plant or more often, variety. The next time you find yourself in such a situation, try the following mail-order nurseries.

✔ **Appalachian Gardens,** Box 82, Waynesboro, PA 17268, 888-327-5483 or 717-762-4312, fax 717-762-7532. Scarce, unusual, hardy ornamental trees and shrubs including many native plants.

✔ **Fairweather Gardens,** Box 330, Greenwich, NJ 08323; 609-451-6261, fax 609-451-6261. Catalog $3. Trees and shrubs. Large selection of camellias, witch hazel, magnolia, holly, and viburnum.

✔ **Forestfarm,** 990 Tetherow Rd., Williams, OR 97544-9599; 541-846-7269, fax 541-846-6963. Catalog $3. More than 4,000 varieties of native and rare plants, with particular emphasis on plants for wildlife.

✔ **Gossler Farms Nursery,** 1200 Weaver Rd., Springfield, OR 97478, 541-746-3922. Good selection of magnolias and other choice shrubs. Catalog $2.

✔ **Greer Gardens,** 1280 Goodpasture Island Rd., Eugene, OR 97401-1794; 800-548-0111 or 541-686-8266, fax 541-686-0910. Catalog $3. Specialist in rhododendrons, but offers other rare and unusual plants.

✔ **Hughes Nursery,** Box 7705, Olympia, WA 98507-7705; 360-352-4725, fax 360-352-1921 or 360-249-5580. Catalog $1.30. Specialists in dwarf, Japanese, and other maples.

✔ **Siskiyou Rare Plant Nursery,** 2825 Cummings Rd., Medford, OR 97501; 541-772-6846, fax 541-772-4917. Catalog $3. Hardy perennials, shrubs, smaller conifers, and alpine and rock garden plants.

Mail-Order Sources for Accessories, Tools, and Supplies

✔ **Deerbuster,** 9735 a Bethel Rd, Frederick, MD 21702-2017, 800-248-DEER, fax 301-694-9254, www.deerbuster.com. A full line of deer fencing, repellents, scaring devices, and other pest control products.

✔ **Design Toscano,** 1645 Greenleaf Ave., Elk Grove Village, IL 60007, 800-525-0733. Classic garden statuary along with garden gargoyles, figurines, and garden gifts.

✔ **Garden Trellises, Inc.,** Box 105N, LaFayette, NY 13084; 315-498-9003. Galvanized steel trellises for vegetables and perennials.

✔ **Gardener's Eden,** Box 7307, San Francisco, CA 94120-7307; 800-822-9600. Stylish garden supplies and accessories.

✔ **Gardener's Supply Company,** 128 Intervale Rd., Burlington, VT 05401; 800-863-1700, fax 800-551-6712, www.gardeners.com. Hundreds of innovative tools and products for gardeners.

✔ **Gardens Alive!,** 5100 Schenley Pl., Dept. 5672, Lawrenceburg, IN 47025; 812-537-8650, fax 812-537-5108. One of the largest organic pest-control suppliers.

✔ **Gempler's,** 100 Countryside Dr., Box 270, Belleville, WI 53508, 800-382-8473, www.gemplers.com. Hard-to-find, industrial-grade tools for horticulture.

✔ **Harmony Farm Supply,** Box 460, Graton, CA 95444; 707-823-9125, fax 707-823-1734, www.harmonyfarm.com. Catalog $2. Drip and sprinkler irrigation equipment, organic fertilizers, beneficial insects, power tools, and composting supplies.

✔ **Kinsman Company,** River Rd., FH, Point Pleasant, PA 18950; 800-733-4146, fax 215-297-0450. Gardening supplies and fine-quality tools.

✔ **Langenbach,** Box 1420, Lawndale, CA 90260-6320; 800-362-1991, fax 800-362-4490. Fine-quality tools and garden gifts.

✔ **Lee Valley Tools,** Box 1780, Ogdensburg, NY 13669, 800-871-8158, www.leevalley.com/lvtmain.htm. Wide variety of tools for home gardeners.

✔ **A. M. Leonard, Inc.,** Box 816, Piqua, OH 45356; 800-543-8955, fax 800-433-0633. Professional nursery and gardening supplies.

✔ **Mellinger's, Inc.,** 2310 W. South Range Rd., North Lima, OH 44452; 800-321-7444, fax 216-549-3716, www.mellingers.com. Broad selection of gardening tools, supplies, fertilizers, pest controls, and plants.

✔ **Natural Gardening,** 217 San Anselmo Ave., San Anselmo, CA 94960; 707-766-9303, fax 707-766-9747. Organic gardening supplies and tomato seedlings.

✔ **Peaceful Valley Farm Supply,** Box 2209 #NG, Grass Valley, CA 95945; 916-272-4769, fax 916-272-4794, www.groworganic.com. Organic gardening supplies and fine-quality tools.

✔ **Plow & Hearth,** Box 5000, Madison, VA 22727; 800-627-1712. A wide variety of products for home and garden.

✔ **Smith & Hawken,** 2 Arbor Ln., Box 6900, Florence, KY 41022-6900; 800-776-3336, fax 606-727-1166, www.smith-hawken.com. Wide selection of high-end tools, furniture, plants, and outdoor clothing.

✔ **The Urban Farmer Store,** 2833 Vicente St., San Francisco, CA 94116; 800-753-3747 or 415-661-2204. Catalog $1. Drip irrigation supplies.

Landscaping Web Sites

The Web is growing — fast — and in the process, is becoming more useful. With these Web addresses (and a computer, modem, and Internet access) you can go straight to information that you most likely never knew existed.

Finding out more about landscape basics

Even though this book if full of step-by-step guides and tips for building your own landscape, if you're an information hound like we are, you may want more. Here are some of the best Web sites for practical, how-to, landscape information. All are produced by university extension service authors.

✔ **Residential Landscaping,** by M. A. Powell, Specialist in Charge, Horticulture Extension, Publication AG-248, North Carolina Cooperative Extension Service, North Carolina State University.

```
http://ipmwww.ncsu.edu/urban/horticulture/
        res_landscaping.html
```

✔ **Residential Landscape Design,** by David Williams, Extension, Horticulturist, Assistant Professor, and Ken Tilt, Extension Horticulturist, Associate Professor, both in Horticulture at Auburn University.

```
http://www.acesag.auburn.edu/department/extcomm/
        publications/anr/ANR-813/anr813.html
```

✔ **Developing the Landscape Plan,** Ray R. Rothenberger, Department of Horticulture, University of Missouri-Columbia.

```
http://muextension.missouri.edu/xplor/agguides/hort/
        g06901.htm
```

✔ **Six Steps To Home Landscaping,** M.A. (Kim) Powell, Extension Horticultural Specialist, Department of Horticultural Science, North Carolina Cooperative Extension Service, North Carolina State University.

```
http://www.ces.ncsu.edu/depts/hort/hil/hil-623.html
```

✔ **Planning the Home Landscape,** William C. Welch, Extension Landscape Horticulturist.

```
http://aggie-horticulture.tamu.edu/extension/
        homelandscape/home.html
```

✔ **Fitting Ornamental Plants Into The Landscape,** Michigan State University Extension.

```
http://www.msue.msu.edu/msue/imp/mod03/01800014.html
```

✔ **Selecting Landscape Plants: Uncommon Trees for Specimen Planting,** Ray R. Rothenberger and Christopher J. Starbuck, Department of Horticulture, University of Missouri-Columbia.

```
http://muextension.missouri.edu/xplor/agguides/hort/
    g06810.htm
```

✔ **Evaluating the Landscape of a Prospective Home,** Donald H. Steinegger, Extension Horticulturist. Roch E. Gaussoin, Extension Turf Specialist. Discusses facts to consider when examining a prospective home's yard and landscape.

```
http://www.ianr.unl.edu/pubs/horticulture/G1209.HTM
```

✔ **Functional Uses of Plants in the Landscape,** T. Davis Sydnor, Ohio State University Factsheet, Horticulture and Crop Sciences.

```
http://www.ag.ohio-state.edu/~ohioline/hyg-fact/1000/
    1134.html
```

Maximizing landscape efficiency

Not so long ago, landscaping was considered so generally benign that whatever was done and however it was done didn't really matter much. Today, landscape professionals are aware — and you probably are, too — of the profound effect that landscape choices have on energy usage and resource conservation. The following Web sites provide both an introduction to key concepts and links to other important books, magazines, and Web sites.

✔ **Landscape Water Conservation . . . Xeriscape,** Douglas F. Welsh, Extension Horticulturist, William C. Welch, Extension Landscape Horticulturist, Richard L. Duble, Extension Turfgrass Specialist (retired), Texas Agricultural Extension Service.

```
http://aggie-horticulture.tamu.edu/extension/xeriscape/
    xeriscape.html
```

✔ **Creating a Water-Wise Landscape,** Diane Relf, Extension Specialist, Environmental Horticulture, Virginia Tech.

```
http://www.ext.vt.edu/pubs/envirohort/426-713/
    426-713.html
```

✔ **Landscape Plantings for Energy Savings,** Ray R. Rothenberger, Department of Horticulture, University of Missouri-Columbia/.

```
http://muextension.missouri.edu/xplor/agguides/hort/
       g06910.htm
```

✔ **Developing A Water-Efficient Landscape,** Dr. David M. Cox, Extension Educator, East Clark County, Nevada/.

```
http://www.intermind.net/mgarden/links/
       Water_Effici_Lndsp.html
```

Getting into planting, irrigation, and weeds

For those occasions when you need to get deeper into a subject, consider the following Web sites, supplementary to the information in this book.

✔ **Preparation and Planting of Landscape Plants,** Mary Ann Rosel and Elton Smith, Ohio State University Extension Factsheet, Department of Horticulture and Crop Science.

```
http://www.ag.ohio-state.edu/~ohioline/hyg-fact/1000/
       1014.html
```

✔ **Evaluating Your Landscape Irrigation System,** Donald Steinegger, Extension Horticulture, Roch Gaussoin, Extension Turfgrass Specialist, Garald Horst, Turfgrass Physiologist. Addresses irrigation techniques and methods that can improve water usage.

```
http://www.ianr.unl.edu/pubs/horticulture/g1181.htm
```

✔ **Weed Management in Landscapes.**

```
http://www.ipm.ucdavis.edu/PMG/PESTNOTES/pn7441.html
```

Gardening information from the authors

The National Gardening Association is the largest, nonprofit association of home gardeners in North America (and is coauthor of this book!). The Web site includes searchable articles from our award-winning *National Gardening* magazine. And if you're a member, you can ask us any kind of gardening question and get an answer fast, usually within 48 hours.

```
http://www2.garden.org/nga/
```

Getting professional help

Check with these groups for guidelines before embarking on a landscape project, or check references of their members.

- ✔ **Improve Net** is the nation's largest independent service helping homeowners find reliable landscape contractors, designers, and lenders. Their database includes thousands of service providers, each of them screened using a proprietary method that checks licensing, legal and credit history, and references.

  `http://www.improvenet.com/`

- ✔ **Association of Professional Landscape Designers,** APLD, 104 S. Michigan Ave., Suite 1500, Chicago, IL 60603, 312-201-0101. Their mission is to establish standards of excellence in the delivery of landscape design services. They can also help you find a qualified designer in your area.

  `http://www.apld.com`

- ✔ **Associated Landscape Contractors of America,** ACLA, 150 Elden Street, Suite 270, Herndon, Virginia 20170, 703-736-9666, 800-395-ALCA, fax: 703-736-9668.

  `http://www.alca.org/`

- ✔ **American Society of Irrigation Consultants,** Box 426, Byron, CA 94514, 510-516-1124, fax: 510-516-1301.

  `http://www.igin.com/asic/`

- ✔ **American Society of Landscape Architects (ASLA),** 636 Eye Street, NW, Washington, DC 20001-3736, 202-898-2444, fax: 202-898-1185.

  `http://www.asla.org/`

- ✔ **California Landscape Contractors Association (CLCA),** 2021 N Street, Suite 300, Sacramento, CA 95814, 916-448-2522, fax: 916-446-7692. The California Landscape Contractors Association is the nation's oldest and largest organization of licensed landscape and irrigation contractors.

  `http://www.clca.org/`

- ✔ **The Irrigation Association,** 8260 Willow Oaks Corp. Drive, Suite 120, Fairfax, Virginia 2203, 703-573-3551, fax: 703-573-1913. The mission of the Irrigation Association, a nonprofit, North American organization, is to improve the products and practices used to manage water resources and to help shape the worldwide business environment of the irrigation industry.

  `http://www.irrigation.org/`

> ✔ **Ontario Association of Landscape Architects,** 2842 Bloor Street West #101, Etobicoke, Ontario M8X 1B1, 416-231-4181, fax: 416-231-2679.
>
> `http://www.clr.utoronto.ca/ORG/OALA/`

Going to landscape school

Okay, you're hooked. You're having so much fun creating your own home landscape that you'd like to try it professionally. Or maybe you're interested in a continuing-education class. Here's how to find what's available.

> ✔ **Council of Educators in Landscape Architecture.** Virtually every U.S. school with a landscape architecture program is a member and is linked from this site.
>
> `http://www.uidaho.edu/cela/`

> ✔ **European Foundation for Landscape Architecture.** This organization represents professional landscape architecture associations throughout Europe.
>
> `http://www.cyberlandscape.com/efla/efla_uk.htm`

Finding landscape links to the world

The following sites link you to schools where you can study landscape architecture or where you can find like-minded individuals.

Austria

Institut für Landschaftsplanung

`http://s11e261gw1.tuwien.ac.at/`

Australia

University of New South Wales. Sydney 2052 Australia

`http://www.fbe.unsw.edu.au/units/Landscape-Arch/`

Canada

> ✔ University of Toronto, Center for Landscape Research
>
> `http://www.clr.utoronto.ca/`

> ✔ University of Calgary, Faculty of Environmental Design
>
> ```
> http://www.ucalgary.ca/evds/
> ```
>
> ✔ University of British Columbia, Landscape Architecture Program
>
> ```
> http://137.82.35.52/landscape/
> ```

France

Versailles National Graduate School of Landscape Architecture, Ecole Nationale Supérieure du Paysage (ENSP), 4, rue Hardy - RP 914 - F78009 Versailles Cedex, 33 1 39 24 62 00, fax : 33 1 39 24 62 01

```
http://www.landscape-architecture.com/ensp/enspeng.html
```

Germany

> ✔ Technische Universität München-Weihenstephan, Lehrstuhl für Landschaftsarchitektur und Entwerfen
>
> ```
> http://www.edv.agrar.tu-muenchen.de/lae/laemain.htm
> ```
>
> ✔ Universität Gesamthochschule Kassel, Willkommen beim Fachbereich 13, Stadtplanung, Landschaftsplanung
>
> ```
> http://www.uni-kassel.de/fb13/
> ```
>
> ✔ Universität Hannover, Information System of the Faculty of Landscape Architecture + Environmental Development
>
> ```
> http://www.laum.uni-hannover.de/welcome-engl.html
> ```
>
> ✔ Universität Karlsruhe, Institut für Landschaft und Garten, Kaiserstraße 12, D-76128 Karlsruhe, Germany, 49-721-608-3175, fax: 49-721-691406, eMail: institut@lug.architektur.uni-karlsruhe.de
>
> ```
> http://www-lug.architektur.uni-karlsruhe.de/
> ```
>
> ✔ U-GH Paderborn, Abteilung Höxter, Landschaftsarchitektur und Umweltplanung
>
> ```
> http://www.uni-paderborn.de/extern/fb/7/
> ```

Switzerland

Ingenieurschule ITR Rapperswil

```
http://www.itr.ch/departments/l/
```

Index

• R •

Notes

SAVE 33% on a one-year subscription to
National Gardening magazine

No other magazine gets to the root of planting and growing like *National Gardening*. That's because here at *National Gardening*, we haven't forgotten what down-to-earth, practical gardening is all about. And we're talking about all kinds of gardening—fruits, vegetables, roses, perennials— you name it and *National Gardening* knows it.

We bring you hands-on growing information you can use to become a more successful gardener. Make smarter variety selections. Time your plantings more efficiently for better results. Extend your growing season. Fertilize your garden more effectively, and protect it from pests using safe, sensible, and effective methods. Harvest healthier, tastier, more beautiful crops of all kinds.

Plus: Swap tips and seeds with other avid gardeners from around the country and around the world. Choose the best, most practical gardening products for your needs. Get expert gardening advice. Let the gardening experts at NGA help you grow everything more successfully!

Special offer to ...*For Dummies*® readers:
For a limited time, you're entitled to receive a one-year (6 issue) subscription to *National Gardening* magazine—for just $12! That's 33% off the basic subscription price. Just fill out the coupon and mail it to the address listed below, <u>today</u>!

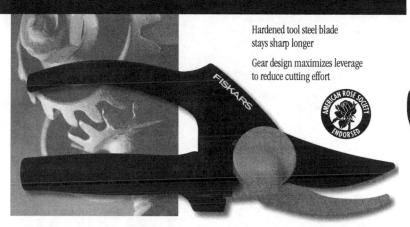